BRAVE ENOUGH

BRAVE ENOUGH

JESSIE DIGGINS

WITH TODD SMITH

 University of Minnesota Press
Minneapolis
London

Published by the University of Minnesota Press
111 Third Avenue South, Suite 290
Minneapolis, MN 55401–2520
http://www.upress.umn.edu

Printed in the United States of America on acid-free paper

The University of Minnesota is an equal-opportunity educator and employer.

24   23   22   21   20   10   9   8   7   6   5   4   3   2   1

Library of Congress Cataloging-in-Publication Data
Diggins, Jessie, author. | Smith, Todd, author.
Brave Enough / Jessie Diggins with Todd Smith.
LCCN 2019036767 (print) | ISBN 978-1-5179-0819-5 |
    ISBN 978-1-5179-0820-1 (pb)
Subjects: LCSH: Diggins, Jessie, 1991- | Skiers—United States—Biography. |
    Cross-country skiing—United States. | Olympic athletes—United States—
    Biography.
Classification: LCC GV854.2.D54 A3 2020 (print) |
    DDC 796.93092 [B]—dc23
LC record available at https://lccn.loc.gov/2019036767

To my family (yes, the dogs, too) for unconditional love and support
and for instilling a lasting love of the outdoors —J.D.

To my parents, Gary and Linda Smith —T.S.

CONTENTS

I CAN DO IT MYSELF

"I can do it myself," I told my parents. "I can carry my own canoe." I was on an epic family canoe trip in Ontario, north of the Boundary Waters Canoe Area Wilderness. Even though I was only twelve years old, average height for my age but gangly and scrawny, I was fiercely determined to portage one of our family's canoes during our trip. Some kids my age wanted a new video game console or to go shopping at the mall. All I wanted was to be able to lift and carry a canoe by myself. What can I say? I was a weirdo.

The Boundary Waters is a large wilderness area in the most northeastern part of Minnesota that extends 150 miles along the U.S.–Canada border, where it becomes Quetico Provincial Park in Ontario, with thousands of lakes and waterways linked by wooded trails. Campers travel by canoe across the pristine lakes and carry their canoes across these trails through the woods to the next lake. Portaging your own canoe is a quintessential Minnesotan activity, and even as a young kid I wanted in on the action.

We were so deep into the wilderness north of the Canadian border that we didn't see a single other soul for the entire week. Which was amazing. I don't think I realized how incredible it was to be out in the absolute middle of nowhere, totally immersed in nature, because my parents took us on these canoe trips so often! I learned how to catch and clean a fish and how to paddle properly so I could actually contribute physically to our daily voyages across the lakes. My younger sister, Mackenzie, and I would put life jackets on and float ourselves down gentle rapids when the water was high, and we thought this was just about the best vacation ever. It was like a sweet water park ride. We'd swim over to the shore near our campsite, run up the side of the river, and hop in again for ride after ride. My mom and dad would be looking on, ready to fish us out, but I was a strong swimmer and fiercely protective of my little sister, and we never got into trouble. But as cool as floating down the rapids was, nothing was cooler than watching my mom and dad carry the canoes over their heads.

"I can do it myself," I repeated my favorite tagline. "I can carry the canoe."

As a toddler, my favorite phrase was "I do it mineself!" I wanted to do everything alone, unassisted. I was energetic, extremely stubborn, and with some hindsight I now feel sorry for my parents. I wanted to know that I could do anything without help, even if I realistically had no chance of doing something without a little boost. This attitude persisted (OK, fine, it's still there even now) as I got older. If an art teacher reached over to adjust my clay pot, I would get unreasonably annoyed. But now it's not my work anymore! I'd think. Now it's not something that was made by me. I'd rather have glaring mistakes and know it was my own work than have it be perfect and know it wasn't mine. This attitude makes up a huge part of my racing ethos today when it comes to doping in sport; I'd rather get last place and know that it was all me out on the course, rather than win and know it wasn't my effort and hard work alone that made it happen.

I also grew up alongside a lot of cousins who were around my age, all boys. I decided early on that anything they could do, I could do too. The more something was labeled a "boy thing" because of how tough or gross or physically draining it was, the more I wanted to do it. Clean a fish and get rid of all the fish guts? If boys do that sort of thing, then I will too. Split firewood and carry all the heaviest pieces? Duh. Get sweaty and tired shoveling snow and mowing the lawn? I don't really feel like it, but I'm going to do it anyway because I'm a girl. To this day, I get involuntarily prickly when guys insist on taking all the heavy luggage and leave me with nothing to carry. Chivalry may not be dead . . . but my acceptance of it needs a little help.

But back to canoeing!

"All right," my dad said after a few days of rapid-fire pestering. As we paddled our way across a lake, he looked over and said, "You can portage the canoe tomorrow at the next crossing. But first I'm going to teach you how to do it, because you don't want to bang it around on the rocks."

At our campsite, my dad taught me how to lift the Wenonah, the lightest of our two canoes. I still managed to make it look painful and awkward! My young age and small size didn't matter to my dad though. He patiently showed me how to prop the canoe up, get underneath it, and lift it onto my shoulders using my legs. I learned how to get it up and how to take it down without damaging the canoe, and that was a big deal for me. And it was an even bigger relief for my parents, as we were out in the middle of nowhere!

I finally got my chance. The next day, we packed up our campsite, loaded the canoes, and paddled across the lake toward the next portage. Thirty minutes later, we pulled up to the far shore and unloaded our gear.

"I got it!" I exclaimed. "I can carry the canoe!" As though my parents would dare suggest that they might want to carry it across.

I picked up the end of the canoe, turned it over, scooched under it, and felt the middle bars dig into my shoulders. Then I bent my legs and hoisted the canoe up, steadying it as it rocked on my shoulders. My dad let me go first on the trail. I gripped the edges of the Wenonah tight and proudly marched my way down the rocky trail, teetering a little. But I steadied myself and kept moving forward, one wobbly step at a time. The euphoric look on my face told the whole story. I still have the photo of me under the canoe, knobby knees sticking out, face glowing as though I'd just won first place.

"Look!" I excitedly yelled back at my mom, dad, and Mackenzie as I made my first steps down the trail with the canoe on my shoulders. I beamed with pride. "I'm doing it!"

• • •

Technically, carrying a canoe in the middle of the summer had nothing to do with my future skiing career. But it also had everything to do with it. The same approach I took in portaging a canoe I would use in sports. If I wasn't completely reckless, if I was smart about my strategy, if I worked really hard, and if I was brave enough to try and was allowed the freedom to go for it, then good things would happen. The results and winning weren't the sole focus either. The process was just as important. It was the doing that gave me the rush of satisfaction, not the potential for a ribbon at the end. For me, the feeling of knowing I had accomplished something tough was always a huge reward.

I also had no way of knowing then how this same perseverance and sheer stubbornness would be called upon later in life—how hanging tough and working through the hard parts would become about so much more than lifting a canoe or grinding through a sweaty, brutal training session. It would become a fight for my own life and my self-confidence as I battled an eating disorder. While in recovery for bulimia, the absolute self-confidence I had on that portage at age twelve was nowhere to be found, and it would take a lot of digging to bring that brave little girl back to the surface.

But like anything worthwhile in life, while I always want to be able to do it "mineself," the truth is . . . I don't have to. I'm not alone. I've never been alone, even when I felt like it while trying to isolate myself. I have found so much satisfaction, happiness, and the feeling of being whole from being part of a team, more than I could have ever guessed. And each team that I've been one little piece of has left its mark on me. Finding my role within the team and developing my own style of leadership are processes that I'm still in the middle of and are ever evolving. I have realized that I don't have to be perfect, as long as I keep working on it.

I have the most incredible team at my side, ready to provide guidance, lift me up, and show me how to navigate this crazy life. That team now includes my boyfriend, the incredible men and women on the national ski team and my club team, and my coaches and techs, but it all started with my family. It was my parents who first taught me how to be coachable, to be able to watch, listen, and learn new skills for myself. (Although I had boundless enthusiasm for lifting our canoe above my head, first someone had to teach me how to lift the darn thing!) They also instilled in me a love for the natural world and being active: through camping trips to countless places, winters spent cross-country skiing, and summer vacations to our family's camp in Thunder Bay, Canada. I was suntanned and sweaty in the summer, and frosty and racing across the snow in the winter. I was forever bruised and scrappy, a kid perpetually in motion, whirling from one adventure to the next. That's still who I am today, scrapes, bruises, and all. Being able to lean on my family for support, trusting that they're always going to be there for me through thick and thin, has been the ultimate gift. Their support lifted me up as I jumped over my own hurdles.

Looking past a gold medal at the Olympics, I know my family's support was just as crucial when I decided to become an advocate for The Emily Program, sharing my history with an eating disorder to help others make it through their own battles. Identifying what matters most to me and then being willing to fight for it didn't come naturally or easily. But as I work with The Emily Program, and as I travel the globe watching the world lose its winters as the planet's climate changes, I see how one can become passionate about many things without being an expert in the field. And help.

This book is the story of my life, or at least all the parts of it that I could fit into these pages. That doesn't mean that it's just the good parts. In fact, you're about to get a glimpse into some of my worst experiences as well as my favorite ones. Why? Because even if you're not an aspiring Olympic athlete, we all have a staggering amount in common. The strength of family and friends supporting you. Learning to love yourself, flaws and all. Finding something you believe in and being brave enough to fight for it, whether that's advocacy work, the promotion you want at your job, or winning back a healthy relationship between yourself and your body. This is my story of pushing past limits and setting new goals . . . but it could easily be yours, too. If you see yourself reflected in these pages, know that at my core I'm an ordinary girl from the heart of the midwestern United States, and if I can battle through barriers here and there, you absolutely can too. And your hotdish will most certainly taste better than mine.

CHAPTER 1

SNOW BABY

I have loved being outdoors pretty much since birth. I was born on August 26, 1991, and was quickly introduced to the wintery world of the upper Midwest. When I was just two months old, Minnesota was pummeled by the legendary 1991 Halloween blizzard, a historic snowstorm so massive it became a cultural icon because it buried the Twin Cities and the whole region in twenty-eight inches of snow.

Our house in Afton, twenty miles east of downtown St. Paul, had been encased by huge, heavy snowdrifts that cut us off from the world. To make matters worse, my dad was away on a business trip and couldn't get back home due to the storm, so my mom was home alone with me, her newborn baby, and had to dig her way out. Even as a baby, I didn't really sleep. I was simply bundled up in a car seat and brought outside multiple times a day as my mom relentlessly shoveled out our house like a badass pioneer woman. Immersed in snow and wind, under the bright-blue Minnesota sky, I became a true snow baby—and have been ever since.

My parents loved being active outdoors every weekend, and having a baby didn't deter their usual ski dates together on the rolling trails in parks nearby. They would just put me in my dad's backpack and off we'd go!

Afton may be only twenty minutes from the Twin Cities, but it is a world away from city life. A combination of farmland, rolling hills, bluffs, and dense woodlands, Afton is a blend of agriculture and recreation, a place with marinas and ski slopes just minutes from each other. It was a rural place to grow up, and our house was set so far back in the woods that we couldn't see the road. We were half a mile from our neighbors on one side, half a mile from our neighbors on the other. The only sounds I heard out the window as a child were birds and the wind in the trees. My parents had a number of bird feeders around the house and a large bird identification book that I loved to flip through. To be honest, I was mostly interested in finding the pink flamingo because it was a pink bird! My favorite birds to see were chickadees, and I would run around calling "chick-a-dee-dee-dee-deeeeeeeeee!"—proud of myself that I was (totally inaccurately) making bird calls.

Our house was on the side of a large hill, with woods on two sides and fields on the other two. Even inside the house I felt like I was still connected to the outdoors through the large windows on all sides, and all I could see were trees, forest foliage, animals, and the ever-changing Minnesota sky. When I wanted to get outside, I'd sometimes go out the door . . . or I might crank open a window and jump out that way. When I needed a break or had to be inside the house, I lived on our three-season porch, where a large hammock hung, its white knotted netting draped between two wooden bars and perfect for a small child to run and leap into easily. I *adored* this hammock. It became a prop for my active imagination, and my cousins and I would play "shipwreck" on it, pretending the hammock was our ship in wild and crazy high seas, swinging it wildly back and forth and flipping it upside down. You were the captain if you could stay on the hammock while it was upside down, and trust me, that is hard to do.

All of the land around our house was my personal playground. Which was a godsend for my parents because as a child I didn't do bored very well. I didn't nap and hardly ever sat down. I had so much energy that when I would go places with my parents where I was required to sit still, they brought a pack of books, toys, and coloring pages they sweetly nicknamed their "arsenal of distraction" to keep me occupied. Otherwise, I was like a racquetball pinging all over the place. To be fair, I *could* focus when I needed to. I loved doing arts and crafts projects and could be totally absorbed in what I was doing, whether that was painting the paper or slowly spreading paint up my arms to my neck. But I had to be invested in what I was doing, and being told to sit still "just because" didn't work for me if I didn't think there was a good reason for it.

While my parents understood this and let me be an active child, my teachers in preschool did not. Every child was expected to take a nap, and I was really worried about this. "But what if I can't sleep?" I asked, and was assured that it was OK, all I had to do was stay on my mat. Hmmmmm. Stay on the mat. Let me tell you, I *never* stuck a toe off that mat! But I *did* do cartwheels, headstands, jumping jacks, and all the gymnastics my little heart desired, right up until the teachers put me in the isolation room. I was given a coloring book and crayons, and from then on, when everyone else napped, I got to stay in my coloring room, a room that conveniently had a window looking into another schoolroom, where the big kids would watch movies during nap time. My earliest sharp memory of "school" was dragging my chair under the window and clinging to the sill, standing on my tippy-toes, laughing along while watching *Willy Wonka and the Chocolate Factory* over the big kids' shoulders.

During grade school, I went to Valley Crossing Elementary School and absolutely loved it. I made friends, and I was fiercely dedicated to having their backs. One day at recess while we were building snow forts, a boy came over and pushed my best friend into the snow. I pushed him back, hard. He fell down and gave himself a black eye with his knee. At least this was how I patiently explained it to the principal when I was sent to his office; if I had wanted to give him a black eye, I would have! I was simply treating him the way he apparently wanted to be treated. This, obviously, didn't work out in my favor. It appeared that pushing back wasn't tolerated, which was probably a good thing. But between you and me, that kid never bothered my friend again, so who really won here? A more self-aware person would have recognized that she had a fiery temper at times and little to no patience, but at a young age I simply described my character traits as "don't mess with my friends, dude."

· · ·

We had one TV in the basement of our house, and it got only two stations: news or sports. But somehow it was only ever showing golf when I turned it on. I never really wanted to watch anyway, so I spent most of every day outside. I was outside so much that in summer I was incredibly tanned and my hair was shock white from being bleached by the sun. My skin freckled, and my feet turned tough and calloused from running barefoot. I was always covered in scrapes, cuts, and bruises, too busy playing to stop and worry about injuries. Honestly, I never cared about getting hurt. My knees are a mass of scar tissue because I was always out doing things and skinning them over and over.

It was a *Lion King* childhood: I was surrounded by the natural world, and all of it was my own imaginary kingdom. My parents never told me that there were areas that were off-limits. I was free to run around our house, into the woods and fields, right into the trees. I was never scared to wander around the woods by myself, and my parents trusted me to not be an idiot and to never climb higher into a tree than I could climb back down.

I often scavenged for fossils in huge rock piles in the middle of the fields around our house, not knowing what might pop out or what I'd find. One of my favorite spots to explore was an old abandoned house a mile down the road. With its creepy, crumbling exterior, the house looked like a set for a horror movie. I would poke through the rubble, finding picture frames with the pictures torn out or burned completely, making up stories in my head about the people who had lived there. I had a lot of empathy, even for people in my make-believe world. Standing in the shell of that home, I wondered if there were ghosts and if I was disturbing them.

I always wanted to know how things worked, and I was relentless in asking questions, even when it was not an appropriate time to be pestering. My mom would laugh, telling me about the time she and my dad took me to see the play *Peter Pan*. I was quite young and super stoked on the whole flying across the stage thing, but I couldn't stop squirming around in my seat, peering at the stage until I figured out how they did it. "Mom! There's wires! They're flying because of the *wires*!" I announced, proud of my detective skills. The woman with kids my age in the row in front of us turned around and angrily hissed,

"Ssshhhhhhh!" It hadn't occurred to me that not *everyone* wanted to know how it worked. Thankfully, for my little sister's sake, I modified my tactics in time for Santa Claus.

• • •

I remember begging my parents for a baby sister when I was in preschool. Most of my friends had a little sibling, and I was so envious! I had this half-formed concept that getting a little sister was about as easy as driving over to Toys "R" Us and picking one out from the shelf. But, you know, a quiet, cute, well-behaved one that I could tote around like an accessory. Not one of the wrinkly, screaming, stinky ones.

When my parents told me I was getting a little sister, I was through-the-roof excited. We didn't actually know if it would be a girl or a boy, but I was quite sure it'd be a little sister (because that's what I wanted, obviously). I was curious about this baby. How did one take care of it? Would it talk? Could it do tricks? My mom showed me how to put a diaper on a baby by putting one on my doll, and after that I put diapers on *all* my stuffed animals and practiced changing them every day. Not even the pink dinosaur was spared this humiliation. My mom did her best to keep a straight face and hold her laughter in when I bossily proclaimed, "OK, Mom. *You* can be *my* mommy, and *I'll* be the baby's mommy!"

Of course, all that changed when Mackenzie Rose Diggins arrived when I was five years old. She was premature, and there were a few complications, and we're lucky to have her alive! My poor mom had to spend a few months on bed rest, and during this time I house-hopped from my grandparents to cousins to other cousins, as I wasn't really sure what was happening and my parents figured it'd be better for me to not spend all my time running up and down the hospital halls. When we finally got everyone home, I was perplexed. Why was my little sister crying all the time? Why didn't she just go to sleep at night like everyone else? And good lord, *why* did her diapers not smell as nice as the ones I changed on my dolls? But despite having the rose-colored lenses off, I loved her and was fiercely proud of my baby sister. After all, she was the cutest baby in the world. She might drive *me* nuts, but *nobody else* was ever allowed to be annoyed by her.

As we grew up five years apart, we often missed each other's phases by a hair. I grew out of Barbie dolls just as she grew into them. We overlapped schools for only one year. I had a short fuse and was quick to anger but also quick to move on, whereas when Mackenzie finally got mad, she'd stay mad for days. But we also had a ton of fun together. One of our favorite games was Mackenzie sitting in the laundry basket while I pushed her in circles around the living room, zooming around like a two-man bobsled team. I'd lie on the floor reading books to her as she sat perched on my back. Above all things, we loved to play dress-up together, and to this day we have a fantastical box of make-believe.

One of my favorite activities (other than being a pirate and running around the house with Kenzie as Tinker Bell clinging to my back) was helping my mom in the garden. I loved being her little assistant, and I desperately hoped my thumb was green as well. She taught me how to find the weeds and pull them out, how to put new flowers in the ground, and what the heck a perennial versus an annual was. I remember the day I learned that you could actually pull things out of the ground and *eat* them. I was dumbfounded. *You mean to tell me you can just eat anything outside?* No, my mom explained, but she did point out all the herbs, rhubarb, asparagus, and chives. When she went inside to wash the dirt off her hands, I started plucking one tall piece of chive after another, eating it simply because I could. When she came back, I smelled horrible, like an onion, and was feeling quite sick.

Later, when I was out of high school, I helped my parents build a bigger garden for all the vegetables we could handle. Dad and I nailed the wooden boxes together, fetched local compost and dirt, and spent hours trucking one wheelbarrow load after another to fill the raised beds. We had to make the fence surrounding the garden high enough to protect it from the deer, but once it was finished, I had so much fun planning which vegetables would go where and helping my mom plant the seeds. Even today, whenever I am home in the summer, I love running out to the side yard with a basket to collect spinach, kale, peppers, tomatoes, sugar snap peas, asparagus, lettuce, beets, and carrots— although most of it is gone by the time I'm back in the house.

CHAPTER 2

WILD CHILD

My weeklong family canoe trips sum up so much of my childhood: time spent outdoors, where I was curious, stubborn, and determined, fueled on adrenaline with a healthy dose of laughter. I was bursting with raw energy, and because of this, I was constantly outside testing my physical and mental boundaries. I always loved a challenge. More importantly, I was raised in a culture where my parents and grandparents taught me that I could do anything I set my mind to regardless of my gender, size, and age. I was always empowered to go outside, try something new, and be fearless.

My childhood adventures in the outdoors would become the foundation for my athletic career—and a lot of that came right from the geography of Afton, Minnesota. Endurance athletes have long flocked to the area to train for marathons, bike races, triathlons, and cross-country ski races, on both the roads and wooded trails. The land is perfect for training athletes of every skill level, and it was literally my backyard. Afton State Park offers great running trails with many hills to push yourself on. The roads that wind through the farmland near my house provide long, peaceful stretches of pavement to put in miles on a bike. As those wide-open spaces get closer to the St. Croix River, the roads transform into a series of rolling hills. My parents' house in

Afton was located right in this sweet spot of forest and fields, of farms and hills, of recreation and serious workouts.

I went from a childhood spent outdoors in a tiny hamlet tucked away in the St. Croix River Valley, to a career as a professional cross-country skier, traveling from one country to the next every week with the World Cup races in Europe. To understand my journey, you first have to visit the places that shaped me. Let me take you on a little tour of the experiences and people that made me who I am, of the town that helped raise me.

• • •

The first stop is smack-dab in my backyard. Walk round the side of the house, through a row of pine trees, and past my two favorite trees. My parents planted two apple trees, one for when I was born (Haralson), and one when my sister, Mackenzie, was born (State Fair). Every year, we'd get hundreds of apples. We literally couldn't eat them fast enough. Growing up, I snacked on so many of those apples as I ran around, or picked them to make apple crisp, apple pie, applesauce, or just anything apple. When we couldn't pick them fast enough, we'd naturally make a little tower out of all the rotten ones and smack it into smithereens with one well-placed golf swing. My mom said it got apple guts all over the yard, but I liked to think of it as composting with flair.

When I was ten, I was running through the yard as usual one day and stopped to grab an apple off a tree. I snapped one off, rubbed it on my shirt (probably made it dirtier), and took a few bites. Then a thought popped into my head. *I should be eating this in a tree house.* Yep. That's definitely what we needed here.

After scouring the yard, we picked a tree in the corner of the side yard, past the apple trees and bonfire pit. It was impossible to see the tree house from the house, which of course made it feel like some awesome secret lair and hideout spot for me and Mackenzie.

We went straight to the lumberyard, and I helped my dad pick out the planks, siding, and two-by-fours and load them into the car. We designed it together, and I was his pint-sized apprentice. Then I decided it needed a little vinyl door flap like a dog flap in a door. My mom and dad tried to talk me out of it (what kind of tree house has a dog flap for a door?), but I was dead set on having one. So OK, maybe I was kind of a poor apprentice, but at least I was learning things!

It was so empowering to help my dad build it, to use the saw and drill and hammer—to have an idea and then create something. The first time I climbed up and stood inside of it, it felt like Christmas bursting in my heart. From that moment I used the tree house every day for two months. I didn't play video games, and I didn't watch TV. I just went outside, enjoying my personal fortress. Even when I was reading a book, I would read it in my tree house. But something was missing . . . a daring escape route.

We had already put in a zip line in the backyard, and I loved it to death. But it wasn't very fast or dangerous, so naturally, it was time to take that baby to the next level.

My dad, being the awesome dad that he was, built a little platform that came off the tree house and hovered ten feet off the ground. Then he hooked up a long cable that started above the platform and ended halfway up the trunk of the large oak tree across the yard. He tested it out himself, and I still have the image of him zooming down the zip line, my mom laughing and me cheering. This was now the coolest tree house in the whole world, I was convinced.

I would spend entire days in the yard using the zip line with my sister. It got to the point where I was really quite creative with it. I had this trick where I flipped myself upside down and then flipped back up and jumped off just before I'd hit the oak tree. That was my go-to stunt. My mom would be gardening in the yard next to me and casually look over while she was weeding and see me flying across the yard upside down, flipping over at the last second to get my feet up just before I hit the tree. I give my parents a lot of credit for letting me be a little bit wild and trusting me to use my best judgment, even when it appeared I was heading upside down toward a hard-earned lesson.

And the zip line was only one part of my one-woman Cirque du Soleil act. Around the back of our house, between the fields and the kitchen windows, stood an old swing set. With my tiny kingdom finally built, I created gymnastics routines on every feature of the playground for hours on end. The slide, swings, bar, and two-person glider swing didn't stand a chance. The little playground grew with me as I got older;

I went from swinging to dragging the hose over to the top of the slide to create a grand entrance for a Slip 'N Slide, to using the bar for pull-ups when I came home from ski camp.

• • •

My raw, natural energy only increased with age. I was either fully on or fully stopped. There was no middle ground. Our neighbors had a trampoline and let me use it, and, of course, that's all I wanted to do once I'd tried it. My mom would walk with me through our side yard, past the tree house and apple trees, along paths my dad had mowed into the grass, past a craggy old crabapple tree, and through a field over to our neighbors' side yard to use their trampoline. Mom spent hours taking me over there and spotting and teaching me how to do a back handspring and then turn that into a backflip. I remember feeling so psyched when I finally did it.

We eventually got our own trampoline, with a protective netting around it. It ended up being the most amazing thing ever because it stoked my bravery, allowing me to get even more ambitious—or foolish, depending on your point of view. With the netting there, I was invincible. I would try to do two front flips in a row or multiple backflips in a row, knowing that if I missed, I'd just fly into the netting and bounce back. I used the trampoline so often that eventually I could do five backflips in a row. I would just flip, bounce, flip, bounce, flip, bounce, all day, and I was *immensely* proud of myself, dragging my parents out to the yard to show off my "gymnastics routine."

Before I realized that skydiving and bungee jumping were super fun recreational ways to scare the daylights out of your parents (sorry, guys), I loved finding ways to be just a little bit scared and get some adrenaline going. Nothing gave me more of a thrill, though, than the feeling of being weightless in the air, of flying. I needed something aerial to push the envelope, so my dad set up a big rope swing in the backyard. It was a disarmingly simple toy, but I loved that thing to death. I'd sprint across the grass, wearing a dirt patch into the ground, delighting in the feeling of being lifted into the air, gripping the rope loops in each hand and kicking my bare feet at the sky.

I never looked at the rope swing, trampoline, swing set, or zip line as a form of training, but man, that's definitely what they were. I was constantly pushing past my comfort zone, jumping farther, climbing higher, getting used to falling down, and taking risks. Everything about the way I naturally played and found delight in being outside was also building my endurance and strength, but I never saw it as "working out," because I was just having fun.

· · ·

With all the extra energy I had, it's no wonder that my parents started signing me up for any sport I wanted to try. I can't thank them enough for this—and for never pushing me to specialize in anything, always letting me try my hand at any activity I wanted.

We signed up for swim lessons early on, as it was important to my parents that I learn how to swim and tread water with as many canoe trips and times at the lake as we had. I was such a water baby, and I would later join the swim team in junior high school through tenth grade, and I even spent a year on the diving team. I loved being airborne so much that learning flips felt like an extension of trampoline time. I also started dance classes at age three. I adored dancing, and although I was never very good, I danced for ten years, eventually giving it up when I could no longer make it to practice because of ski races. I still seek out local dance classes whenever I'm traveling, because I still love to learn how to groove! Soccer was never my calling as I never really knew how to handle the ball, but, man, I could run forever, so for the years I played soccer, I basically ran around getting in the way and having a ball (pun totally intended). I went to rock climbing camp one summer, which I absolutely loved.

Surprisingly, when I tried gymnastics for a year at age five, I hated it. Don't get me wrong, I loved the routines, and my hyperflexible body was well suited to the sport, but the other girls weren't very nice to me, and I quickly decided this wasn't somewhere I belonged. I took ice skating lessons for a summer, which was pretty fun, but I had even more fun running the spotlight for my sister's ice skating show, perched high on scaffolding above the rink. I steadfastly ignored the advice to evenly distribute the spotlight on all the girls and made sure my little sister shone for every step of her routine.

Most people are surprised to learn that I've only gone alpine ski-ing about ten times in my life, but I don't think it's all that shocking, because whenever there was snow on the ground, cross-country ruled my world. It's ironic that I never tried cross-country running in school, because now for training I go on trail runs anywhere from one to five hours long. But back in junior high, I absolutely loathed running and would do anything to avoid it.

I'm so grateful to have had all these other sports in my life. They kept (and keep) me balanced, and I do mean that literally, as being able to move in multiple different ways has been one of the best things for my skiing career. Most of all, I'm grateful because as I got to experience so many different sports, when I made skiing my focus, I really knew it was out of love for the sport.

• • •

My first Olympics was the 2014 Winter Games in Sochi, but long before that I was in another Olympics . . . of sorts. When I was twelve years old, I had an Olympic-themed birthday party in my backyard, complete with cheesy little plastic medals. Every year I'd get so excited to plan my birthday party, and every year had a different theme. Some of the great-est hits include rollerblading with glow sticks and neon clothes (not in an ironic, cute throwback type of way, but because I actually thought it was awesome) and rock climbing at Vertical Endeavors all day. I believe that one year the theme was simply "everything has to be pink."

My mom is terribly creative and always helped me create an all-encompassing day of events at our house. She was straight-up amazing and would spend hours organizing these wild scavenger hunts for me and my friends for my birthday parties. She would make these clever little riddles and hide them all over the property, in the fields and in the woods. We'd have to find them in order and solve all the riddles to find the "treasure," which, funny enough, always included chocolate. The riddles were something like "What is a home away from home?" Then we'd all run across the yard to the camper and search through it for another hidden riddle. Tucked inside a cabinet in the camper, we'd find another clue, which read, "I'm a rope that does not tie but helps you fly."

Then we'd run to the tree house and find another riddle attached to the zip line. It was amazing.

The year I turned twelve, my birthday party coincided with the summer Olympics, so that became the theme. My mom set up all these stations where we had different summer Olympic sports. The trampoline routine was for our gymnastics floor routine, and we had to end our routine by posing in every direction to thank the judges, and everyone got to hold up their scores. We had track and field events in the fields behind our house that included a three-legged running race (so what if they don't have that in the actual summer Olympics . . . yet?), sprints, and all sorts of fun, silly races. Every girl got a medal, of course. Funny how that worked out.

Every one of my birthday parties ended with a bonfire, and this one was no different. Bonfires were such a big deal at our house. Every couple of weeks we would burn all the buckthorn brush we'd hauled in from the woods. Hauling brush was a monthly chore for me, but we made it a family affair, and it was actually pretty fun! We had our friends over and hosted them in the side yard, and the bonfire would get to ten feet tall because we had so much brush to burn.

For my twelfth birthday, Mom led us in a ceremonial lighting of the Olympic torch—the torch in this case being a huge bonfire, where we roasted s'mores.

CHAPTER 3

SUPER SPEED

While summers at our house in Afton were a circus act of sorts, winters were just as adventurous. There was no time to hibernate away from the cold and snow where I grew up, especially because our house was at the top of the greatest sledding hill ever. It would have been a crime to let it go unused.

Down the hill from our house we had a garage, where we stored canoes, kayaks, the camper, camping equipment, and the lawn mower. Built into the side of the hill, the old garage roof sloped down to the point where it was only a foot from the ground. Naturally, I would scamper onto the roof, where I could stargaze, contemplate life, do my homework. And when winter rolled in, the roof was where I'd go sledding, because why wouldn't you sled off a steep roof? I'm sure this was terrible for the shingles and not exactly healthy and safe, but my parents were tolerant of my wild schemes. When it snowed—this was when we actually had real winters—I would go sledding off the roof for hours.

My sister and I were sledding aficionados and took sledding seriously. We discovered that sledding through the yard and then straight down the driveway was terrifyingly fast, and that's all that mattered. Speed was the ultimate goal—unless, of course, there was a jump involved. Then big air was the goal, until our butts were too bruised from hard landings on the plastic sled. We had multiple sleds for different conditions and a big, long toboggan. My friends, my sister, and I would pile onto the toboggan and get enough weight to go nuking down the driveway.

The end of the driveway emptied out into the street, however, so we had to take precautions. Per my parents' request, we always propped a big sled in the snow at the end of the driveway so that cars on the road would know there were kids sledding. The one rule was that we had to come to a stop before we got to the street. Rather than sacrifice precious speed, we'd come bombing down the driveway, and then everyone would scream "Bail!" and throw themselves to the side off the toboggan. Hats and gloves, scarves and bodies would spill out over the driveway and yard. Then we'd pick up the toboggan and the clothing that had gone airborne and run back up and do it all over again.

• • •

My parents have always loved winters and the changing seasons. No matter the weather, they both were always out there working in it and enjoying the snowy months. My dad is from Thunder Bay, Canada, and my mom grew up in Canada and Duluth, Minnesota, and they have had winter in their bones since they were kids. Thanks to their love of the outdoors, I grew up believing the best thing you could do with your family every weekend was to get out of the house and appreciate nature.

Growing up in Thunder Bay, my dad lived and breathed hockey and was into everything outdoors: fishing, hunting, hiking in the woods. One winter, while skating at the outdoor rinks with his buddies, many of whom were Finnish, he was persuaded to try this other winter sliding sport, called "cross-country skiing." The Finns assured him he'd love it, and even if he didn't, it'd be awesome cross-training. My dad instantly embraced it.

The technical aspect of gliding across the trail, the graceful movements combined with endurance, speed, and power—this was a sport he knew he'd love his entire life. His dad was a doctor and his mother a nurse, and when a position was offered in Minnesota, his parents moved to the United States, and the whole family got green cards. My dad was about to finish his final year of high school, however, and he wanted to graduate with his friends. One day after hockey practice his coach called him into the locker room and told him to sit and take some tests he'd need if he wanted to apply for schools in the United States. In his sweaty hockey gear, my dad sat down and took the SATs. I now laugh at how casual it all was, as I think about the weeks and months of prep that students undergo for the SATs these days! After finishing school, he moved to the States to play hockey and go to college at Gustavus Adolphus in St. Peter, Minnesota. And there, with a black eye from a hockey game, is where he met my mother.

My mom was also born in Canada, in Senneterre, Quebec. Her dad was stationed there with the Royal Canadian Air Force in ground search and rescue, and had met her mother when they lived in Windsor, Ontario, where they grew up three streets apart. When my mom was three years old, the family moved to an air force station near Duluth and eventually settled on Pike Lake. She spent the majority of her life there and eventually became a U.S. citizen.

And the majority of her time was spent outside on the lake, paddling and swimming in the summer, snowmobiling and ice skating in the winter. Similar to my dad, she loved every part of being outside. My mom was really well rounded and played a few different sports, was in theater, played violin in the orchestra, and graduated an honor student. She was also great at prank wars with her younger brother. After graduating high school, she also went to Gustavus for college.

My mom is not shy at all, and I am happy that I inherited that trait from her. She marched right up to my dad one day and said, "Hi, cutie!" They're my mom and dad, but man, they are so stinkin' cute together. My dad got my mom to try cross-country skiing by bribing her with a wine and cheese picnic, which they enjoyed sitting in a tree on the side of the ski trail. Gentlemen, take note: it worked.

When my parents got married after college, they decided to hike and backpack through Europe and Australia before having kids. I'm so glad they did, because as a child I'd sit on the lid of the white rectangular box that held the trash and recycling bins in the corner of the kitchen, thumbing through old albums filled with photos of my parents hiking in the Alps, meeting kangaroos, and setting up tents in big, tall woods.

There were photos of my mom hiking up a steep trail with a huge back-pack, and of my dad with his curly head of hair, sitting on the deck of a hut in the mountains, sipping coffee. I didn't know the word for it back then, but two things became evident to me: my parents were total badasses, and traveling the world was something I desperately wanted to do as well.

My birth didn't stop them from going out on the trails. They had a backpack carrier they would put me in, all bundled up. When I got a little older, I learned that you told sled dogs to mush, and so, by exten-sion, I told my dad to mush. I'd yell, "Mush, Daddy, mush!" as he skied along, with my mom trying hard not to laugh. My other saying was "I want to go super speed." *Super speed.* I always wanted to go faster, and my dad got an amazing workout skiing because I was always pulling on his hair and yelling at him to go faster. But the entertainment didn't stop there. I would sing songs, too, treating my audience to renditions of "Twinkle, Twinkle, Little Star" while they were skiing, which I'm sure was very annoying!

• • •

When I was older, I spent a lot of my childhood winters on the ski trails at Willow River State Park, twelve miles north of Afton. The Minne-sota Youth Ski League had a branch there, which is funny, because the park is actually in Wisconsin. I joined the Minnesota Ski League when I was three years old; we joined as a family, and my parents got me my own little pair of skis with three-pin bindings. We mostly played games like soccer or tag on skis, waddling along with our poles flailing around in the air. We'd have so much fun, but at the same time, we were also learning basic skiing skills: balance, how to deal with the cold and wind, how to coordinate arms and legs, and how to deal with different kinds of snow. Most importantly, I was making friends and being active. It was kind of childcare, too, because when the parents weren't helping coach the kids, they could go and enjoy the trails while knowing their kid was having a blast with the other little skiers. It was a cool, forward-thinking program as it taught entire families how to ski, so it could become a lifetime sport they all could share.

We went to the Willow River ski league every Sunday afternoon in the winter. We'd get up, have a big pancake breakfast, and then I would have to do my chores. As I got older, that was how I got my allowance. I eventually worked my way to where I could vacuum the entire house and wash all the windows. Our house had a *lot* of windows. I had to wash the dishes every night from the time I was eight years old. When Mackenzie turned eight, she had to join the party, but then it really did become a party because we'd play what we called "the Disney game" while washing up. She'd say a rather obscure line from some film, and I'd have to guess which character said it and in which movie, then we'd switch roles. Our parents swore we were speaking our own language, and I'd often interpret things for my parents, such as "Oh, Kenzie wants to volunteer to scrub the toilet because that's what Cinderella had to do. Only she needs a pink dress in order to do it." So guess what? She'd get the dress *and* get to scrub the toilet, dressed up like a long-suffering Disney princess with her hair tied back in a handkerchief.

Then we'd go skiing for the afternoon. The parents at Willow River would bring food to eat in the warming hut after the ski. We'd go out in our age groups, play games to warm up, and then ski on different trails, coming back to enjoy cookies, orange slices, and a *lot* of hot chocolate.

I was never super competitive, except for when it came to the Medals for Miles part of the program. Actually, that name makes no sense, because it was really "pins for kilometers," but somehow *that* name never really caught on! After every Sunday afternoon ski, kids in the club would record the kilometers that they had covered. At the end of every ski season, pins were given out to each skier according to how many total kilometers they had skied that year. Bronze pins were for 25 kilometers and under, silver pins were for 25 to 50 kilometers, and gold pins were for 50 kilometers or more. We would ski circles around the building the day before pins were given out if we were tragically short at 49 kilometers, because, darn it all, a gold pin was super cool! Even more fun to flaunt was an actual medal given to the skier who had covered the most kilometers that winter. Receiving the pins was such a great way to see how hard we had worked all winter and gave us each a sense of accomplishment regardless of our total number of kilometers. But let me tell you, when it came to tracking kilometers, I was in it for the medal. To be fair, the real reason I was there at all was for the sledding we would sometimes do after our ski group was done. I wasn't interested in skiing for the pure graceful, mindful connection to nature. I was like any other little kid, interested in the hot chocolate, sledding, and going super speed on the downhills.

Each trail had a different color, and I got to know them all by heart. The Blue Trail went to a gorgeous series of waterfalls, water gushing beneath frosted pillows of blue ice stacked up the steep hill. It was a long ski, so if you made it all the way to the falls and back you could totally brag to your friends. As a kid, I loved the Purple Trail because it went down by the river. Once a year, my mom would come to practice early and add a treasure hunt, hiding stuffed animals in the trees and bushes. Sometimes there'd be a little cache of Hershey's Kisses the group would find to snack on at the end of the trail. I'll never forget the year I finally put two and two together and realized that it was *our* stuffed animals that were hiding out in the woods. I'd always thought, wow, what a coincidence! The park has the exact same pink and purple spotted dinosaur as I do! I mean, what are the odds? Also, I never found it strange that alongside the stuffed bear and squirrel, I was scouting out dinosaurs, koala bears, an ostrich, and a platypus in the trees. I just thought all the animals belonged there, because they were friends. I love little kids' logic.

As I grew more advanced as a young skier, I loved the Brown Trail because it had the biggest hills and fastest downhills with swooping turns. I'd follow my dad as I learned how to tuck as tight as I could, rushing down the hill and seeing how far my momentum would carry me up the next hill. It was like a roller coaster, and although powering up over the hills was sweaty work, the uphills were a means to an end: the fun downhills. That was my first experience learning how to carry speed from one section of the course to the next.

I also learned how to navigate the downhills from my dad. He has amazing balance from playing so much hockey, and it made him a fearless downhill skier on cross-country skis. When I was still a kid, my parents competed in citizens' races. My parents were always my heroes in races, and when the course happened to be a sheet of ice, my dad's mad skills came out to play. He figured out how to ride a ski and carry that speed and balance without wasting much energy or falling. I eventually started to learn how to do this too, and now downhill working sections are my biggest strength at World Cup races. I ski a lot like my dad, and to this day, my "race face" is exactly like his.

• • •

Growing up, my dad had a collection of VHS tapes of World Championship and World Cup ski races. He'd buy them at a local ski shop months after the actual race happened, and this was our way to see what World Cup racing looked like. And I'm not going to lie . . . I wasn't all that into it. I thought it was kind of boring, and decided I'd rather die than wear those one-piece race suits. But Dad would sit me down and explain which racers I should watch, why it was fun to follow each of them, and how the timing checkpoints worked. Suddenly, I thought ski racing might kinda maybe be a tiny bit cool, but I was still highly skeptical.

When my parents went to their races, there was often a little-kids category, sometimes called a "mini-loppet": a 2K kids ski, or a 1K fun run in the summer. I was super hooked on the idea of getting a medal once you crossed the finish line (see? Medals for Miles! It worked!), but even more so, I was interested in seeing if I could make it to the finish line. What would happen if I raced a longer race? A new distance challenge? Could I really race that far?

I did 3K to 5K mini-loppets every year until I was eleven, when I raced the 13K Vasaloppet in Mora, Minnesota, for the first time. My mom laughs when she remembers when I started to get really competitive in that annual race.

"I was out warming up for the 35K race," my mom said. "Then all of a sudden somebody came up to me and said, 'Jessie's skiing with the lead pack of boys! And she's *leading* them!'"

She ran over to look, and sure enough, there was a little blonde ponytail bobbing up and down in front of a pack of boys. I finished only twenty seconds back from the lead boy, and they were a little pissed about it.

I also loved to do the Kortelopet every year, the shorter, 25K version of the famous American Birkebeiner ski race. I desperately wanted to do the full Birkie 50K distance, but you have to be eighteen years old to compete. However, the Birkie and Kortie skiers started in the same place at the same time, so one year I decided to try to sneak onto the Birkie course where the Kortie cuts off. Someone with a bullhorn shouted out so everyone could hear, "Hey, *you*! Girl in the *Kortie* bib! Get back onto the correct cutoff!" And then, because this is the Midwest, that person added a nice "Please!" Because the Birkie always coincides with World Cup and, usually, either the Olympics or World Championships, I've never completed it, but I look forward to the day when I can finally experience the biggest race in North America.

One year my dad and I headed up to Giants Ridge, Minnesota, to do the Pepsi Challenge, a 50K race for my dad and my first-ever 25K race. It snowed eight inches during the race and was freezing cold. I was so tired that I stopped at every aid station to unwrap a Snickers bar. Honestly, I was in heaven. *No wonder everyone likes ski racing! You can just stop and eat candy every 5 kilometers! This is fantastic!* My dad finished his race and went to look for me, certain that I'd be in tears or at least extremely grumpy after slogging through inches of new snow for hours, but when he found me, I was all "Hi, Dad! How're you doing? Wasn't that great! We should do this next year!" It must have been the sugar buzz.

I also remember the first time I had an asthma attack during a ski race and learned that I had inherited my dad's exercise-induced asthma. I was twelve years old, doing a race at Trollhaugen in Wisconsin, and there was one long climb that was steeper and bigger than anything I'd raced up before. Because it was so cold, I was wearing a neck gaiter, often called a buff, and as I struggled up the hill, I started to panic. Why did it feel like my buff was getting tighter and tighter around my neck? Why was I making these horrible rasping sounds, and why did it feel like I was breathing through a cocktail straw? I couldn't get enough air, and because I had no idea what asthma was, I thought I was going to die. Convinced my buff was choking me to death, I stopped in front of my mom, only fifty meters from the finish line, sobbing between each ragged breath and clawing frantically at my buff.

My mom tried to reason with me and said, "You're OK, calm down, we'll take the scarf off. The finish line is all downhill from here."

She knew I'd be super pissed if I dropped out of a race I was winning with fifty meters to go, but in that moment I was furious with her for not being more pitying of my imminent death by buff. I couldn't wear a buff for nearly ten years after that, and I still can't race with anything touching my neck. Luckily, we learned about my asthma early on, because this would have been a serious problem for me throughout my ski career. It was terrifying at the time, and feeling like I had no control over my body and my lungs made me think hard about doing another race. But once I got help from a specialist and learned that with the proper inhaler I could get back to a normal level of breathing, I was once again excited to challenge my body and keep racing.

By the time I was ten, I had run out of Minnesota Youth Ski League levels to complete. Every year, once you learned a new set of skills, you'd move up a group, like in kids' swimming classes. My parents eventually took over Silver Skiers, a group for the older kids who had completed all the levels, and they taught us more advanced techniques and elements. They took us on field trips to races so we could experience racing a 5K together, and it was my first involvement on a team. I started to do more and more races and was placing with the high school girls as a sixth grader. I began to realize that I didn't want to finish just to see if I could anymore—I wanted to cross the line first.

• • •

As counterintuitive as it sounds, skiers are made in the summer. Doing cardiovascular and strength workouts during the off-season is crucial to improving your performance, and nothing comes as close to using the same muscles as roller skiing does. Roller skis are about eighteen inches long, with one wheel at the front and one in the back, and a binding mounted on the ski so you can click your boots into it just like you would a normal ski. Classic roller skis have a ratchet in one of the wheels, so they will only roll forwards, and you can "kick" the skis to mimic the motions of kicking your wax down into the snow to propel yourself forward. Skate wheels, however, are skinnier and harder to balance on, and they roll both directions. The best part (or worst, depending on your attitude) is that roller skis don't have brakes, so you have to learn to control your speed by "snowplowing" or stepping down the hills. Generally, we never go down a hill that we haven't scouted before, and most of the time you just coast to a stop at the bottom. I've gotten up to fifty-two miles per hour on a downhill while drafting one of the bigger guys, though, so if you're thinking of taking up roller skiing: when it doubt, stop and walk down the steep hills!

To be a competitive cross-country skier, you have to log long hours on the road, running on trails, and lifting weights in the gym during the summer. As a young kid, I had a great introduction to the culture of cross-country with my parents and friends at the Minnesota Youth Ski League. With that genuine love for the sport in place, my skiing career really began to take shape when I decided I wanted to train in the off-season the summer before seventh grade. At that point in my life, I wasn't serious at all about ski training in the summer, and most of my time was spent playing soccer on a rec league team, swimming in the river, and trying to learn how to high-jump as part of a local track team. (Spoiler alert: I was never meant to be a jumper.) But I wanted to give roller skiing a shot because I'd seen my parents doing it, and it looked like a ton of fun.

My parents took me out for my first roller ski on a flat, paved stretch of road near our house. I wore these big, chunky knee pads, elbow pads, and a dorky helmet. I had thin wire glasses at the time, so I couldn't even depend on a pair of sunglasses to counteract my stunning uncoolness. There was no doubt in my mind that I wasn't cool, but the best part of that age was that it never occurred to me that I was supposed to *want* to be cool. Mackenzie was also in knee pads and elbow pads, but she was going to rollerblade alongside me. We went as a family down the road, my parents watching out for cars. I was this gangly stick figure with terrible technique, flailing all over the place like a baby deer on ice. But I loved it, and miraculously, I didn't fall down! (Don't worry, the falls and epic road rash come later.) From that point on, I often joined my mom and dad when they went roller skiing. It was three miles from our house to Main Street in Afton—and, more important, to Selma's Ice Cream Parlour—and that became the route that now is etched into my heart. I got to know all the best routes, and I could go on my own while my parents skied longer loops.

The energy that I possessed as a little girl found this awesome outlet in roller skiing, and that, in turn, began to fuel my cross-country skiing. It took me a while to find my rhythm, but I began to log more and more time on roller skis. And I wasn't coddled at all. My parents took me out when conditions weren't always perfect, in all sorts of weather, and I began to learn how to deal with discomfort and adverse conditions. It was always my own choice to ski, but they showed me that I could handle whatever the weather threw at me. If I wanted to ski, it could be done, rain and wind be damned. I also learned that it wasn't advisable to go out in humid heat wearing a cotton T-shirt! We roller-skied in the steamy, humid Minnesota summer and straight into the icy teeth of fall midwestern winds.

My adventures in the outdoors of Minnesota helped lay the blueprint for my future skiing career. But there was another special place that helped raise me too. Everything in my young life—strong family connections, all of my raw energy, my accidents, my triumphs, and a new found competitive streak—all of it came together for me in Thunder Bay, Ontario. Born to a Canadian citizen and an American citizen, I knew growing up that I was a "dual citizen"—whatever that meant. To me, it meant I was the luckiest girl in the world, because I got to be half Canadian and claim it, too.

CHAPTER 4

THUNDER BAY

Our family cabins were on Silver Beach, two of them right next to each other, on the edge of Lake Superior near Thunder Bay, Ontario. A little creek ran through the property between the cabins, and there were two cute little wooden bridges to walk across the creek, although we always used to get a running start and leap over it. My dad had been going to these cabins every summer since he was six years old. As a little kid, I went there every summer as well, sometimes twice a summer, usually for a week or two weeks. Many happy childhood memories were formed at these cabins, which we simply called "camp."

Mary Island was about a quarter mile offshore from where our cabins overlooked the beach. Every summer, we'd go out and take a sunset paddle around the island. I get why it was one of my parents' favorite ways to end the day, because it was gorgeous, the sun setting over the lake that stretched to the edge of the horizon, sunlight dancing on the waves. It took forty-five minutes to paddle out through the rolling and rocking waters of Lake Superior and around the whole island. But best of all was that there was a sunken tugboat named the *Gordon Gullion* only fifteen feet from the edge the island, on the side facing the beach where all the camps were. It had burned and crashed many years ago. Everyone just called it "the sunken tug," because when you're that famous, you don't need a real name. Sort of like Lady Gaga. As kids, we would paddle out there and then go diving to explore it.

To dive down and see this cool wreck, you had to pay a price. Even in summer, the water was punishingly cold, ranging seasonally from 32 to 55 degrees Fahrenheit. Absolutely freezing. For reference, when athletes use a cold bath to help with muscle soreness after a hard workout, the recommended temperature is between 52 and 60 degrees Fahrenheit. Within seconds of diving into Lake Superior, the frigid water raised goosebumps and seriously challenged one's commitment to swimming. It wasn't a temperature I would have picked for a relaxing vacation swim by any means, but I knew that if I wanted to see the boat and explore—and, most important, last as long as my cool older cousins—I had to deal with the goosebumps.

I would dive down and swim around the sunken tug in my goggles, holding my breath until the very last second when I could no longer stand it. You could see the boiler of the tugboat, the pipes, huge wooden beams with spikes driven through them. Of course, divers had already taken anything small and had picked the whole boat apart. But there were parts of it that were too big to take. It's not very deep, maybe five to ten feet under the surface of the water.

When I was sufficiently creeped out by all the dead bodies I was *certain* were hiding underneath the boiler, I'd come shooting out of the water and climb back into the boat. My lips would be purple, my skin bright white, and I looked like Rose from the *Titanic*. My parents would wrap me in towels and hug me to warm me up. The minute I felt warm again, the minute my blood began to recirculate, I'd dive right back into the water.

The best reward of all for enduring the freezing water was my dad, uncle, or older cousins getting the sauna going on the shore. We had this little bathhouse at camp, where we stored our boogie boards, wetsuits, and paddles. It had a little bucket outside where we had to dip our toes to wash the sand off (or else risk Nana's scolding when she swept the floor clean later), but best of all it had a wood-burning sauna. We'd paddle back into camp and run straight inside the sauna to warm up. We also loved to take saunas at night, when the sun was finally starting to set around ten thirty. I'd stay in there until I couldn't take it anymore, and then one of my cousins would yell, "One, two, three, go!" and we'd all burst out the door and sprint into Lake Superior. I'd run with high knees as long as I could until the water would catch me around the ankles. Then I'd fall and go splashing into the freezing water. I'd repeat this four or five times, and then finally, mercifully, crash into bed for a glorious and cozy sleep.

When we weren't playing games on the beach, my cousins and I would be picking our way through the rocks, searching for amethysts to present to Nana so she could decorate her garden. As little kids, my cousin Bill and I would wade around with nets, catching minnows and crayfish, and keep them in buckets. Mackenzie was impervious to the cold water as well, and we would paddle this big inflatable tube out into the lake, jumping off it over and over again. Kenzie, being her Disney princess self, would do these dramatic, awesome belly flops we called "mermaid flops." She'd perch on the edge of the tube, and I'd yell, "Meeeeeeermaaaaaaid floooopppppppp!" and *splash*, she'd soar into the lake. When it would rain we played the games Risk and Monopoly like there was no tomorrow, and at night we'd have big epic games of capture the flag. During one of these games, I was running for my life through the woods wearing, stupidly, only a thin pair of flip-flops. Suddenly I noticed a piece of old wood was coming along with me. Thunk, thunk, thunk, it clanged along with every step as though it was attached to the bottom of my foot. I lifted my foot. The board came with me. A nail from the board had come up through the bottom of my flip-flop and into my heel. Shit. We were often getting into little scrapes like that, but we looked out for one another and learned a few good lessons about proper footwear along the way.

• • •

Over the course of my childhood, there was a baby boom along the shoreline of Silver Beach, and there were many families with kids around our age. All of my cousins were there too, and every summer we would form these roving bands and play outside from morning until sunset. We would play at the beach, run around the woods, and a day was considered wasted if you hadn't gone swimming at least three times. We would save our loonies and spare change and bike to the candy store three miles away, where they had rows and rows of five-cent candy jars. We'd pick out our sour candies, fuzzy peaches, and skull candies and then bike back and try to make them last until the end of the day.

During my summers in Thunder Bay, adrenaline became a big thing for me. All the zip lining and sledding I did in Minnesota was perhaps me trying to get as close as I could to the feeling of flying through the air and the surge of happy adrenaline that I felt when we went cliff jumping at the cabins. In our usual large pack of kids, we'd ride our bikes to the Silver Harbour quarry to jump off the cliffs where they had blasted away large chunks of rock into Lake Superior below. It was the safest place to cliff jump I think I've ever seen . . . and I've seen a lot of them. You'd just have to step off the clean-cut edge, and there was no way you could get hurt. The water was twenty feet deep. Believe me, we tested it! We were always trying to swim down to touch the rocks at the bottom, but no one ever could.

My cousins and I would go jumping nearly every day. Sometimes our parents would come too, though my Nana never loved it. She'd sit on the deck back at camp as we were leaving, arms crossed, and proclaim, "I don't know what you're doing, and I'm not looking!" We'd all climb up, scampering over the rocks to the top, and throw ourselves right off the edge. There were many different heights to jump from, so we simply progressed up to the top as we got older. There was one ledge a foot off the water. Then there was a rock that was three feet off, one that was five feet off, ten feet off, and fifteen feet off. The highest one was around twenty-five feet. By the time I was eight or nine, I was jumping off the twenty-five-foot one because my older cousins were doing it, and darn it, I was going to do it too.

• • •

On a long holiday weekend each August, the adults would host this huge Camp Games for all of the kids. It was our favorite weekend of the summer, filled with races, swimming, and field events. The first day was the long-distance swim, down the length of the beach in the freezing lake. Depending on the day, it might be a little warmer and tolerable, or it might be windy with hard, cold waves splashing us in the face every time we tried to breathe. Swimmers needed a boat alongside them to make sure they had an out in case they got too cold or tired. But I was absolutely determined to never have to climb into my parents' canoe! Honestly, just making it to the finish in waters that cold was an accomplishment unto itself, which is probably why they created trophies for not only the fastest male and female finishers but the oldest and youngest finishers too! And the biggest trophy one could earn was—you guessed it—The Youngest Finisher. The names inscribed on each trophy go way back to my parents' days, and it was so fun adding our names to the tradition.

My competitive side really started to come out during these races. At the start, I just wanted to challenge myself and go up against the waves, the cold, and the long distance. I wasn't trying to beat anyone, I just wanted to make it to the end! I'd stand on the beach before the swimming events started, goosebumps already covering my arms, and I'd secretly ask myself, *Can I do this?* But as I got older, I stood there on the beach and told myself, *Now I want to win. Now I want to be the fastest.* A flame had definitely been sparked. It was the first time in my life that I was really competitive about something—even if that something was the lake itself.

The second day was all the games, and these were important not only for bragging rights (a force unto themselves), but because, from a little kid's standpoint, you could basically get rich. If we won an event, we got a ribbon stapled to a little brown-paper package. This tiny thing would have money inside! There was a looney for first, fifty cents for second, and a quarter for third. So we could make serious candy store money from being quick. Which basically made us pro athletes starting at the tender age of five. There were multiple swimming races, which were spaced out by age groups. My favorite was the race where we started chest deep, and at the blow of a horn, we had to get back to shore as fast as possible, however we could. I loved the feeling of swimming as hard as I could and then launching out of the water into a dead sprint to the finish line on the beach.

There were boating events too. We had to bring our own boat or canoe, and we always fought over who got the lightest one. We rowed different races, such as a hundred-meter dash and long-distance sprints.

Then there was the partner canoe row where pretty much none of us kids had any concept of steering, and canoes would go zigzagging down the beach with the adults laughing and cheering, cameras in hand.

In the afternoon, we would participate in the field events in the old park, which boasted a lumpy tennis court, a playground, and a basketball hoop next to a large open field. That was where all the really fun things happened. Parents would line the edge of the field in camping chairs, with coolers of drinks and otter pops nearby. There were sack races, three-legged races, egg tosses (yuck), and water balloon tosses. There was a hundred-meter sprint where we had to stick our faces in a pie tin of whipped cream, find the bubblegum buried inside, and blow a bubble to win. Last but not least was the shoe toss, which everyone in the camp participated in, including all of the parents and grandparents.

The shoe toss was quite a huge deal. Kids practiced a week out for the shoe toss, including me. I really didn't want to be the dud who flopped her shoe over her head and behind her for negative points! I'd loosen the laces of one shoe, put it perfectly on my toe, take a couple of big steps, swing my foot as if I was kicking a soccer ball, and flick that shoe as far as possible. During the event, shoes would all simultaneously fly two hundred meters into the woods.

Looking back on my childhood, I vividly remember that feeling of kicking my shoe as far as I could, joyously sprinting after it to see where it landed, then standing proudly by it as a marker, in a swirl of the fun hooting and hollering, thrilled by the friendly competition and a chance to win some more candy store money.

• • •

Although today I'm a competitive athlete who travels year-round with a rigorous training schedule, I feel so fortunate to have started out like every other kid on the street. I played outside, made friends through sports, skinned my knees a lot. I dabbled in a wide variety of youth sports and activities, and though I was never cut out to be a ballerina or pole vaulter, it wasn't for lack of trying! I wasn't made to be a one-sport athlete before I was emotionally and physically ready for that decision, and I truly believe that this saved me from a possible early burnout. I'm a person who has always been hot or cold, and if I had specialized too early in skiing, I would have run the danger of burning that passion too quickly and not letting myself grow a deep, lasting love for the sport.

I was allowed the physical and mental freedom to explore. My career as a competitive athlete actually began in my backyard when I formed my own stuntwoman Olympics. It began by cross-country skiing with my parents on the weekends and looking for saggy pink dinosaurs hidden in the trees. It began by roller skiing in the summer down to Main Street for ice cream. It began by riding bikes and jumping off cliffs with my cousins, by swinging in the trees and swimming in Lake Superior. And yes, it began by carrying a canoe.

All of these things were the foundation for my athletic career. Because of all the love, laughter, encouragement, empowerment, and patience I received from my parents and extended family, that passion for sport grew organically. In time, my competitive nature sparked and came alive. I was ready to start racing more competitively because I wanted to push myself—and not because anyone pushed me.

CHAPTER 5

THE STILLWATER WAY

April 2018. I hadn't seen the purple Nalgene water bottle in years. In the midst of unpacking some of my suitcases, bags, and a few boxes, I spied the water bottle tucked into a box in the room I'd shared with my sister at my parents' house. The bottle stopped me in my tracks. I turned it over and over in my hands, the memories of how I got it as strong as ever.

After spending the previous five months in Europe competing in World Cups, traveling to South Korea for the 2018 Winter Olympics, then going back to Europe to finish the World Cup season, I had finally returned home. I had lived out of a rolling duffel and absolutely humongous backpack for half the year, traveling by van, bus, train, and airplane as I competed in over a dozen countries. But now it was time to unpack and sort it all out. Ugh, the worst part!

The box had found its way into the mess of suitcases, bags, and boxes in front of me. I recognized the box almost instantly because I've used it to hold various mementos, worn-out old T-shirts from different sports team, and memories from my high school skiing career. Basically, this cardboard box is my high school athletic scrapbook. Super classy and organized, just my style.

The first item I found when I opened the lid was the purple Nalgene water bottle. On the front of the bottle it reads, "Goldilocks Award, J

Diggs." The bottle was an award that was given to me when I was in seventh grade by the senior girl captains from the Stillwater High School cross-country ski team. It's funny because even though I'm somehow now the owner of a gold medal, a historic, life-altering event, in holding the purple water bottle I was reminded of how much that bottle and award meant to me too. The bottle represented where my career as a competitive cross-country skier began. More important, it represented the "older girls" including me as part of their group. It represented my adoration for them, how I looked up to them and wanted to be part of that team so badly that I was ready to work my butt off to get there. It represented the camaraderie and culture that the Stillwater High School team was made of. It may look like an old and beat-up water bottle, but for me, it was a keepsake, a major part of my history.

I sat on the floor underneath the bright-yellow loft bed that I'd helped my dad measure, build, and paint, strolling down memory lane. As I reminisced, my dad popped into the doorway and asked, "How's the unpacking going?"

"Ummmm. . . . I've gotten farther than it looks, I swear. And I'm finding lots of stuff!" I said excitedly, waving the water bottle at him.

"Oh, wow, I remember that bottle." he said. "We're going to get dinner going in about an hour. Does that work?"

"Awesome," I said.

My dad left, and I sat there staring at the old box, procrastinating. My life through junior high until graduation—the good, the bad, the stressed out, and the crazy—all of it was right there inside the box. I glanced around at all the other suitcases and bags and boxes littered before me, the ones that I should be unpacking and sorting through. I also desperately fought the urge to take a nap or kick back and watch something on Netflix. I took another long look into the old box and couldn't resist going through it instead.

• • •

Ironically, I almost didn't join the cross-country team in seventh grade. Yes, that's right! Absolute madness! I'd heard that the team practiced six days a week, and my first thought was *How am I ever going to get all my homework done? When will I practice violin? I don't know if I can do six days. I mean, skiing is fun and all, but that's a big commitment.* Oh, the delicious irony. I loved skiing and doing the occasional citizens' race here and there, but I wasn't sure I wanted to start racing *all* the time. Thank goodness for my friends, who had all joined the team and convinced me to get on board, because I absolutely loved it from the first week.

Suddenly, I was surrounded by like-minded people, all excited about getting outside and improving one day at a time. I started branching out and making new friends. Somehow, with a group of friends around me, even interval repeat workouts became fun, because I had someone to high-five afterward, share the suffering with, and complain to about how sore my legs were! I learned that I really loved the feeling of sore muscles (despite also loving to whine about it, just for fun) and the "runner's high" that came after a hard workout. Oh, the euphoric feeling of the runner's high! I can't begin to describe how and why it feels so good to feel so terribly bad, but something about the adrenaline rush and the feel of endorphins flooding through tired muscles was addicting to me. I began to crave the feeling of pushing myself harder, of challenging my body.

The other cool thing about the Stillwater High School ski team was that everyone was welcome, regardless of size, strength, or previous experience. Unlike sports where some might have to wait their turn on the bench, everyone went to every workout and did every minute of it! Whereas some people might see that as a major turn for the worse (We don't get to rest? What the heck is this sport?), I saw that as pure awesomeness because I would never get bored. As I was new to the team and in seventh grade, I placed myself with the junior varsity team with about a hundred other kids. The varsity team wasn't officially selected until conference championships and the end of the ski season, and anyone with the right attitude who could keep up and wanted to train a little more seriously was welcome to train with the varsity group. This generally consisted of the top ten to fifteen girls and boys, and I wasn't sure that I was ready to venture into varsity territory. Because no matter which team we were on, we all got to start every race we wanted! At the end of the season, in Minnesota high school racing, the top seven skiers from each school would make the section team and then, hopefully, go on to the state meet. This was where the competitive racing side of the sport really started for me.

Even in the fall, when the trails were covered in muddy wet leaves and there was no sign of snow, I loved training with the JV crew for the sense of camaraderie and team bonding. In November, we'd grab our bounding poles (a little shorter than classic poles so they're easier to hike, run, and bound up hills with), cram all hundred-something of us into two big buses and head to one of the nearby parks. We'd self-seed into smaller groups by ability, and once the snow arrived we'd start skiing in these groups as well. We were fortunate enough to have all these amazing volunteer coaches as well as the head high school coaches there to run the workout and teach us proper ski technique. The team was made up of all levels, from beginners who had moved to Minnesota and never seen snow, to varsity athletes who were competing in junior national competitions in addition to the high school race calendar.

I was doing well racing with the junior varsity, but to be honest, I was less "in it to win it" than I was in it to make friends and run around outside. The desire to win races would come gradually, around the same time as the desire to score as many points for my team as possible so that we could win the meet as a school. But for now, I was thirteen years old, and I didn't have a lot of patience, and therefore I didn't have great technique, especially in classic skiing. I would try as hard as possible, but sometimes just trying hard without proper technique resulted in me flying down the trail, limbs flopping everywhere, kicking up snow with my skis. You could practically *see* the wasted energy flying in all directions!

Oh, and I was kind of a hot mess. I had glasses and braces at the same time (yeah, I know), and I often wouldn't braid my hair for a race. It was this wild, long mess of hair flying around everywhere as I skied. I looked like a crazy Viking lady barreling down the trail. I don't know why I didn't just pull my hair back in a tight ponytail. Usually I did, but I think I forgot sometimes because I was just bouncing around and so excited to race. Later in the year, a sophomore named Maddy Wendt noticed my hair flying everywhere and sat me down before the race to braid it back out of my way, saying, "Hold still for a second, this is going to make you faster!" That began a big-sister friendship where Maddy became one of my mentors and very good friends, and every race until she graduated she gave me my lucky race-day braid. At some point I had to learn to braid my own hair, but I kept up the lucky braids . . . a tradition that I continue to this day on the World Cup!

Besides the hair flying around in my face, let's take a moment to talk about the fashion aspect of skiing. I'm sure you're wondering . . . how did a girl who wore baggy track pants and cotton T-shirts reading "I finished the 5K Turkey Trot!" ever come to terms with wearing a spandex race suit, top to bottom? Well, I did not. Not for a few years, anyway. My first day of practice, I picked out a locker in the very back of the locker room, looked around, and wondered, *What's the deal with all these tights? Why would you ever wear those? Oh, but look . . . everyone's putting shorts over their tights. That's cool, I guess.* In the time-honored tradition of being an awkward teenager, I didn't really understand why I dressed the way I did, I just started wearing tights with shorts overtop to practice because everyone else did! By the time I was a junior and senior, I had finally come to accept that wearing tights *without* shorts to practice was going to be OK, but it took me a while to get there.

Once I realized that pushing my body hard in races felt good and that working to race faster and faster was something I enjoyed, I started to embrace the racing side of being part of the ski team. I started to place higher and higher on the JV results list, even winning the JV division a few times. But I got my first big break (of my entire career, you could say!) at the big conference meet, which was the lead-up to the section meets, which was where skiers qualified to go to the state high school championship. In Minnesota, high school state competitions are *everything*. And I really do mean everything! Up until last year, people were still saying to me, "Yes, yes, you've been to the Olympics and won World Championships. But you won state, right?" It's such a huge deal and a big part of the Midwest ski culture. In other words . . . if you had even a single competitive bone in your body, you desperately wanted to make state.

At our conference meet, one of the senior girls on the varsity team got sick and couldn't race. I wasn't supposed to race until the junior varsity races, which were hours later than the varsity competition. So, there I was, sitting in the lodge at Trollhaugen ski area eating a

Snickers bar and cheese puffs (the concept of performance nutrition hadn't quite sunk in yet). Then Kris Hansen, the Stillwater high school varsity coach—who I didn't know super well at this point—walked into the chalet and found me sitting on the floor, eating snacks.

"Hey, Jessie," Hansen said. "Ashley's sick, do you want to race varsity today?"

"Yes!" I blurted out through a mouthful of Snickers. Then I threw the bar down to show my determination.

"Great! Well, the race starts in ten minutes . . . so, you've got to warm up now! Go get jogging," Hansen said.

I stood up, squirmed into my faded yellow and black Salomon "bumblebee" boots and sprinted out of the chalet. "What should I do to warm up? Should I test my skis?" I asked Bill Simpson, our longtime coach of the high school team and the absolute legend in charge of junior varsity. He was applying wax to my skis on a bench in the parking lot. "Nope! No time, just keep running, you'll be fine!" he told me as I started running circles around the parking lot. I pulled up to the start line, and Bob Hagstrom, one of our volunteer coaches known for always wearing his big red snowsuit, gently wrapped a blanket around my little shoulders to keep me warm before the start. It was an individual-start race, so I sprinted away from the start line by myself, separated by thirty seconds from the person in front of me, and by thirty seconds from the next starter. There I was, in my first varsity race! I was so excited! I was just a little seventh grader going up against juniors and seniors in high school, but I had been skiing my whole life, and I placed fifth in the varsity 5K skate race. Honestly, to me this is more a testament to the miracle that is a young athlete's ability to get off the couch, barely warm up, and then throw herself into an all-out effort. If I did that today, *especially* after eating cheese puffs, you'd have a different outcome. After the meet, the first report I had ever gotten from a coach about my skiing ability summed it all up.

Kris Hansen said, "Jessie's got some serious energy, really sloppy technique, but she's got something."

It felt like being called up to the big leagues. Here were all the older girls whom I had idolized and somehow feared at the same time because they were so sophisticated. To a seventh grader, a senior looks very, very put together and mature. As it happened, these students were exceptional young women who really were standouts in every way, furthering my natural idolization of them. As I lined up to race that first varsity meet, I thought, *Oh my gosh, these are such strong women . . . I will never be like that.* But I was so excited to compete, and for the first time I had the chance to contribute points to the team score. The top four varsity racers' points are added into a school's total points, but all seven racers displace on the results sheet, so every person I could pass really counted for something. So, I just went for it.

Remember my earlier reservations about wearing spandex head to toe? Those vanished the moment I was handed one of the Stillwater varsity team's spandex race uniforms. I was so amazed that I got to wear the fancy-pants spandex race suit! It was red and black . . . like a superhero, or Deadpool! The suit that I was given at that moment in seventh grade I kept for my entire high school career, which worked for me because I never grew any taller. I'm humbled to write that the suit was eventually retired and is now framed in the Stillwater ski team wax cabin. Which, to my mind, is a better honor than I could have ever received from any hall of fame!

After my first varsity conference meet, I went back to my normal training sessions with the junior varsity. There was no snow that year, which was why all our races were held at Trollhaugen, a downhill ski area with a 5K cross-country race course covered by snow guns (Hello, climate change? Is that you I see coming around the corner?). Between races, we'd go back to dryland training sessions as usual. I was with my friends, running around in the muck with poles. Then Emily Ranta, one of the senior girls, came up to me.

"Hi, Jessie," Emily said.

"Yes!" I said excitedly. *Oh, my god! She knows my name!*

"We want you to come train with the varsity girls," Emily said. "Feel free to join our session tomorrow."

"Oh, OK, cool, thanks!" I said. *This is the biggest moment of my life! They want me to come train with them!* They were so open and inviting, and I became their dorky little sister. I got to train with the varsity girls for the rest of the season and the rest of my high school career.

Oh crap . . . how am I going to get to practice? The varsity team some-times drives to Trollhaugen to train on snow . . . and I can't drive!

Luckily for me, Gina Elmer, another sophomore, was incredibly kind and started picking me up from the junior high and taking me to practice and races with her. That was the year I learned the subtle art of changing into your spandex suit in the car, and grew to love country music.

For the section meet, I was the alternate for the varsity team. But Ashley got sick again—poor girl, that was tough. However, it gave me an opportunity to race with the varsity team. I did well in the race and qualified for the state meet through the skate race.

At Minnesota high school meets, there's a 5K skate race in the morn-ing, followed by a 5K classic race after a few hours break. The classic race is started pursuit style, with the winner of the skate race starting first and everyone else chasing her down, starting however many sec-onds back they finished in the morning's race. Whoever crosses the finish line first wins the combined pursuit event, although the winner of the 5K classic race might not be the same person who wins the over-all. When I was in seventh grade, you could qualify for the state meet by placing well in either skate or classic, so you'd qualify for just that event, or maybe both if you did well. Later on it was changed to quali-fying based on your overall placing, and you'd automatically race both races at the state meet. Similarly, they used to recognize a winner of the skate, a winner of the classic, and the overall winner, but that was later changed to just recognizing the winner of the overall pursuit race.

So, there I was, a seventh grader at the state finals getting to race with the big kids. I didn't race particularly fast, but I remember being so excited that it didn't matter!

At the end of every season, the Stillwater captains of the team gave out fun awards—MVP, Most Improved, and all sorts of fun things. They made up an award for me, the Goldilocks Award, because of my blonde hair flying everywhere. They called it the prodigy award as well because it was the first time that a seventh grader had made it to state. I also made the all-conference team and the section team. Normally, an ath-lete had to be in the sport for two years to letter, but they gave me one anyway, and when I walked up to receive it, my face flaming red from embarrassment at being onstage in front of everyone, I realized that I wanted to keep working as hard as it took to keep making teams.

I felt that cross-country had always been something fun I did with my family. It was our weekend thing. I loved the peace in the winter woods and the hot cocoa afterward and the yummy, warm crock-pot meals. But I was starting to recognize that I liked racing too. I was also realizing that I was good at the sport, and that brought me so much joy. Cross-country skiing was something that I could possibly find success in. I was still an awkward seventh grader, but skiing was the sport where I made friends and people appreciated me for who I was, braces, baggy track pants, shorts-over-spandex and all, and that feeling of acceptance was awesome. And that's what the purple Nalgene water bottle represents.

I was learning how much being on a team meant to me. All of those older, senior girls and boys on the varsity team could have been closed off to me. They could have easily shunned me and not wanted this little kid in their group, especially one who hadn't yet paid her dues. But they didn't do that at all. They were completely open. They brought me right in. That was the Stillwater way.

CHAPTER 6

PAIN CAVE

Having become part of a team, I was making lasting friendships and really starting to learn leadership skills. My life in sports was evolving and growing, but there were also some fierce changes internally at work, and I was developing as a racer too. A lot of that had to do with my growing tolerance for pain and for pushing past what I had previously thought of as my "limits," hard barriers that I was initially scared to approach during a race.

The first time I entered the pain cave, I was fifteen years old. It felt like all of my muscles were simultaneously melting and stiffening into rigid boards, like my very brain was melting. The pain cave is the loving nickname we crazy endurance athletes give to that special place that we go into during a competition when every inch of our body hurts. For me, it only occurs when I've pushed myself past my breaking point, typically during an entire race, on a huge hill, or in a dead sprint to the finish line. Located at the convergence of mind and body, the pain cave is an aerobic mental and physical torture chamber. A torture chamber . . . or a place of honor that few are willing to experience, depending on your point of view. For me, it's a metaphor for how I survive this intensity of physical hurting, for where I go not to escape it but to deal with the pain in my mind. My ability to suffer in it, to straddle this threshold between courage and collapse has become one of the defining characteristics of my athletic career.

I was in ninth grade and competing for Stillwater. It was a team relay in a big conference meet, and I loved relays. Absolutely adored them. And I was the anchor, so I was excited to be helping score some points for our team! Up until that point, every time I skied intervals in practice or raced, I skied really hard. Well, at least, I *thought* I had skied hard. I would say to myself, *Oh, this really hurts, but I can handle it.* I had never truly pushed myself to the breaking point. I would push myself close to it, but I never crossed it. To be honest, I think I was scared of what would happen if I seriously broke through my limits, charged ahead into unknown territory. Ski racing was supposed to be uncomfortable, and I was hurting a little, so I thought I was doing it all right, you know? Who needed to really know what lurked beyond their limits, anyway? This particular race changed all that.

We were racing against Forest Lake High School. We had been duking it out with them all year. The Forest Lake and Roseville programs were always very competitive with Stillwater, and I was so grateful for them! It was an awesome, respectful rivalry because we pushed each other to new heights. In this race, the final lap came down to Stillwater versus Forest Lake. We were down by a little bit, and as the anchor I had to pass a specific Forest Lake girl for us to win.

My coaches and teammates were talking to me as I waited to be tagged to get in the race. They repeatedly told me that I had to pass this certain girl on Forest Lake. They gave me a description so I would know which skier I needed to pass.

"Got it, pass Forest Lake skier in the green race suit. Got it," I said, my voice popping with excitement. I wasn't listening well. Oops.

I got tagged and took off, guns blazing, on a mission.

Stillwater and Forest Lake were big teams. And when I say, "big," I mean they each had around 120 kids, so each school had multiple relay teams in each race. Seconds outside the tag zone, I ran into a serious nightmare. To my dismay, Forest Lake had twenty kids racing on the course, and *all* of them were wearing the exact same green race suit.

As I raced down the course, I couldn't remember who it was that I had to pass. In front of me, all I could see was a sea of green race suits!

Some were leg three instead of leg four, but because it was only a 2.5K loop, the trail was crawling with skiers all clamoring to get around as quickly as possible. It was like trying to find Waldo in a sea of red-and-white-striped shirts.

So, I told myself that I had to pass all of them, just to be sure. Just in case.

I killed myself trying to do just that.

The second I passed one girl in a green spandex suit I would look up and see another one. Then another and another. It was a never-ending game of whack-a-mole. I kept hunting each one of them down. My inner monologue was as simple-minded as a dog playing fetch with a ball.

You have to pass Forest Lake!

I'd come up to a hill and see two more in front of me.

You still *have to pass Forest Lake!*

I ended up passing every single skier in a green suit. I was so single-mindedly focused on my task that I never paid attention to the alarm bells going off in my head telling me to slow down, or else I'd push past my limits. I knew I was in a lot of pain, but I felt that slowing down simply wasn't an option . . . not when there was another green suit just thirty feet ahead of me! I just kept pushing, and pushing, and pushing, throwing myself headlong down the track in spite of the agonizing feeling of lactic acid building up in my body. In doing so, I entered a world of pain that I had never experienced before. I had finally entered the pain cave.

I had my first out-of-body experience as I was racing the final half a kilometer. I thought I was going to die. My vision got blurry. The world suddenly had a pink tint to it, as though I was wearing rose-colored glasses. My hearing got fuzzy. There was a bonfire in my lungs, and it felt like I was breathing through the tiniest of straws. There was a bloody, acidic, metallic taste in my mouth, like sucking on a copper penny. I had stabbing, fiery pain in my legs caused by lactic acid building up. But not to fear! The longer I went, the better it got, because I started to go numb from my toes up to my knees. What a relief.

I crossed the finish line, and there was an explosion of pain like I had never felt before. During the race, I had something to focus on, but once I collapsed into the snow I could no longer ignore the desperate warning signals my body was frantically sending my brain. It's quite possible that I cried, but I can't really remember, because I was on the verge of blacking out.

I had not only passed the green suit I was *supposed* to pass, but we had won by almost a minute.

After a few minutes of frantically trying to suck air back into my lungs, I was able to stand up again and breathe normally. Although in the moment it felt like I would surely die from the effort, I realized I could push myself past the breaking point and live. As clichéd as it sounded, pain really *was* only temporary. I couldn't wait to try it again. If I could suck it up for fifteen, maybe twenty minutes during the race, I was in for the craziest endorphin rush of my entire life. More important, if I could will myself to deal with it, I could become the relay anchor I'd always dreamed of being.

After that race in ninth grade, I knew where my true breaking point was, and I discovered that I could push past it. I felt like I had been let in on a great secret, that I had slipped into a world that allowed me to go faster and harder than I ever thought was possible.

• • •

My dad was actually the first person to show me the pain cave. When I was a child, I watched and cheered as he competed in a lot of different citizens' races. He ran Grandma's Marathon in Duluth, Minnesota, and the Twin Cities Marathon, and he skied the American Birkebeiner many times. My dad wasn't winning any of these races, he was just competing for his own personal best time. He was in it for the epic challenge, the experience, the thrill of pushing his limits, and every time my dad competed, he always left it all out there on the course. My mom and I would stand on the side of the course, Mom holding a water bottle, me sprinting alongside yelling, "Goooooo, Dad! Go, Dad, go!" If I had known the word for it then, I would have announced to the world that my dad was an absolute badass.

By watching both my mom and dad train and then test their skills in races, I learned to not fear the pain that came when I pushed myself. In fact, being a little uncomfortable was simply treated as part of the process. It could be exciting, even, a way to acknowledge to yourself that you were truly pushing your limits. My young, impressionable eyes saw that all athletes have to work really hard to finish a race, and that when they did, they had the right to be extremely proud of their efforts, regardless of where they placed on the results sheet. After all, the right to be proud of a race isn't reserved only for the winner, and the person who pushed the hardest and reached far past his or her limits may not be the person standing on top of the podium. You always have the power to be the person who gives the most, who pushes the hardest. Through watching my dad, I decided I wanted to always be that person.

After watching my parents compete, I soon wanted in on the action. Put me in, coach! I began doing countless little-kid races. We have photos of me when I was five years old at my first mini Mora Vasaloppet, which was a 5K race for kids. I was scooting along on my skis, straight-legged with terrible technique, plowing ahead. My mom was behind me, cheering her heart out, "Yeah! You're doing great." She was doing it with me to cheer but also secretly making sure I didn't get overexcited, tip over, and die in a snowbank somewhere.

I scrambled and powered my way to the finish line, so pumped that I was working hard, just like my parents! I vividly remember the feeling of crossing the finish line on Main Street in Mora, Minnesota. It seemed like the whole town was out cheering us on as I skied right down the middle of the street. Church bells clanged in celebration. The crowd roared with applause. And I remember the 5K being a lot of work . . . especially for my little legs, encased in cozy snow pants caked with snow clumps. But it was unquestionably worth it. *Especially* when they stuck a shiny plastic gold medal around my neck, and I could show it off to my grandma as we baked cookies later that afternoon.

As I grew older, I would eventually inherit my dad's high tolerance for pain. I also inherited my dad's race face. Which is hilarious and, well, quite fitting. We share the same zoned-out, yet zeroed-in facial expression when we are racing hard!

I basically absorbed my dad's pain tolerance through desperately wanting to be like him. I saw the positive attitude, determination, and fortitude that he displayed when he dealt with an injury or adversity. One day, he was running in the park and was ten miles from his car when he broke his foot. My dad gutted out the ten miles back to the car. When he got home from the doctor with a boot on his foot, he told me, "Well, the doctor ordered me to stay off my broken foot. So . . . I guess I'll start swimming now." That was my dad. He just kept pushing forward, a little bit each day. It was incredible to witness as a child. He never complained once. I never heard him complain about anything, actually.

It wasn't that his injuries didn't hurt, or that he didn't experience pain in a race. They all hurt. What separated him from others was how he dealt with them. His tolerance and acceptance of the pain without complaint made him a superhero in my eyes. My dad figured out a way to keep going forward. I grew up admiring that and wanting to be just like him.

By watching my mom, I learned that when you really want something, you have to roll up your sleeves and go after it, no excuses. When I was in high school, my parents bought a franchise store of Slumberland Furniture, located in Red Wing, Minnesota (this is *totally* a plug for the Red Wing Slumberland, by the way. I'm shameless like that). My mom was the owner and in charge of getting the place up and running at speed, and she worked so incredibly hard that it left a lasting impression on me. She would work seven days a week, ten hours a day, pouring her heart into making the store a great place for her employees and the community. I would see her come home late at night, tired and exhausted after a busy day at the store, and she'd still find the energy to make me laugh and check the spelling on my homework, help Mackenzie with her projects, and watch her practice her newest dance routine. Then she'd be up early the next morning, ready to go back at it all over again.

I saw how hard my mom worked, and how even when she was tired, she'd find a reserve of energy to get shit done when it needed to be done. She was (and is) an absolute superhero in my eyes, and I decided at a young age that if I could have even half of her work ethic, then I'd probably do great in the game of life. I wanted to be just like her, working hard at something that I love. Through these traits and many others, both my parents gave me all the tools that I would need to become the best cross-country skier that I could be.

• • •

At the end of almost all my races, you'll see me collapse to the ground. This isn't for show or because I love having the snow melt into my suit and make me wet and cold later on. It's because I can't stand up. When I've pushed myself that hard, laying it all out there in the final kilometer coming in to the finish, it's as though a switch flips in my brain the second I cross the line, saying, *Now* you can finally rest! Stop moving! And just like that, I'm down, like a marionette with its strings cut.

But every time, eventually, all of that pain passes. Thirty seconds and suddenly my breathing starts to slow from its frantic gasps to a steady intake of air. I start to calm down and collect myself. Then a syrupy and warm wave of endorphins and euphoria washes through me, and I'll sometimes have the sensation of floating. In that moment, nothing can ruin my day. Even if I didn't have a good race and I'm disappointed, it's hard to feel bummed when I have a happy drug coursing through me.

Sometime later, though, reality sets back in. Hours after the race, my body will feel like it has been liquified. My muscles turn into jelly. My legs feel weird, and my stomach aches. I'll be walking around on wobbly sea legs, constantly on the verge of tripping over nothing, hungry but not really feeling like eating.

OK, kids, now who wants to become a cross-country skier?

It's so awesome, I swear. You'll love it. Promise!

CHAPTER 7

THE GREAT BALANCING ACT

Tucked into the side of that same box in my bedroom was a post-card from West Yellowstone. It was bent with a few creases on it, bought yet never mailed, serving as a little memento of my first trip to West Yellowstone with the Stillwater team. I remember how excited I was, looking forward to this trip for weeks, thrilled to get a chance to basically have a huge sleepover party with all my best friends (and go skiing too, I guess).

I was in tenth grade when our varsity coach Kris Hansen started organizing this annual training and team-bonding trip. We'd go during fall break so we could have five days to make the most of it. We weren't the only team with this great idea. The Yellowstone Ski Festival was a gathering of teams traveling there to train on early-season snow from all over the country, from high school to college and professional teams. We'd go to the expo and collect posters of our favorite athletes from different ski brands that had set up booths showing off the latest equipment and giving away posters and autograph cards of the nation's top athletes, and my posters of Liz Stephen, Andy Newell, Kikkan Randall, and Kris Freeman still adorn the walls of our family's wax room.

As fun as poster collecting was, we were there to ski, and every day we would log hours and hours of skiing on the vast trail system. It was a great way to kick-start our team fitness and technique at the start of each season, but even more important, it was amazing team bonding: a five-day sleepover in which we would reconnect, get to know new team members better, and gel as a group.

We'd ski for three hours in the morning and come back and eat everything in sight. Then we'd go out and ski again in the afternoon, switching techniques and doing some drills. At night, we'd watch movies together and eat popcorn and fall asleep spread out across the floor of our rental house, bonding over the shared experiences of sore muscles, fatigue, skiing through the woods in awe of the beautiful trails, and agreeing that Ryan Reynolds was the hottest actor alive. I was inspired by skiing somewhere new and also by seeing some of the best skiers in the country up close. For the first time, I got to watch the elite athletes who were going to be racing the SuperTour races. And I got the opportunity to see exactly how hard they trained and how professional they were.

• • •

I pull an old high-school report card from the box, and it reminds me of just how hard it was to balance my schoolwork with my increasingly busy schedule of competitive skiing. Behind the report card I see the buildup of anxiety, stress, and worry that I wasn't ever going to get it all done. Because of my rising skiing career on both local and national levels, I was gone from school for long stretches, missing sixty days of school my senior year. I would disappear from school for one to two weeks here and there, always for a training camp or a competition such as the Junior World Championships, Junior National Championships, and Senior Nationals. I missed so much school that I was often thought to be a new student who had transferred in midterm, an easy mistake for fellow students to make in a school with over eight hundred kids in a graduating class.

The report card does not just represent how hard I worked as a student. It also represents how hard my teachers worked to make it possible for me to pursue my cross-country skiing. My AP chemistry teacher, Miss Swanson, had just had a baby, but she would get a babysitter and open the lab at six in the morning so I could do my lab when I had missed it. My AP calculus teacher, Miss Gunvalson, saved me too! The last month of school I had mono and couldn't go to my final competitions of the year. I was a mess mentally and physically, as my poor body just couldn't keep up and I desperately needed to pass my AP exam to make all this hard work worth it. Miss Gunvalson opened her classroom an hour before school so I could come in every day for a month to get tutored, catch up, and figure out the material, which was extremely hard for me. Mr. Weaver always went above and beyond to make AP biology exciting and applicable to real life. In deer hunting season, we'd all get to see firsthand a dissection of an animal slightly larger than the cookie-cutter formaldehyde cat! He also understood my crazy schedule and was willing to work around it with me. Mrs. Stippel was an English-teaching goddess who not only granted me the flexibility to turn in my papers from the road but challenged me to keep writing at a higher and higher level. She always wanted to know if I'd kicked ass like I wanted to in skiing and took a genuine interest in me as a person, which made me feel supported in my quest to balance it all. I had so many teachers who played extremely positive roles in my life that I can't list them all here, but the overarching theme was that instead of checking out on me when I presented my "I'm going to miss a week of school" slip to them, they would say, "OK, this is going to be a lot of hard work, but you can do this. Here's how you can turn the work in." I can't thank them enough.

By my junior year, I realized how much school I was likely to miss if I qualified for all the international races I was eyeing. I started looking into how I could finagle my schedule so that I would have more time to train and ski. The summer after my junior year I took online government and economics classes, allowing me more freedom my senior year.

I would also go to a soundproof music room in the music hallway to study before school. I would lock myself in and work on homework, or I would practice violin. That was the goal anyway. But some mornings, I'd be so tired from waking up at five thirty in the morning to train that I would sit down, prop my head on my elbow, and fall asleep while trying to read my biology textbook . . . and sometimes drool on the textbook. Mr. Lindsey, the band director, would walk down the hallway, look in the window, and say, "What? Diggins is asleep again?" Or I would get woken up by the bell and have to run to my next class with crusty sleep in my eyes, crease lines all over my face, and homework still left to do.

• • •

At the bottom of the box is a pair of plastic neon sunglasses, a memento from when we won the state title my senior year in 2010. The last race of my Minnesota high school career was epic and one of the closest finishes in Minnesota high school history. I had missed competing in the state championship my junior year because I had qualified to compete in the Junior World Championships in France for Team USA. Anne Hart from St. Paul Academy won the state championship that year, and she was so amazing. During my senior year, Annie and I began a friendship that would last our entire careers when we competed together at the Junior World Championships in Germany. But when we got back to Minnesota, we had to compete against each other in the Minnesota state championship. There was this big imagined rivalry, but privately we found it hilarious and high-fived each other about it.

The state championship took the combined time of the 5K skate and the 5K classic. I was really strong in the skate portion (thanks, Dad, for teaching me!), and it gave me a fifteen-second lead heading into the last event—Annie's strongest. As the race went on, I knew that lead would not last, because Annie was really coming on strong. She caught up to me within 3 kilometers, and I hung on for dear life. We were both digging as hard as we could. With the finish line in sight, I swung out from behind her on her left side. I dug deep and then dug a little deeper. We were ski to ski, not giving an inch to each other. Two state champions going for the finish line in a dead sprint. In the last few meters, I could feel my entire body flooding, but I kept double poling at a furious pace. In an instant, I took the lead and won by a single ski length. I ended my high school career with a state championship, but the hug I got from Annie at the finish line meant just as much.

Although the state titles were cool, it was the camaraderie of the team that made it so special. We were learning how to race, but most important, we were learning how to have fun, be great teammates, and be leaders as we got older. Every year we piled into dorm rooms for our Giants Ridge training camp for three days of crazy workouts, late-night sledding on greasy pizza boxes, hallway dance parties, and crazy night sprints under the stadium lights. Every week of training during the year involved some practical jokes, some hugs, and some heartfelt team-bonding moments.

It was bittersweet my last year, as I was certain that nothing was going to ever feel this special, that nothing could come close to this team and experience. And of course, I was proved wrong. The national team was not more or less amazing, it was just as different and unique. I still found that sense of camaraderie, fun, and belonging to the group. But the culture that Stillwater team had was truly special, and it really cemented my love for skiing.

• • •

The jump rope that I kept in the box is a clear reminder of my grueling morning workouts my senior year. Twice a week in the mornings before school I would wake up early, drive to the school gym, and do strength training. Each workout began with jumping rope to wake me up, then I moved to weights and exercises. I'd been to a few national-level camps and training with some professional teams, and I saw that they were lifting weights, so I felt that I should start doing that too.

Kris had written my training plan for me, which was huge. She was an amazing part of my high school career because she helped me balance being a skier and a person. Beyond skiing, we became good friends, and I found in her a compassionate and caring mentor. When I graduated, we continued to grow our friendship. Kris would join me on early morning training sessions, helping me with technique and taking video for me to review later. Our favorite thing was the long Sunday morning "overdistance," or OD, skis that we shared, because it was our time to catch up on everything. We still get together for workouts every time I'm in Minnesota.

Sometimes sport brings you to the most incredible people and helps you make connections and friendships that last a lifetime, and I'm so grateful to skiing for bringing me to Kris. She became my coach but also my friend, mentor, ski mom, and a person I could share every-thing with as we skied all over the roads in Afton. She's one of the first people I told when I started to write this book, and I ask for her advice on everything from writing to gardening to travel plans. It's impossible for me to accurately describe the depth of my admiration for her as a human being, but having her and her family in my life is a total ray of sunshine.

Besides helping me balance missing school to go to all my national and international competitions, Kris helped me figure out how to be at every high school event I possibly could. I missed very few high school practices and races, because it was so important to me to be part of the team. These were my people, my "ski family," and I didn't want to miss a moment of it. Kris helped me navigate that space so I could always be a part of the team and be there for my teammates. She never made me feel like I had to choose between the skiing and normal high school kid stuff. She always said, "Let's help you do both and love it."

I wanted her help all the time, trying to figure out how to balance my life. I also wanted her help in taking the next step forward with my training, as I was getting more and more serious about ski racing. So, she helped by writing me a personalized, efficient training program that I used daily to maximize my time. She was also the first person who impressed upon me the importance of keeping a training log, so I could look back and see what I had done for training and start looking for patterns of what was working best for me, since no two bodies respond to training the same way.

Perhaps most important, Kris gave me my first introduction to sports psychology, long before I even knew that that's what it was! She simply taught me early in my career that it wasn't the *result* that defined my race, it was *how* I raced that mattered and should dictate whether it was a "good" race for me. After every race, before I checked the results, Kris had me mentally list three things I did well during that race (for example, maybe I remembered to take an extra push over the top of a hill to gain speed, or maybe I had used my arms and lat muscles really well in my climbing technique), and list three things I could improve on for next time. I learned to understand that no race was either fully "good" or "bad," but that in every race there was something to be learned and improved upon. Simultaneously, there were always going to be things I did well that I needed to recognize so I could repeat them and focus on the positive.

With Kris's help, I started to improve my mental training, and I started to get fitter and stronger in the off-season by working her plan in the mornings before school. Stillwater High School has since been remodeled, and it now has an incredible state-of-the-art gym. But back then the weight room was kind of a dingy space that smelled like football-pad sweat, and it was, honestly, disgusting. It felt like one of those training sessions in the movie *Rocky*. I loved it.

Most mornings, I'd be the only person in the weight room. Instead of feeling lonely or like I was sacrificing so much to be working so hard, I was psyched because, finally, I could choose the music! It was never a "poor me, this is so tough" attitude, or even a "wow, I'm so hardcore, I'm working so hard" thing for me. It was simply a "I'm checking this workout off my list, so I can get stronger and improve" mentality, and when I was the only one in the room, I could dance and boogie around to the music between sets as much as my heart desired! Sometimes the principal would come in and lift weights too. I would be trying my best and doing all these weird skier jumps and weight-training exercises that don't look normal, and across the room there was the principal doing bench presses. He was always supportive but did his own thing, which I appreciated because I didn't want to feel self-conscious about all the hops and jumps I was doing.

• • •

The training was working well, and I was winning almost every race I entered. Kris would look for ways for me to keep challenging myself, so one day I raced as part of the boys field. We were having a friendly skiathlon race with two other schools, which is where skiers do the first half of the race classic style and then switch to skate gear and skate the second half of the race. I definitely had an advantage because I had done this race format before, at World Juniors. But, you know, I had a lot less testosterone than the boys, so I figured we were even. As we lined up, I heard whispering right behind me: "Break her poles" . . . "No, dude, I'll break them once we round the corner." I took off as hard as I could, reasoning that they could break my poles only *if* they could catch me. I crossed the finish line forty-five seconds ahead of the first boy. I'm still grateful for their rough style of racing, because nothing could have better prepared me for the anything-goes feel of the World Cup. Unfortunately, I was never allowed to race with the boys again, because no other coaches were willing to crush their boys' egos.

At that point, I had gone to the junior national camps, where all the nation's top skiers are invited to train and compete together. I went from being a big fish in a small pond straight into a large pond overflowing with big fish. Really shiny, pretty fish, too, that looked a lot more sophisticated and put together than my frumpy, little goldfish self! I quickly learned how nice they were, though, and started to make strong friendships that would last me through my career, and it was a wonderful feeling to have friends around the country. All the girls at the junior national level were such amazing skiers and were so talented. When I won a few junior national races at fifteen years old, it was surreal. That was the first time that my dad said that I had "some magic." That was nice to hear, of course. But I took it with a grain of salt. Plus, he's my dad . . . he's *supposed* to be biased!

At national-level camps, I realized quite clearly that I had to keep working really, *really* hard to keep pace with all the talented skiers in the country. There was no time for ego, no place to rest on my achievements. I trained like I had never won anything in my life.

I learned that there were a lot of girls who were better technical skiers than I was. Many were more gifted than I was, and some of them were faster. But I also learned that I couldn't control any of that. I couldn't control what others were doing. What I could control was how hard I worked. I made a pledge to myself that nothing was going to hold me back in the gym and in training. I was willing to commit to the minutes, hours, days, and months that it took for me to get stronger. I made a commitment to be coachable, a good teammate, and the hardest worker. I was going to commit everything I had and follow the training program. That's what I could control, so that's what I did.

CHAPTER 8

TO SKI OR NOT TO SKI

The weight of all of the time I spent training, studying, competing, and traveling can be measured by the little planner and organizer where I scribbled out my days and weeks toward the end of high school. There was just so much information to juggle, and it seemed like every minute of every day was planned out. I also had a separate training log for all the hours I spent in the gym, roller skiing, and on the snow. I had to balance my monthly race schedule on top of training, and there were cross-country skiing camps to prepare for as well that required a labyrinth of travel accommodations, flight departures, and arrivals. Looking back, I wonder how I got it all done.

I wonder how *any* high school student gets it done. There's so much pressure to have perfect college applications, all the right extracurriculars, and great grades while participating in clubs and sports. I loved all the various activities I was involved in, but there simply wasn't enough time to devote to each one. I sure tried to overpack my schedule though. It makes sense that a few times per year I'd inevitably have a mini meltdown where my mom would find me at the kitchen counter, sobbing on top of my planner, paralyzed by my own stress and anxiety over getting it all done. Let me tell you, the stress and pressure I felt as an Olympic medal hopeful paled in comparison to the crippling anxiety

I felt as a high school senior trying to balance skiing with school and everything else.

Those miniature panic attacks definitely served a larger purpose. They helped me come to the conclusion that I couldn't keep up the act, that I couldn't continue to pursue so many different areas of life at full throttle. I wasn't able to fully realize my potential in every area that I reached toward, but I wasn't OK with backing off from anything. I was a very "all or nothing" personality, and when I thought about what I wanted to put it all toward, it came straight back to skiing, every time. This self-reflection helped me realize something big: I didn't want to go immediately to college after I graduated from high school. I wanted to take a gap year and see if I could ski full-time and become a professional. A year to see what I could accomplish when I wasn't juggling so many different things. To see how fast I could race when I wasn't having meltdowns from overreaching and overextending all the time. I loved skiing to the extent that I wanted to pursue it as a career, and I loved the competitive side of racing so much that I knew I didn't want to just make a World Championships team someday—I wanted to stand on the podium. At the time, I remember looking at my planner and seeing all the dates and times and months and realizing that trying to balance a full collegiate schedule with a full training schedule while getting the sleep I needed every night was simply not going to work. Something had to give. I wanted a full basket of one thing, not half baskets of two separate things. I needed to put college on hold.

My parents believed in me and my decision, but they didn't just say, "OK, sweetie, follow your dreams!" No, first they sat me down and asked to see the road map, the path I was going to lay out to take me to my dreams. There had to be goals, steps to take along the way, a solid plan—and an even more solid plan B. If I was going to ski full-time, I had to figure out a plan for how to fund my career. My parents were going to help me put together sponsor pitches and make the connections needed to pitch my dream to companies looking to partner with athletes, but there were hours and hours of filling out grant applications, fundraising, and rejections ahead of me. My parents supported my dream, but they said I would have one year to live at home and then I needed to have a solid funding foundation, because their daughter was *not* going to be "thirty and living in the basement, thanks very much."

"We'll help you get on your feet, but after a year you need to make this your career if skiing's what you want to do," they promised. I'm forever grateful that they said that, because it taught me early on how to work with sponsors, create my own brand, and start marketing myself. Throughout my career I have received so much support, both financial and emotional, from the community around me, but it all started right there in our kitchen.

As college was my (very strong!) fallback plan, I started looking at universities, deciding where I wanted to apply based on the ski team they had and the training opportunities they offered. Eventually, I settled on Northern Michigan University, or NMU, for its ski team and the feel of the campus. I had also been offered a generous academic scholarship from them, which made the choice even easier, as between that and skiing I wouldn't have to pay a single cent for school. I figured I'd be going only if skiing wasn't working out for me at the highest level or if I didn't enjoy professional racing, so I wanted the biggest part of my scholarship to be academic-based to take the pressure off ski racing, should I choose to go to school.

The plan was to take off the year following my high school graduation, join a professional ski team, and race around the country with them while declining any money I might win to preserve my NCAA status and keep the university option open. It seemed a foolproof plan, and we all felt good about it. Interestingly, although my own parents trusted the direction I was going and many of my teachers at school were excited for me, I had to endure the sideways glances and the "Oh, *really,* you're not going right to college?" judgmental speeches from strangers and other people's parents. I realized then that I grew up in awesome but cookie-cutter neighborhoods, where all teenagers are expected to go the same route, want the same things, and follow "the path." My announcement that I was taking out the machete and cutting my own path wasn't widely accepted, so I didn't announce my plans loudly! In any case, the U.S. Ski Team coaches had told me off the record that I'd been doing great and was expected to be nominated to their development team, so although I had my plan B, I was forging ahead, dead set on plan A working out.

That is, until my faith got rocked just a few weeks before graduation, when the U.S. Ski Team got much of their funding cut after the 2010 Olympics. Instead of letting me know, they never responded. So when I was making decisions about whether it was worth it to pursue skiing full-time, I was waiting on this potential nomination and all the funding benefits it came with. I finally called one of the national team coaches, and it took all the guts I possessed to make that call to ask where I stood on being named to the development team. His response was that I needed to "make my own decisions and do what I needed to do," because there wasn't going to be a development team that year, and they didn't know when a development team would be funded in the future. My mom still remembers me hanging up the phone and breaking down and crying hard, as she hadn't seen me do that very often. I felt like all my dreams had come crashing down and I hadn't been given any hope for what I might have in the future. That feeling of not being good enough fed right into my dangerous desire to be perfect all the time. Instead of blaming budget cuts, I blamed myself for not making the team. *If I had just been better, had raced faster, had won high school meets by two minutes instead of one minute, maybe I would have made it.*

The point is, few people get the straight line forward. Many people looking back on my career assume it was easy for me and that I just leapfrogged my way from one lily pad to another until I reached that pot of gold under the rainbow . . . but it wasn't exactly like that.

Back then, with nothing promised, I was left with me and my determination to do this no matter what. I still decided to ski and shoot for the moon. My parents gave me the freedom to make the decision, but it was still my choice to make, and they never pushed me one way or the other. But after the ski team's handling of the situation that spring and the lack of funding opportunities, my parents found it harder to feel good about what skiing could offer me in the United States. I made the leap not only with no real safety net but with what appeared to be a ripped and broken net below me.

As it turned out, that next year the national team would get more organized, be better funded, and revamp their development side of the program, and they would in fact add me along with a number of other young athletes to the team. But I had no way of knowing at the time how it would work out, or that I even had the ability to make it, when I was making those important choices coming out of high school.

I decided I wanted to blaze ahead with my plan to pursue skiing to the best of my ability, national team nomination be damned. I got accepted to NMU and deferred for a year, and everyone was on board with this plan. I realized that at the end of the day, pursuing excellence in ski racing was incredibly satisfying and fulfilling for me, and I knew I would never be happy unless I had truly tested my limits and seen how far I could take it. And I still had belief and support from my parents and little sister, the people who mattered most in the world to me.

"If you want to take your skiing to the World Cup level, I believe you can do that. If you want to take your skiing to the Olympics, I believe you can do that. And if you want to win them someday, I also believe you can do that," my dad told me. "I have no doubt that you have what it takes, and the work ethic to make it happen."

Love and support from the people closest to you are powerful things indeed.

CHAPTER 9

SLOW SPIRAL

During my senior year at Stillwater High, it looked like I had everything going for me. On the outside, school and sports and dating were going great. But on the inside, it was a whole different story. I was carrying a dark secret with me. By the end of my senior year and into the summer this secret, left to its own devices, might have killed me.

In my senior year of high school, I was trying so hard to be perfect, with that type A personality of mine. I was getting straight As, taking multiple AP courses, getting college credits, and taking honors classes. I had a great group of friends. My cross-country skiing was really taking off, and by my senior year, I was winning races by around a minute.

My family life was amazing. My parents supported me in everything I did. They were so proud of my good grades. But they never pressured me into any of it. It was never like, "Let me see your grades" or "You have to do this!" If I was happy with my grades and skiing and with my level of effort and commitment, then they were happy too.

• • •

I had everything in the world going for me and nothing to complain about. Which is why when I started to struggle with an eating disorder, I felt such shame. Why did I have this problem? I didn't have any reason to have an eating disorder (so I thought). But eating disorders don't discriminate. They can show up in anyone. Skinny teenage girls represent only 10 percent of eating disorder victims. Boys can have eating disorders. Old people, middle-aged people, young people starting at eight years old, and people from every religion and every skin color can struggle with eating disorders. It can be hard for friends and family to help when the stigma is "only skinny white teenage girls deal with this."

Bulimia crept into my life underneath all of my success in skiing and school. It was a silent disease that no one at home, at school, or on the ski team saw coming.

During my senior year of high school, I was putting a lot of pressure on myself. Everything that I did needed to be all or nothing, 100 percent of the time. Which I now know is unrealistic! But at the time, I felt that I could give a 100 percent effort in everything I did . . . while doing everything under the sun.

School got out around two fifteen, and then I would train with the Stillwater ski team. After being gone all day, I would arrive home and eat a huge snack because the workout would make me so hungry. But then I would feel bad about eating so much and go for an extra run. In my mind, I felt that I had justified my "extra" eating by training more.

In hindsight, the snack I ate wasn't more than I should have been eating, not even close. I was a growing girl in high school and an endurance athlete. I knew that after training, I needed to give my body both carbohydrates and protein so that my muscles could rebuild. So a bowl of grain cereal with a banana was something that my body needed to refuel and rebuild! But somewhere in my mind, a voice was telling me that I couldn't let myself sit still with "all that food" inside me, even if rationally I knew I needed it to survive. It made me feel icky inside, and I couldn't stand myself. So I'd go running. This in itself was disordered eating behavior, but I didn't realize it at the time. I just thought I was trying to be a really fast athlete. That second workout would make me hungry all over again. Then I would make something much less healthy—like cookies—and eat a bunch of cookie dough. Again, that's what kids do. But I would feel bad about it. Someone else might have been able to just shrug it off: you're a high school kid. You're working out. You're still growing. You need calories, and that's fine. But me? I would spiral into guilt and feel that I was now a bad person and poor athlete because of what I had eaten. I didn't realize that attaching such strong emotions to food and seeing it as "good" or "bad" were early warning signs of an eating disorder.

What also freaked me out was my changing body. A teenage girl goes through puberty at age twelve to fourteen—everyone knows this. And yep, the stress, the teenage angst comes in like a storm. Then you kind of settle into your rhythm. You're still growing taller, and you get boobs and hips and stuff. But then girls go through a sort of second round of puberty when they're eighteen to twenty and put on a little more weight. Most women I've talked to have acknowledged that this same scenario happened to them. Young girls go through this second round of puberty, and it's a normal thing (although it kind of sucks, as your perception of yourself and your body shifts). But it freaked me out. It was scary to gain a little bit of weight. I gained just ten pounds, not a crazy amount. I'm sure that some of it was fat, but also some of it was muscle, as I'd been starting to strength train in the gym. And hey, wasn't that the whole goal? Build some muscle? I was OK with the *idea* of it, but when the muscle actually came, I was suddenly *not* OK with it. What's really heartbreaking is that now when I look back at photos of my senior year, I see a totally normal-looking, strong, athletic girl. I felt like I was way too heavy and not fast enough, but I looked like any other athletic kid. I never saw myself clearly, not even close.

I used to have a pretty skinny frame in my early years on the Stillwater team, and I was cut straight up and down, without any curves. I'd heard the older girls in track and field talking about how they used to be so fast in ninth grade, before they grew hips and boobs, and how they could never get back to the times they used to run. I never wanted hips that would slow me down, and my eating disordered brain processed the information as "hips, boobs, fat . . . that will all make me slow and tank my skiing career." I knew that eventually I wouldn't have a skinny, little-boy frame anymore. But as an endurance athlete and as a perfectionist I felt it wasn't right. I wasn't worried about looking normal or even having a healthy body so I'd be able to have children someday if I wanted. All I could see was the extra weight that I thought was going to ruin my career. And to be clear, what I thought of as extra was actually what made me healthy. My definition of a perfect lean athlete was an emaciated runner's body. I had no realistic idea of where my body was supposed to be anymore, and I thought of myself as completely over-weight even when I was exactly healthy. Those ten "extra" pounds car-ried a much heavier weight in my mind, and they began to lead me down a dark and scary path.

I'd get stressed out about being lean, so I trained all the time. But these extra workouts would only make me hungrier. The stress would compound, and it would make me eat too much, and then I'd lace up my running shoes and head out the door again. All of this was happen-ing the second half of my senior year. At this point, I was compulsively exercising and had begun to form a terrible relationship with food, but I hadn't yet thrown up.

• • •

Near the end of my senior year, I began a slow spiral. My school life, skiing, puberty, and my disordered eating twisted together in a really bad way. All these outside stresses in my life that I had put upon myself began to build up inside of me. I was taking one too many AP classes. The demands of violin training were there. I was becoming a nation-ally recognized skier. The ten pounds or so that I gained over the year became an anchor, a weight that pulled me into this mental and physi-cal spiral. I knew that I couldn't directly control how fast I raced against the best in the nation. I might make a few mistakes while playing in orchestra, might miss a point here or there on an AP test. But maybe, just maybe, I could be in control of my body. Get skinny? Sure. That's one thing I *could* do.

I wanted to be really, really good at skiing, and I believed that to do that, I needed to have a super-lean body. I was now following FIS World Cup Skiing closely. Among all the skiers from different countries, there was every sort of body shape. But that's not what I saw. It appeared to my impressionable teenage-girl eyes that all of the popular athletes and champions who won the medals were very lean. Now, this wasn't true of course; athletes of every size and shape were, in fact, winning races. But it was incredibly easy for me to think that I had to be lean to compete, to focus in on that one fact that seemed so easy to control compared to everything else. I thought that to be successful as a skier, I needed to have no body fat. This misconception was the starting point where my life began to spiral.

You can't give someone an eating disorder, and you can't get one from simply wanting to be skinny. As the saying goes, "Genetics loads the gun, environment pulls the trigger." Eating disorders are a mental illness, and they're not a choice or a behavior issue. I was already programmed to be likely to develop an eating disorder, and the desire to be lean for skiing was just the trigger that pushed me over the edge. It would begin with the desire to be skinny for skiing, and as a coping mechanism for stress and all the uncontrollable factors in my life. But once my eating disorder grew, it began to take on a life of its own, and it slowly began to control mine.

Of course, I didn't know all of this back then. I just thought I wanted to be a better athlete! Over time, though, I grew to think that something was wrong with me and I had a behavior issue. The entire time, I thought it was my fault. It would take years before I could actually forgive myself and see my eating disorder the same way I would see having cancer or a broken leg.

My mom could see the first spins that I took in my spiral. She knew something was off. This was long before my eating disorder really started to control my life. I had had a minor breakdown over trying to finish all my school projects and study for all my tests. So, one day my mom sat me down to talk about it.

"You know, I've noticed that you've been kind of stressed out with school," my mom said to me as we sat in our kitchen, drinking tea. Sunlight poured in from the wall of windows on the west side of our house. It was a perfect, cozy place to talk.

"Oh my God, I signed up for too many classes," I blurted out. For a brief moment, I felt the spiral slow just a little.

"OK, well, let's prioritize," my mom said kindly. My mom was trying to help me, walking me through it. "What do you have to get done? What projects must be done? And can you let the rest go? Could you drop a class?"

"No way, I have to do everything," I said, feeling the current of the spiral tugging me back in. "I can't give any of it up!"

My mom calmly said, "I've noticed you've been training a lot and under a lot of stress. You'll have a big snack and then go out for an extra run. Jessie, I'm kind of nervous about where this is leading."

My mom saw the signs that an eating disorder was growing. But in that moment, I believed eating disorders only happened to *other* people. I didn't know who those people were. But it certainly wasn't me! I was an honor roll student, good kid, and an athlete. I told myself, what kind of person doesn't have the self-control to not eat too much? I also believed that I could be perfect at everything else if I just tried hard enough. I believed that if I did, in fact, have an eating disorder . . . which I certainly did not . . . that I could be perfect at fixing that too. I told myself that I just wouldn't eat so much (and by that, I meant that I'd effectively starve myself) and then I wouldn't have to go for an extra run. I didn't want to hear my mom's doubt and worries.

"No, Mom, I'm fine," I told her.

"OK. I just want you to know that you don't need to do that. You don't have to go for a run every time you eat," she said, reaching out to hold my hand. She was supportive and said all the right things. But I began to feel a little guilt because I thought that I had let her down. I felt awful for making my mom worry so much, especially since I had been a perfect child up until that point.

I was totally in denial that I was using disordered eating. I was still winning all my ski races. I was in tremendous shape. But I would constantly feel bad about my body image. I felt icky in my own skin. I didn't feel pretty. I didn't feel sexy. I was ashamed of my muscles. I was ashamed that I wasn't super lean. I was just ashamed of it all. The shame was now a living thing that swirled around inside me. Sadly, I didn't do anything about it. The spiral just built up inside my brain and was gaining speed with every day. I would "overeat" and feel bad about it and then exercise more and then eat again and feel bad all over again.

Another big issue for me surfaced at this time too. It gave the eating disorder spiral the fuel it needed to finally take over. I was starting to feel off during training in the week leading up to the Minnesota state ski meet. I was feeling quite awful and depleted. Slow. Sluggish. I chalked it up to being too fat to be fast anymore (I wasn't very nice to myself back then). But I rallied my strength, dug as deep as I usually could when faced with adversity, and barely eked out a victory.

After the race, my lethargic feelings got worse. I was eventually diagnosed with mono nearing the first week of March. I had qualified for junior nationals, which was a highlight. But I had mono and obviously couldn't go. This was supposed to be another year for me to go win some more titles and get my name cemented in the national program. All my friends were going to junior nationals, and I was left behind. I was emotionally gutted. These emotions all came pouring out to an unsuspecting police officer when I got pulled over for rolling a stop sign the same day I found out I had mono. The poor guy never saw the tears coming. But he panicked and let me go with only a warning, frantically saying, "And you don't even have to tell your parents! Just please stop crying!" I cried harder. I felt like I deserved the ticket.

Winter became spring, and the end of the school year was close. At this point, I knew that I wanted to defer a year of college and try to become a professional skier, but I couldn't exercise, because of the mono. If I couldn't exercise, I couldn't become a lean athlete. If I couldn't be lean, then I couldn't be a top skier. If I couldn't be an athlete, how could I ever deal with all the stress in my life? So, I ate my stress and put on another pound or two, and I began to lose control of what "normal" felt like. I suddenly couldn't remember a single thing I liked about my body. Near graduation, a moment that was supposed to be one of great celebration, I was happy on the outside. But things were coming to a head.

• • •

A week after I graduated from high school, I made myself throw up for the first time. It made me feel empty. The act of throwing up hollowed me out emotionally as well as physically, and honestly, it felt like a huge relief.

All of the stress that had been building and building for months— school exams, graduation, mono, training for nationals, college choice—was suddenly nowhere to be found. When I threw up, all of those bad feelings were mercifully gone, and I didn't feel anything anymore. I just felt numb. For a single moment, the spiral inside of me slowed, and I was now on solid ground. I stopped spinning. I was free from the weight of training and the expectations of continuing to be an elite-level skier and the goal to have a perfect body.

That first time I made myself throw up I was on my way to work in Red Wing, Minnesota, a forty-five-minute drive. I worked as a stock boy at my mom's business (I called myself a stock boy because I was the only girl and I thought I could lift as much as the guys). I helped load mattresses and things in her store. I was going to work there for the summer while I was training, and I was stoked about it. My mom was also the only person who would hire me with my crazy training schedule.

Before I left for work, my family had a big pancake breakfast at our house in Afton. I ate a lot of pancakes, and again it was not so much that most anyone else would have felt ashamed of it. But I did. Sitting there at the table with my family, I began to feel super guilty about eating a few extra pancakes, especially because they were made with white flour. I wasn't even eating "good athlete food." I couldn't remember when I had started to strongly attach labels to food, to decide whether they were good or bad, but by this point I would feel intense guilt over anything that wasn't a complex carbohydrate, protein, or veggie. Then my mom had to leave to drive to work, and I was going to leave a little bit after. I drove for fifteen minutes and began to feel these awful toxic feelings of shame stirring inside of me. They made me emotionally sick. And that's when I thought to myself, well, what if I could just make it go away? Clean the slate? What if there was a way to just start over?

I pulled into a gas station, went into the bathroom. I had heard you can just stick your finger down your throat until you throw up. I paused for a few seconds. *No! What the actual hell? You're not actually going to make yourself puke, are you?* my subconscious screamed at me. But the voice of my eating disorder came uninvited into my head, and it was screaming a whole lot louder. *You have to! You can't let that food just sit there! You're gross. You're nothing. You don't even have the self-control to not eat pancakes.* I felt such intense anxiety, shame, and unrest that I couldn't think straight . . . so I did it. I stuck my finger down my throat. And I felt an instant relief that I had gotten the pancakes out of me. I felt this sort of numbness. Because when you make yourself throw up, it's a release in one sense. The voice in my head went silent.

I looked up at myself in the mirror. There were tears streaming down my cheeks, but my face was oddly calm, devoid of any emotion. Suddenly, I felt nothing. I started to understand why people are alcoholics or addicted to drugs. Because the ability to suddenly feel nothing was amazing. The ability to not have to face your emotions, to not have to feel shame or guilt or fear about the future and always wonder if you're doing the right thing, to suddenly get rid of those feelings was such a euphoric thing. But the feeling doesn't last long. I quickly began to search for that numbing feeling again and again.

I drove to work and started to feel the guilt creeping back in. I was haunted by the thought that I now had an eating disorder. Or did I? There was no denying that I made myself throw up. I thought, oh, that was bulimia. What I had just done was literally the definition of bulimia: you eat, you feel shame, and you throw up. But other people suffered from this thing, not me! I didn't really have an eating disorder . . . that was just a onetime offense. Next time, I simply wouldn't eat the pancakes, and there would be no need to throw up, I told myself.

Nobody noticed. Because why would they? Why would one of my coworkers suddenly go, hey, Jessie Diggins, the "stock boy," you have the look of someone who just ate a bunch of pancakes and felt a ton of shame and then threw them up in a gas station bathroom? It wasn't written on my face. I wasn't drunk. I wasn't high. There was no scarlet letter pinned to my uniform shirt.

I worked just like normal. I moved mattresses and boxes and furniture, and nobody noticed. At the end of my shift, I drove home past the gas station and thought, gosh, that's so embarrassing that I made myself throw up. I'll never do it again. I'm not going to be someone who has bulimia. I can't be one of those people who has an eating disorder. That happens to other people. But not me. I told myself I would never do it again.

But I didn't stop.

• • •

I had a serious problem. As the internal stress in my life continued to build, I went looking for the numbness I'd felt in the gas station bathroom. I would eat too much of this or that and think, well, I could just make it go away. I could get back to zero here. So I did.

There weren't any telltale signs that I was continuing to make myself throw up. I was not super skinny. I was still eating food. Unlike anorexia, which can sometimes be obvious when it's advanced, with bulimia you don't usually have any idea. At some point, people very close to a bulimic can often figure it out. There are signs, like the person disappearing after meals, having hair falling out more, and being vitamin deficient. But the only sign someone could see in me was in my eyes. After I threw up, my eyes would be a little bit red rimmed because it would make them water. If you throw up violently, sometimes you can burst blood vessels in your eyes. Eventually, later on, I burst a blood vessel in my eye right before a big training camp, and I had to lie and tell everyone that I'd been sick and was coughing violently or something. It was embarrassing because I was sure people would see it written on my forehead: Jessie Diggins makes herself throw up! But, just like at work, people never noticed and were just sympathetic and would say, "OK, I'm sorry you were sick."

I was a truthful kid and never lied. To this day, my eating disorder is probably the only thing I've ever lied about. You tell the white lie; oh, thank you, I love the present, that was exactly what I wanted for my birthday. But my eating disorder made me really, truly lie. It made my entire life a lie, and I was so ashamed because of that. But I was unwilling to face the fact that I was not perfect anymore.

I felt like I had figured out a way for me to be able to eat pretty much whatever I wanted until I was full, because I could just throw it up. I realized I wasn't able to simply starve myself, but this way I wouldn't have to feel bad about eating a normal meal (remember, what most people considered a normal meal, I thought was way too much for me). It also felt like I was still in control. Instead of having to worry about not eating too much, I now had the power to eat whatever I wanted to. Throwing up became an absolute crutch. I realized that I had a serious problem, but I was unwilling to fix it. I didn't want to get better. Throwing up was my solution. It was how I was going to train hard while still eating, which was going to make me a better skier. It was how I was going to feel numb when life got too stressful. It was how I was going to be perfect.

• • •

The summer after I graduated from high school, my bulimia really started to escalate. I would eat my breakfast and go for a two-hour roller ski. I'd come back and eat my lunch. I'd eat some snacks and maybe some chocolate chips, whatever I wanted, really, since it wasn't there to stay. Then I'd throw it all up. I'd feel that adrenaline surge of wiping the slate clean. Then I'd feel that euphoric numbness. I would be hollowed of stress and pain and anxiety. I'd drink a ton of water because I wanted to stay hydrated. I wanted to be a good athlete, right? It's amazing, the irony. I thought, well, I'm bulimic, but I'm also going to drink electrolytes because I'm a good athlete. I was living at home that whole summer. I was training and purging almost every day, while my family was gone for work or school. I thought I was hiding it pretty well too.

After I attended a national team camp and came back home, things escalated quickly. I was throwing up after lunch, after my afternoon snack, and after dinner. I would get so hungry because there wasn't anything ever permanently in my system. I would eat something and then feel good about it because I told myself I was refueling. But then the shame of eating would spiral me down again, and I'd throw the food up. I had initially thought I was in complete control of myself and when I would throw up, but gradually my eating disorder took over until I felt compelled to throw up nearly every meal, even the "perfect athlete food" that I actually *wanted* to keep down. I burst blood vessels in my eyes once or twice. My eyes were red rimmed a lot. My mom and dad started to figure it out. But I couldn't stop.

I had my little rituals. I would always try to purge as soon as possible after eating. Because the longer you wait, the harder it is to get the food up. I would keep throwing up until I knew I had gotten it all out. I felt that I couldn't live with the feeling of having the food in me. I couldn't stand it. The feelings were so strong inside me, the spiral twisting with such force that I couldn't sit still, couldn't concentrate, couldn't move forward with anything in my day until I had thrown up. At that point, I had gotten pretty quick, and it would not take me long to throw it up.

It was somewhat easy to hide bulimia. Most people normally take a few minutes to use the bathroom. But in that same time someone who is bulimic can have thrown up and then quickly wiped the toilet seat clean, and you'd never know. At the start, you make gagging noises. By the time you get to the advanced stage of bulimia, it has become scarily natural. You learn what foods are harder to get up than others. A lot of bulimics really like ice cream because it's very easy to get up.

I began to eat only food that I could get up quickly. I knew that I had gotten it all up when I started throwing up just bile at the end. At the start of my eating disorder, I was throwing up normal meals. But after a few weeks, I would eat just whatever would come up the easiest. The crazy thing was what it started to do to my body. I got a little bit skinnier but not much. Somehow I'd still digest some of it. But my body went into survival mode. You see this in people with disordered eating, and not just in the more extreme cases like bulimia and anorexia. If you're not providing your body enough calories, if your body isn't getting enough food, the body goes, well, holy shit, I don't know when I'm going to get food again. So I am going to cling to this small portion of food for dear life. Even if you're just not eating quite enough food every day and you're not throwing it up, your body will hang on to it. Your metabolism slows to a crawl. It becomes harder and harder to lose weight.

• • •

People couldn't tell anything was wrong with me. But my parents figured it out. My boyfriend at the time knew. My sister knew. They were all as supportive as they could possibly be. My parents are really smart, sharp people. They did a little Internet research on how to identify bulimia and how to identify eating disorders. They were reading the signs, like the disappearing act, the eating more ice cream than I normally would, and one day I didn't quite clean up every last throw-up mark in the toilet.

My voice would get really raspy because there was stomach acid touching my esophagus. I would always brush my teeth after I threw up, because I was terrified of ruining my teeth. When people have bulimia for a long time, it ruins their throat and teeth. Most people don't brush their teeth three to five times a day, so that seemed a strange habit to pick up.

There were a few times that I would start throwing up blood because I would try so hard to make myself throw up. Throwing up is pretty violent when you think about it. I would either accidentally scratch my throat with my nail, or maybe it was too much stomach acid. But I would get some blood in my throat from it, which scared the hell out of me. I knew this could only end badly. I had this crazy red mark in my eye from bursting blood vessels.

I knew my eating disorder could kill me. But I couldn't stop.

Bulimia was quickly becoming my silent killer. My pH balance was all off. My electrolytes were out of whack and now were in dangerously low levels. I was putting so much additional stress on my heart that I knew I might die. I knew all of this.

I'd researched the facts of my own eating disorder. There was nothing you could tell me that I didn't already know.

My parents were trying to tell me all of this too.

"This is so dangerous," my mom told me one night in another one of our talks. "I don't think you understand the risks."

"I know all the risks," I said, confessing to my serious addiction. "I just can't stop."

• • •

There was an intervention. I was in tears because I was so ashamed.

"No, I'll do better," I sobbed. "I'll stop. I can stop."

"Yes, we believe you want to stop. We're just not sure you can on your own," my mom said. "We're just really worried. People die from this."

I'd done all the research. My parents had too. We all knew I needed to stop because I could really die. That was the reality. I was an endurance athlete who was training for three hours a day and also a bulimic who made herself throw up multiple times a day. If I kept going, if I kept doing this to myself, it was going to end tragically. There's a reason people with the flu sometimes have to go to the hospital . . . and I was essentially living with the flu for months on end. But I had no idea how I was going to stop.

I *said* I was willing to try and stop. I *said* I wanted to get better. But I wasn't really sure if I wanted to.

I was worried that if I got better, if I sought out treatment or a therapist, I'd have to stop training and change my eating patterns. I was terrified that if I got help, I'd become fat, and that then I'd be slow, which would mean I couldn't ski as far and fast as I was capable of. If I couldn't be a great skier, I'd lose everything.

The more out of control my eating disorder got, the more I thought I was in control of it. Even at my worst, I thought I had it all together. I thought everything was going fine. I was so delusional. But that's the way eating disorders work. They create a scary spiral of delusion and anxiety and fear.

"You know, I think it would really help to get you a therapist that you can talk to," my mom suggested one day. I was kind of ashamed to talk to my dad about this because he's a guy, and I believed that maybe he wouldn't understand that I felt fat.

"That's a great idea. I'm willing to try it," I said. "I want to try it."

"I looked into getting help for eating disorders, and there's this place called The Emily Program located right here in St. Paul." My mom handed me the phone.

CHAPTER 10

THE EMILY PROGRAM

I called The Emily Program with my parents by my side—it was the most terrifying phone call of my life. Remarkably, I had an appointment just two days later. There wasn't a long wait time like there usually was for a regular doctor's visit. I was so grateful for not having a delay in the whole process, because every day mattered.

I honestly don't think I could have gone to that first meeting alone. I was scared, angry, and defiant, still unwilling to really truly acknowledge deep down that I needed professional help, because that, of course, would mean admitting that my eating disorder was something that had really taken over my life. I was doing this to make my parents happy, but I wasn't going there with the intention of actually giving up the thing that I now believed was my only way to survive.

My mom drove with me to The Emily Program in the Como neighborhood just west of the Minnesota State Fairgrounds. I was scared of what I was about to do: admit to someone outside my family that I had an eating disorder. Worse still, the admission would possibly derail my whole skiing career—something I had worked so hard for.

It's so sad to think about now. But at the time, I truly believed that to become a pro skier, I needed my eating disorder in my life. Without it, I would eat food and not have a way to get rid of it. Then I'd get fat and slow and my career would die. The fact that I knew my eating disorder would likely kill me or even make my racing worse didn't add up in my brain. It doesn't make any sense at all, but then, eating disorders rarely do.

I distracted myself by concentrating on the sights all around me. The Como neighborhood looked like a movie set: there were blocks of small businesses and a nice coffee shop, a public library with park benches out front that were surrounded by a beautiful garden, and people walked their dogs and greeted their neighbors. The Emily Program sat right on the corner of a busy business street, housed in an old bank.

I was struck by how normal and cheerful everything around me appeared. *Don't they know what a freak I am?* I felt out of place, like there was a sign on my forehead stating that I was about to get treatment for an eating disorder. I felt like everyone must know my secret. But of course, nobody did.

I stood at the front door next to my mom, who has loved me all my life through all of my ups and downs, took a deep breath, and tried to stay positive and find the courage to go inside. I reminded myself that I was brave enough to actually make the phone call and ask for help. That's a huge thing to do! Even if I was doing it to assuage my guilt at the intense worry my eating disorder was creating for my parents, I'd still done it.

Now, I would have to be brave enough to take the next step and talk with someone. I'd had moments of bravery throughout my whole life—in fact, I prided myself on being fearless. I went cliff jumping without a second thought, raced gutsy races all through high school, traveled to new countries, and met new friends. I tried out for solos in orchestra in front of all my peers, and if I could survive playing violin with palms *that* sweaty, I could surely survive this. Or could I?

I was fearless in many areas of my life, but at that moment, I was terrified to take that step forward. My eating disorder had taken my brain and my feelings hostage. It had created such insecurity that I wasn't sure if I could survive without it. I reminded myself that even if I didn't want to be here for *me*, I was doing this for my parents and their peace of mind. I put my hand on the front door and opened it. I didn't know it at the time, but when I walked into The Emily Program, it was the first step on my road to recovery.

• • •

In the front lobby was a beautiful staircase made of wood and glass that reached upper and lower levels. Staff breezed by us as we walked through the lobby. Every person acknowledged us, said hello, and directed me to where I needed to check in. There was a small piano against the wall that had a sign on it that invited people to play. *Wait . . . what kind of doctors' office has a piano in it? How are people so cheerful and happy? What is this place?* I walked into the main-floor office and reached a reception area with a high counter, where I imagined a former bank customer would've made a deposit with a teller. *Let me deposit my life's problems with you,* I thought. I was greeted at the counter by a friendly receptionist.

"Hello," a young woman said. "How can I help you?"

"I have an appointment," I said tentatively. "My name is Jessie."

"Hello, Jessie, it's nice to meet you," the receptionist said and smiled. She looked at her computer and said, "Yes, I have you right here. You're all checked in. If you want to take a seat and fill out these papers, someone will be out shortly to get you."

I sat down on a comfy couch in the waiting area, close to my mom. She helped me through the paperwork, and I was reminded of how extremely lucky I was to have such a great support system. Then a fresh wave of guilt washed over me. Here I was, taking up my mom's day with all of my self-induced problems after weeks and months of snapping at her out of anger and crying on her when I was tired and hungry from throwing up. And here she was doing whatever necessary to give me the chance at a healthy life again, including paying whatever out-of-pocket fees insurance wouldn't cover and doing the paperwork to boot. *What kind of horrible child am I, anyway? I don't deserve this help!* Have I mentioned that my eating disorder caused me to hate myself?

As scared and immersed in self-loathing as I was, I noticed that there was something different about The Emily Program. I was expecting a cold and sterile medical clinic. But it wasn't a regular doctors' office at all. The waiting area was warm and inviting. The walls were painted soft colors. There was a large vase filled with small scrolls with a sign that read, "Take an inspirational quote!" There were half-finished puzzles on all the tables, and the scattered pieces invited you to contribute. I nervously played with a puzzle piece. Then a woman approached me in the lobby.

"Hello, are you Jessie?" the woman asked. She was older with short salt-and-pepper hair. Her voice was calm and friendly.

"Yes," I squeaked out. "Hi." *Why was my voice suddenly three octaves higher?*

"My name is Dr. Joan Caillier. I'll be meeting with you today."

I set the puzzle piece on the table and stood up. Dr. Caillier put out her hand, and I extended mine. We shook hands. I think she must have been used to some seriously sweaty-palmed, nervous first-time patients, because to her credit, she never flinched.

"Hi, nice to meet you."

It was now official. The reality of my life was now right in front of me. I was about to share my deepest secrets with this doctor. Or was I? I still could barely admit out loud to myself that I had bulimia. Would I be able to tell a stranger? Dr. Caillier smiled at me and said, "My office is right down this hall. Shall we?"

My mom smiled, assured me that she'd be there waiting for me when I was done. So I followed her down the hallway, one foot in front of the other.

•   •   •

Dr. Caillier's corner office had large windows that looked out at the library across the street and the garden out front. The entire atmosphere was bright, friendly, and welcoming, which was the opposite of how I felt at the moment; if her office was a sunny day, I was a nervous tornado circling round and round. I sat down in a chair across from her.

"Jessie, thank you for coming here today," Dr. Caillier said.

She told me a little about her background and her career. There were plaques and awards on her desk behind her. She was clearly smart, an expert in the field of eating disorders. Dr. Caillier looked at me with kindness in her eyes and simply asked, "So, Jessie, why are you here today?"

Where do I start? I asked myself. I was overwhelmed because there was so much to say and I didn't want to say any of it.

"Um . . . because . . ." My voice trailed off. *I couldn't bring myself to say it. How could I tell this woman what a monster I was?*

Dr. Caillier smiled and reassuringly said, "I want you to try and tell me the story of how you came to The Emily Program today."

Her words were sincere and made me believe that she truly cared, that she honestly wanted to help me. So, I took a deep breath, and I told her my story. Well, at least, I planned to tell her the parts I could bear to say out loud. I told her all about my skiing career. That part was easy; there was no shame in that. I told her all about the stress of trying to become the best skier I could be. I told her about my pressure-packed senior year in high school. This was harder to talk about, but still, I felt that I had been a good kid through this part of my life. Then I told her how I would throw up to relieve the stress.

I blinked my eyes every few seconds because I was trying to suppress tears of shame, but she never looked at me with anything but understanding and trust, and that unconditional kindness helped me have the strength to keep talking. I told her that throwing up and numbing myself were now controlling my life in almost every way. The entire time, I felt this intense guilt and shame and was too embarrassed to look her in the eye. While I didn't want to share anything about myself, the rational part of my brain reminded me that Dr. Caillier had seen hundreds, maybe thousands, of people just like me. She'd probably heard it all.

For an hour in that first intake meeting, Dr. Caillier asked me all the questions that I never wanted to answer. And when I answered them, she never judged me once. It was very open, and I felt very accepted by her. Which was unbelievable, considering I was mortified by the knowledge that if most people heard the things I was saying, they would judge me harshly for what I was doing. Especially myself. Nobody on the planet could have been a more merciless judge or jury than my own cruel brain. But Dr. Caillier didn't flinch. She only wanted to help, especially when she could tell that I was withholding some of the truth because I was so embarrassed.

"For example, the other day after my training session, I was really hungry. So I ate a snack. But then I felt bad about eating the snack, because I shouldn't be eating before dinner time. So I went for another training run."

"Why did you feel that you needed to go for an extra run after the snack?" Dr. Caillier asked.

"I feel like I need to be skinnier to become a better skier. I felt like I couldn't stand sitting there knowing I'd eaten something. I tried to just do my homework, but I couldn't focus on anything. So I got up and ran as long as I thought I needed to in order to burn off the calories."

"Jessie, what happened next?" Dr. Caillier asked calmly, gently guiding me toward the truth.

"The extra run made me hungry again. So, I ate another snack."

"What did you eat?"

I looked down at my lap. Fidgeted. *If I was a better skier, I wouldn't have eaten anything at all. I'm such a failure.*

"I made cookies."

"Anything else?" *Crap. She knows!*

"Yes," I said. *How did she know I ate something else?* Then I paused and took a breath. "I ate some ice cream."

"After your extra run, you ate cookies and then you ate ice cream," Dr. Caillier said, gently pushing forward. In that moment, I could tell that she was playing the role of detective, too, and digging for information. It started to feel like she was grilling me, and my palms got sweaty. Even though she was my partner, I didn't see it that way at the time. "I'm curious, Jessie. Did your feeling of shame come back after you ate the cookies and ice cream?"

"Yes," I admitted. *How did she know it came back?*

"Can you tell me why you ate the ice cream?" Dr. Caillier asked.

I paused. It was so hard to admit the truth.

"Because it's easy to get up. I . . . I didn't ever plan on keeping it down." I said.

"Yes, ice cream is very easy to get up," Dr. Caillier said calmly. "You are not alone in thinking that, Jessie. Ice cream is a very common food item for people with eating disorders. Can you tell me what happened next?"

I kept talking, and although I hated myself for what I was saying, Dr. Caillier understood every word. It was a liberating experience because I was no longer speaking a foreign language. She knew all about the anxiety and panic that drove me toward the eating disorder. She knew intimately how purging created my feeling of release, euphoria, and eventually numbness. She also understood that wanting to become emotionally numb became my addiction. She understood that when I felt I couldn't handle my emotions, I needed to feel nothing at all, which is when I turned to throwing up.

For the first time since confiding in my parents, I felt a small dose of freedom. I also felt my eating disordered brain rebelling against this help, this kindness. *What will happen to you without me?* it asked me. *You'll be nothing. You'll get fat and lazy, and you'll never race fast again.*

But what if I actually do need this help after all? I fought back. *Let's just try this, even if it's to get my parents off my back about trying to get healthy again.*

Along with help from my family, I felt like I had found a doctor and a clinic that would help me fight my bulimia. I now had teammates in my goal to get healthy, which was something I truly understood. I was still scared to unpack it all, of course. I was scared to share every small, humiliating detail of my eating disorder. But sitting in her corner office, making the decision to go to my first appointment, I felt a small weight leave my shoulders.

After our intake meeting, Dr. Caillier made her assessment.

"Jessie, I'm very glad that you came in here today. I know it can't be easy to talk about your eating disorder, but I'm proud of you for sharing with me so that we can help you. It is my recommendation that you should meet once a week with a therapist, who can help you work on your recovery. We have a therapist right in Stillwater, and I can help you get started with her."

I nodded, wanting deep down to feel better but still feeling unsure about this whole thing. What if I didn't like my therapist? *What if she didn't like me?* I left The Emily Program that day with my mom, reluctantly taking a few more steps away from my eating disorder. Or so I thought.

.   .   .

Over the next few months, I met once a week with a therapist in her office on the third floor of an old building in downtown Stillwater, Minnesota. Even though the office was only a twenty-minute drive from my house, I dreaded that drive every week. I was still in a place where I wasn't yet ready to let go of my eating disorder. *It had only been a few months! What damage could I be doing to my body in the long run, really?* I thought I could become the one person with enough control to live with an eating disorder in moderation. You know, like that one friend who uses cocaine every second Tuesday, just for fun.

There were three main factors that held back any progress I could have made in the two months in which I saw the therapist in Stillwater. The first was that I wasn't there for me, I was there for my parents. I needed to be able to look them in the eye and say, "Yes! I'm working on getting better! I haven't missed an appointment ever!" I hated lying to them about my eating disorder, so this was a way for me to go through the motions of recovery without having to put my heart and soul into it. The second issue was that I never really clicked with this therapist. There needs to be a real bond between an eating disorder patient and the therapist. There needs to be enough trust for the patient to really lay it all out there without any reservations. For whatever reason, I just didn't have that much-needed connection with the therapist. But since I was new to this whole "therapy" thing, I didn't realize I was missing a key ingredient.

The third problem was that I was still training full-time and going to ski camps. Just like I wasn't ready to let go of my eating disorder, I wasn't ready to back away from a single minute of the incredibly intense training regimen I was putting myself through. So, without telling any of my coaches or teammates, I still went to team training camps, and my rate of throwing up climbed higher and higher.

I was invited to train with the U.S. national team during this time as a guest. The team invited me to a camp to introduce me to what they were working on and the latest thoughts about technique. The national coaches would give their input on drills and ways for me to improve. I went to that camp filled with extreme anxiety because I wasn't officially a part of the team. I shouldn't have had anxiety, because the entire team welcomed me into the program. But I was secretly carrying a lot of shame about my eating disorder. I was not yet ready to face it, and I was so worried the team would find out. *What would they think of me? Will they kick me out? Will they send me home? Will they hate me? Will they think I'm stupid?*

The camp was really hard with my eating disorder. I spent a lot of time alone in my room, sadly, because I would eat lunch and then tell the coaches and skiers that I was going to take a nap. Then I would go throw up my lunch, retreat to my room, and sit alone. I didn't have great confidence. It was hard to not compare my fitness level in the summer and my body shape to other skiers'. I hadn't yet learned that no one's body is going to look the same, especially among skiers, where there is no one ideal body type. I was an insecure teen, and my brain was filled with toxic thinking. *I'm not lean enough! I'm not strong enough! My muscles aren't big enough! I'm too short . . . but also somehow too tall! You're never going to make it.*

I don't know how I made it through even one day, let alone a two-week training camp with what I was doing to myself. I'd eat a normal small breakfast, just enough to get me through the morning training session. Starving, I'd eat a huge lunch, then disappear to throw it all back up. My afternoon snack was much of the same; eat a big cup of ice cream so I could easily throw it back up again. Somehow, I absorbed just enough sugar to drag my aching body through the afternoon workout, and then at dinner I'd either keep some of it down or none at all. It was like having mild food poisoning all the time.

It wasn't working. I wasn't training well or living well, and I was generally unhappy all the time even though I tried to force a happy face on whenever I wasn't alone. At the end of the summer, I hit an all-time low point of purging five times a day. I was throwing up every meal I ate.

My parents figured out how badly I'd been lying to them about my so-called recovery and called in another intervention. Things had gotten really, really bad, and my parents totally knew it.

"No, no, I'm doing better," I tried to tell them, even as I was starting to spin out of control.

My parents knew the truth, though. My mom called my bluff.

"OK, wait a minute," my mom said, confronting me. "No. You're not doing well. You can't do this. I noticed you showed up to work with puffy eyes, and your cheeks were a little swollen from having thrown up. You need to be honest with yourself. You need to be honest with me."

She was totally right. I couldn't be honest with her, because I couldn't be honest with myself. I was scared to live without my eating disorder. I was scared to lose control. I was scared to get fat and slow—I would lose everything. I was scared to die. But I knew I couldn't stop. *The voice in my head wouldn't let me stop.*

At that point, again, I thought I wanted to get better. But I was really only 80 percent sure I wanted to be healthy. I wanted to get better without having to let go of my eating disorder. I wanted to get out of my marriage to my eating disorder but still date. I wanted to divorce him but still live with him. In reality, that wasn't possible. But I still believed I could live with it.

"You need to go back to The Emily Program, meet with them again, and be honest with how much you're throwing up."

"I'm going to go. You're right," I told my mom, trying to convince myself and her. "You're right. I need to go."

My mom paused for a short time. Then she laid out some hard truth. "We can't watch you live in the house and destroy yourself," she said. "This is hard on the whole family."

"I know I can't live like this," I finally confessed. And this time I meant it. "I know you can't live like this either."

•   •   •

At the urging of my parents, I went back to The Emily Program and met with Dr. Caillier again, confessing that I was still throwing up and getting worse every week. This time, I was honest about the fact that I was throwing up almost everything I ate. I was honest about the fact that sometimes, after hard training, my heartbeat would pick up and feel out of control, hammering away at my ribs, even when I wasn't working hard anymore. She knew it, and more important, I knew it: my body simply couldn't take a whole lot more of this.

"Jessie, you are coming very close to something we call 'the edge.' When you have an eating disorder, you never really know how close you are to the edge of a cliff, because you can't see yourself clearly. But sometimes people fall over this cliff even when they think they are 'doing OK,' because their body just can't handle the stress they're putting on it anymore." Dr. Caillier told me after our second meeting that "everything that you've gone through and the emotions behind those actions have led you here. It is a very dangerous place to be for someone with an eating disorder."

Dr. Caillier continued, "We want to shine a light on what is causing you to head for the edge, and by doing that, help you walk back. We want to get you to a safe place. You have a serious eating disorder, and you need more intensive care."

I took tissues out of a box in front of me.

"It is my recommendation that you should enroll in our intensive day treatment residential outpatient program. This means we would like you to be here five days a week from 8:00 a.m. to 2:00 p.m.," Dr. Caillier continued. "This would become your full-time job. You'll be under the care of a medical doctor, a nutritionist, and a therapist. You will be able to continue your career as a cross-country skier too. But you need to be here five days a week and fully commit yourself to getting better."

Dr. Caillier was right. It was still hard to hear. But I was at the edge. I honestly didn't know how much longer I could've stayed there before I went over. I tried to summon the courage to be brave enough to take the next step. I had to admit the truth and finally commit myself to getting better. My eating disorder wasn't going away. I told myself to start with just one step.

"OK," I said, tears bubbling in my eyes. "I think I can do that."

•   •   •

I began my intensive treatment in The Emily Program immediately, attending group therapy sessions Monday through Friday as recommended. Our group sessions were in various rooms; one had the vibe of a college rec room, and another room was in the old bank vault. I didn't think an old vault could be made to feel welcoming, but they work miracles in that building, so in hindsight I'm not surprised at all. The huge bank vault door was still there and left open, used as a magnet board for people to leave positive messages.

My group sessions were often in a large room with lots of tables, chairs, and couches. Art done by patients decorated all the available wall space. A huge floor-to-ceiling dry erase board was at the head of the room, filled with brightly colored scribbles of lists, bullet points, and information.

At my first group session there were eight of us. There were men in the program too, but this particular group had only women. We weren't the only group that met in the program, and at any given time there were multiple groups going on. But I think they put us together because we were all experiencing similar things at this stage in our lives. In my first session, I thought, well, by virtue of being there, they all knew something about me, and I knew something about them. Which was terrifying. I was still filled with so much shame about having an eating disorder. I still felt that I had nothing to be sad or anxious about. I was an honor roll student and a competitive athlete with a great family life. *What did I have to be sad about? Maybe I didn't deserve to be there getting help, because this was something I'd brought entirely upon myself!*

On my first day, I burrowed into the corner of a couch off to the side. There were lots of pillows and blankets near each seat, and my fellow patients and I used them as armor. I also wanted to cover up as much of myself as possible, as though by covering up my body I could cover up the selfish monster I thought I was. As we sat in a loose circle, most patients were almost in a defensive crouch and protected themselves by holding the pillows on their chests with their arms folded across, or they were tucked behind a shield of blankets. It was as though the weight of our eating disorders was causing us to fold in upon ourselves. Also, many of the girls were so severely underweight that they couldn't stay warm without layers upon layers of clothing, so the blankets served a dual purpose.

The tables were filled with things for us to fidget with, such as stress balls, knitting baskets, cups of tea, and Rubik's cubes. This helped me because I was extremely nervous and emotional about having to share my soul with a bunch of strangers. In that first group session, though, I saw for the first time that eating disorders could affect anyone. ED (eating disorders) wasn't a discriminatory guy. Sitting there on the couch, squeezing a stress ball to within an inch of its life, I realized that eating disorders didn't affect just stressed-out, type A endurance athletes like me. They affected women and men, rich and poor, people of every color and background, every sexual orientation, young and old.

Over the course of a few days, I began to share my story. I sat there quietly at first and was pretty shy. I'm not a shy person by nature, but I couldn't bear the thought of these strangers seeing this terrible, horrible side of me. I've always been someone who wants everyone to like me, and if I'm in a room full of a hundred people, I'll focus on the one person who doesn't seem to like me. *Why won't you talk to me? Why can't we be friends?* I was so desperate to be accepted that I would go outside with the girls who smoked on their cigarette breaks, even though I'd never smoked anything in my life, just to talk to them and be part of the group activity.

I gradually started to open up, and as I shared more of myself, I became friends with the other girls. Nobody judged me like I'd feared. They just accepted me for who I was, flaws and all. I learned their hopes and dreams and life stories. We were all from different parts of Minnesota and the Midwest. We all had vastly different backgrounds and upbringings. But we were all married to ED in our own way.

At first, I flirted around the edges of my life, painting my life story in broad strokes that they all could see. But after a few days, I felt more comfortable telling the group about my career as a skier and the level of competition that I was doing. But I did not talk about the level of training. During the group session, I was acutely careful about what I'd say because I didn't want to trigger someone else. I wouldn't talk about a specific three-hour run because then the girl sitting next to me might go, "Oh my God, I didn't run for three hours, and I also ate breakfast. Do I not deserve to keep that food in? Should I go run?"

We were being honest, but some things we simply didn't talk about. We never talked about food, unless we were learning about nutrition or how food could positively fuel our bodies. We never talked about using symptoms in detail. That's the way we would describe our self-harming actions: using symptoms. Symptoms of an eating disorder could include restrictive eating, binging, purging, throwing up, compulsive exercising, or any combination of those. The exercising part was extremely hard for me to navigate, though, because of my career choice. The way I exercised and trained could by definition be considered compulsive exercising. We had to rewrite the definition of that symptom. Compulsive exercising, for me, meant anything beyond my carefully mapped-out training plan. So while I would share if I engaged in compulsive exercise, I never talked about my normal training regimen. Often, I simply shared the emotions and anxiety of what it's like to be a competitive athlete.

"Well, I had a training camp, and I felt like I had to perform well in a time trial. It made me feel anxious," I told the group. "I used symptoms the night before, and because of it, I didn't have enough energy and strength. Then I felt very guilty and ashamed of myself that I was sabotaging my training. But I felt like I couldn't stop."

"Wow, that's very brave of you to share that," the woman next to me on the couch responded.

"Thank you for being so honest, because I also feel those emotions," someone would add. "Sometimes the guilt is too much for me as well, and knowing that I used symptoms, I then decide that the day's gone to shit so I may as well use them again."

I learned that my problems were confusing only to me. As patients in The Emily Program, we were often so close to our own issues that we could not see them clearly. Many of us struggled with the same exact set of feelings, and we could be incredibly harsh on ourselves. Yet hearing someone else describe what we, too, were feeling, we'd realize that we would never put that same amount of criticism onto their shoulders. It took a while to subtly sink in, but after a few weeks I started to get the point: that nobody deserves to feel this way, and if I could find such compassion for other girls, why couldn't I extend the same courtesy to myself?

This was why the group sessions were so important for all of us. When a patient shared her story, others could see it, and we began to support that person as a group, with a therapist leading the discussion. We would talk through the reasons why we were feeling like we had to continue feeding our eating disorder, and would try to get down to the very root of it. Often, we'd notice the small details that other patients missed in their own stories.

In one session, a patient told a story about using symptoms, and in the middle of her story, she dropped in a small clue.

"You mentioned your parents were arguing a lot," a woman in the group said. "Do you think this might be connected, because you mentioned your mom and dad were getting a divorce? Do you think maybe you were unintentionally or subconsciously putting shame on yourself?"

The patient looked up surprised and said, "Oh, I didn't think about that, but yes, now that you say that, it's totally true. My parents are going through a divorce. I wondered if it was my fault, and I felt stressed about that, and I needed to use symptoms."

We were in the fight together, and the giant dry erase boards reflected that message every day. Each week, we wrote our name and then listed five goals for the week. It was a group activity, and the lists were all side by side and lived together on the board for the whole week. While we may have had different goals and were there for different reasons, the board was our way of seeing that we were in this fight together. Because of the honesty throughout the group, my fellow patients were no longer strangers, and we quickly became friends. Within days of being at The Emily Program the people sitting in my group session knew more about me than most people ever would. And I knew more about them.

I would often arrive home in tears, exhausted emotionally from group session. I felt such enormous, crushing guilt. But now it was for a new reason. Many of the girls in my group had developed eating disorders as a protective coping mechanism for some serious abuse that they'd suffered in their life. Many of them had such tough life circumstances or such a rough family life at home that they used symptoms to help them navigate. I had no terrible incidents in my life. My life had been perfect! Why did I deserve to get help from The Emily Program when I had no real reason at all for having an eating disorder? Of course, I still had so much to learn, but at the time I would return from group depressed and sad from hearing such tragic stories and feeling like there was nothing I could do to help. I liked the girls in my group, but still I dreaded going every day because I knew I would have to face so many emotions without being able to numb myself to get through it. This was perhaps the hardest part; after months of numbing my emotions and feeling nothing, letting it all flood back in was terrifying. Experiencing the intense emotions from not only my own struggles but those of a roomful of women, at times I would feel like I was being crushed by the sadness of it, but at other times, I was lifted up by all the hope.

• • •

I had a lot of unpacking to do. No one likes moving furniture and boxes, but this was even harder. I was unpacking my thoughts and emotions and moving them from the deepest, darkest part of my brain and out into the bright, open space of The Emily Program. This unpacking process was where I took major strides down the road of self-discovery.

For pretty much everyone at The Emily Program, it wasn't really about food. Yes, we were in a clinic that handled eating disorders. But our treatment wasn't focused solely on food and eating. Our group and individual therapy sessions were more about unpacking our own history. It wasn't so much about what symptoms we were using but more about the emotions behind our actions, the reason we were using those symptoms in the first place. Often, it wasn't even about getting skinny. Some people had an eating disorder because they'd been abused. Other patients had eating disorders because they didn't want to look pretty. They didn't want to look attractive because they were terrified of it. For some people, it was about handling stress from work or school or athletics, and that was exactly why I was there.

The unpacking process was exhausting for me. I was encouraged to talk about how using symptoms made me feel and what led up to it. My emotions were packed away in a series of tightly connected boxes like Russian nesting dolls. They were stored in the back of my psyche, and some emotions fit inside other emotions. Every time I would bring an emotion out from the deepest, darkest spot of my brain and into the light of The Emily Program, another emotion would reveal itself. Soon, the boxes were stacked up all around me. I worried that if they toppled over, they'd bury me alive.

"Everyone's favorite question to ask an athlete is about what we can or can't eat," I said in one group session as I began to unpack an emotion.

"They always ask me, 'Can you eat dessert? What do you have to eat? Are you on a special diet? Oh, you're going to eat *that*?' People are always asking what I'm eating and question if I should be eating it," I told the group.

"So, now, I question whether I should or shouldn't eat the food in front of me. I'm questioning myself at every meal, especially if I'm eating in front of teammates who are watching me. I feel so guilty about the amount I'm consuming because I'm an athlete."

The guilt was now unpacked and out in the open space of our group session. The light allowed me to discover another emotion inside of the one I had just revealed. Heck, I didn't even know it was there. But I now knew that this feeling haunted me.

"At first, I felt guilt about what I ate. But then I realized that I also felt ashamed and completely unworthy because here I was, trying to become a pro athlete, following my training plan perfectly . . . and I can't even extend that same attention to detail with my diet. I feel like maybe I'll never be enough, that I won't be good enough to make it."

Unpacking that memory led to a discussion about how my eating disorder was tied to my athletics and how I created very restricted eating ideas, but we also talked about how my quest to be "perfect" was creating really rigid walls for me as well. Our group therapist led a discussion about how all foods do fit into everyone's diet, and that allowing yourself to be who you are is key to being able to be at peace with yourself. I began to think maybe perfection didn't need to have so much control over my life.

In those first weeks at The Emily Program that was exactly how my recovery went. I still felt guilty and ashamed for needing to be there at all, and it was confusing. But I also felt relieved. I was sharing my secrets for the first time, and that made me feel brave. While a large part of my brain that was still controlled by my eating disorder screamed at me to quit, a smaller, much quieter part of my brain was jumping up and down, waving banners, and cheering for me as I slowly came around to the idea that I might not always need my eating disorder. I was unpacking all those emotions that I was so ashamed of, and the people sitting next to me were so supportive, and as they listened, they offered insight. Most important, I felt supported in my quest to open up and figure out why I used symptoms.

•   •   •

I began to make breakthroughs. Besides my therapist meetings, my parents were actively trying to help me. My mom bought me the book *Life without ED* by Jenni Schaefer. This extremely well-written book is about how one woman declared independence from her eating disorder, and I highly recommend it for people struggling with an eating disorder and anyone close to them who wants to understand what they're going through.

Schaefer likens having an eating disorder to being in an abusive relationship, which is very much what it is. In many abusive relationships, the victims think they need the abuser. The victims are not willing to leave because they're too scared to think about what it's going to be like without the abuser. It's a really good analogy because with an eating disorder the one thing you think you need the most is the one thing that hurts you the most. It might kill you someday. While you're in the relationship, you don't believe it's really going to kill you. Because that only happens to other people. You don't think it will ever happen to you. Your marriage, your relationship with this eating disorder, is fine. You think you have it all under control. Nothing bad is going to happen.

I continued to have private sessions with a therapist outside of our group sessions, and this time I met with a new therapist, Angie Scott. I instantly clicked with her. She had this air of warm, caring calmness about her, and for the first time in private sessions, I truly believed that I could share everything I felt and thought.

These intimate, raw conversations turned my life around. They helped me separate who I really was from who I was with an ED. Angie was very motherly, and her aura reminded me of one of my grandmas. She helped me gain the tools to cope with the stress of being a competitive athlete. Using symptoms was currently the only tool I had in my toolbox, but Angie helped me figure out that I had many other, less self-destructive ways of dealing with stress. Every week I practiced a new tool, such as taking my dog outside to play when I felt the urge to throw up, calling a friend, or watching a show that would distract me. I had no idea at the time, but the tools Angie gave me during those sessions at The Emily Program were ones that could help me throughout the rest of my life. Most important, Angie helped me figure out my struggles weren't about the food and that it wasn't all my fault.

Before I met with Angie, I thought there was something wrong with me, that if I was just a better person, I wouldn't be struggling with an eating disorder. As a result of this assumption, I felt shame and embarrassment that caused me to not act like myself. I was always such a truthful child that I never had a curfew. My parents just trusted me to use my judgment and come home at a reasonable hour. And I always did! I was so intense with my ski training, so focused on school and getting into university that I never considered staying out late, partying, or lying to my parents about anything. However, when my eating disorder came along, I found myself lying for the first time in my life. I became a different version of myself.

My eating disorder took a strong hold, and from there on it did whatever it had to do to survive, like a parasite that's taken over its host. Lie to my parents, saying I wasn't hungry at dinner because I'd already eaten? No problem. Be angry with my parents for trying to talk to me about my eating disorder? Piece of cake (figuratively speaking). Cry irrationally and become overly emotional at the smallest things? Of course, that's what happens when you're trying to function on, shall we say, less than optimal nutrition. Whenever someone was trying to help me, my immediate instinct was to push the person away, even if a small corner of my brain was still crying out for help. The larger part of me that was controlled by my eating disorder was terrified of accepting help of any kind, so taking any steps whatsoever toward recovery was like dragging a ball and chain behind me.

I've always been such an intense person, and that's been an incredible thing for my ski career. My ability to focus in on one thing and stay on task until I am finished is simultaneously my best and worst character trait. And my eating disorder absolutely thrived on this intensity.

"Genetics loads the gun," Angie explained. "Environment pulls the trigger."

I learned through the experts at The Emily Program that bulimia is a mental disorder. Much the same as alcoholism, depression, or anxiety, it's something you feel you cannot stop. It's part of your genetic makeup, and you're predisposed to suffer from that condition. If you're someone who is predisposed and at risk for an eating disorder, it's likely going to surface at some point. It might surface very early if you're a super type A athlete in a really stressful situation, or it might surface much later in life. Maybe it'll never surface, or maybe it surfaces quickly, and you get treatment and you get better fast. Or maybe it takes a long time. It's different person to person and case to case.

The environment I was in, one with a lot of stress, brought everything to a head. Let's face it, high school is stressful for almost everyone. And the stress I was under with school, skiing, violin, AP tests, and applying for college is what pulled the trigger on my loaded gun and set me off into an eating disorder. It's hard to explain how much this knowledge helped me let go of some of the intense guilt and shame I felt. All along I'd been thinking I had a behavior problem, that I just wasn't strong enough to not use symptoms, that I was a bad kid. Learning that I hadn't done anything wrong to deserve this helped me start to have compassion for myself.

Stress was at the root of my bulimia. So, Angie set out to help me handle stress, because I had never known how to deal with it well. Now, I know that when I'm really stressed, I can call my mom and talk it over. I have a sports psychologist I can hash it over with. I can talk to my coach, Cork. I can talk to a teammate. I can talk to my boyfriend, Wade. I can go for a walk. I can do yoga. I can watch *Grey's Anatomy* on Netflix. There are a million tools in my toolbox now because Angie helped me put them there. I've also learned that if you just need to be sad, that's OK too. You can be sad! You can be anxious. You can be worried about something. You can be nervous about a race. It's human, and if I learned anything at The Emily Program, it's that I want to let myself feel the whole range of incredible emotions we humans experience.

I was always such a happy-go-lucky kid. When I was eighteen years old, a time when everything was going right for me, I felt that I had no right to be nervous or anxious. So, I didn't know how to deal with stress and adversity. Angie changed that. She helped me figure out that life is about facing and channeling that stress. We would talk about everything in life and talk about symptoms and what my eating disorder was doing to me. She would break it all down to the smallest box to find the truth.

Two weeks into my residency at The Emily Program, I felt that I was beginning to heal. I started to see things more clearly from the mental health and emotional side of things. But I still needed to conquer the next stage.

I had to keep the food down. I still didn't want to eat.

CHAPTER 11

NEVER ALONE

The Emily Program dietitian determined how many servings each patient needed. I had individual meetings with my dietitian, Rasa Troup, every week. She had been an Olympic athlete competing in track and field, and I could tell she was well versed in every aspect of sports nutrition from both being an athlete herself and studying it. Every week, I brought her my training plan so she could determine my caloric needs for the week, and the meal plan she wrote was designed exactly for me. While at the beginning I struggled to trust that this plan wasn't going to make me fat, Rasa simply asked me to do my best and give it a fair shot, and after a few weeks the rational side of my brain could tell it was going to be OK.

At group meals you didn't get to say how much you were going to eat, because everyone there would have said, "I'll take a leaf of lettuce. Thanks." We needed a serving of grains, calcium, and a protein. We also got a serving of healthy fats. But each patient's meal plan was designed for their specific needs. In my case as an athlete in training, I might have needed three servings of grains, whereas someone else needed just one.

The kitchen and the dining room were located in the basement level in a large, open area near the old bank vault. There was no physical separation between the kitchen and dining room, and one flowed right into the other. We always ate together as a group. We'd stand in a line that ran parallel to a long buffet counter, which was on an island in the kitchen area. That sounds easy and straightforward, but it was terrifying for all of us. This line was paralyzing.

Our line was formed where the carpet of the dining area ran flush into the tiled floor of the kitchen. All we had to do was line up at this seam and take one step off the carpet to serve up our food. The space between the seam and the buffet counter was no more than four feet. But it might as well have been the Grand Canyon. We just stood there on the seam, terrified by the bowls and trays full of food on the counter before us. Because once we stepped onto the kitchen tile, it was for real. We had to get the food, and we had to eat it. People without eating disorders often say, "What's the big deal. Just eat a hamburger." If only it was that easy.

My eating disorder had hijacked my brain so severely that when food was in front of me, all I heard inside my own head was a warning to not eat anything. It wasn't that I wasn't hungry, but as soon as I thought about having to keep the food down and live with it, eating lost all appeal. The voice in my head was not polite either. It was screaming. I heard only all-or-nothing scenarios. The screaming told me if I ate certain foods, my world would end, or some dire circumstance would happen. More important, I believed it—I truly believed that everything would fall apart if I ate a pancake or had white bread on my sandwich. These were my normal emotions when it was mealtime: fear and self-loathing. With the recent brain research into eating disorders, all this screaming finally makes sense. We now know that the brain of someone with an eating disorder is unable to make sense of the messages coming in about food. They sound like noise—loud noise—and they stop only when you aren't eating. That makes it really hard to do what needs to be done . . . to eat!

There were two main rules during mealtime at The Emily Program. The first rule was that we couldn't look at another patient's plate. Everyone would get a tray of food, and we'd all sit down and eat a meal together just like normal people! Score one for us! One of the huge hallmarks of eating disorders is checking out everyone else's plate. We look at what other people are eating and become competitive.

What are you eating? I'm gonna eat less than you. I should be eating less than you because I'm smaller. I want to have as little as possible. How are you hiding your food?

We could look at each other's plates in a natural way. I mean, we couldn't just put horse blinders on! But the rule was we could not scope out what other people were eating and then compare our food to theirs. Comparison was not helpful for anyone, because everyone had a different metabolism and everyone had different needs.

The second rule was that the bathrooms were locked for thirty minutes after meals. We could not get up to go to the bathroom during that time, because we needed to keep our food down. We needed to rewire our brains and learn that we could keep a meal down, and life would go on. The world would keep turning even though our brains screamed at us that it surely wouldn't. Sitting through a group mealtime was my new training session, my practice of rewiring my hijacked brain.

At breakfast there might be oatmeal, biscuits, pancakes, fruit, and French toast. If we needed three servings of grain, we could take one of each or three of one, player's choice. However we chose, we had to get our allotted amount, and the dietitian would help walk us through it. Besides the nutritional benefits we got from eating a balanced meal, our dietitian was trying to also help us have a healthier relationship with food. So, she'd say, "Well, what do you want to have? What do you enjoy? What do you feel like this morning?" This seemed like such a normal question, but to me it seemed foreign. I hadn't allowed myself to feel like I wanted anything other than the oatmeal that athletes were "supposed" to eat. The dieticians never gave advice about which food was better for us or what had more or less fat. They would simply say, "Well, if you want to have a piece of French toast, you may have that!"

As a group, we learned life skills that would help us when we acclimated to the outside world. We learned that everything in moderation was fine, and that all foods fit into a healthy life. We learned that no food was off-limits as long as it was in moderation. I mean, even carrots are bad for you if that's all you eat! We learned that we could have the alcoholic drink, we could have the dessert, and we could have the hot dog. We learned how to simply talk to people as we ate. We learned how to be social and eat our food without obsessing over it. Essentially, we were working toward eating the way we did when we were ten years old: without being self-conscious or hyperaware of how many calories we consumed, but simply eating when hungry and stopping when full. Over the course of several months, I began to take back my own brain. Taking back my own body was next.

· · ·

Once a week, I had a checkup with Dr. Mary Bretzman. The medical side of my treatment was extremely important for getting my body on the road to recovery and making sure that I wasn't continuing to put myself at risk. Almost all patients at The Emily Program were facing health issues that were related to their eating disorder. While that knowledge was scary, the medical rooms at The Emily Program were unlike any doctor's office I had ever been in. It didn't feel clinical. Everything felt safe. The walls weren't painted bright and blinding white but a soft green color. The rooms were kept at a warm and comfortable temperature.

A small detail at The Emily Program that had a huge impact on all patients was that our weighing was handled privately. The scales were not in an open hallway like they typically were in a regular medical clinic. In normal medical clinics, a patient's weight is in public view and discussed in these open spaces or casually talked about by doctors and nurses. As a patient with an eating disorder, getting my weight taken at a medical clinic could be a devastating experience. When I stepped onto a scale, my weight was more than just a number. Tied to that number were my emotions, anxiety, and shame. Those feelings could swing wildly up and down as I gained and lost weight. So whenever we were weighed, only the doctor, nurse, or dietitian saw the digitally displayed number on the screen. All the staff at The Emily Program were trained in handling this stressful situation, and they never made stepping onto the scale a tougher experience than it already was.

Although I was making breakthroughs in my group and private therapy sessions, I was still using symptoms when I wasn't at The Emily Program. My bulimia continued to have destructive effects on my body, and the medical staff closely monitored my body's deterioration. I underwent weekly tests, such as blood work and EKGs. This was because an eating disorder puts so much stress on the heart that it can cause arrhythmia, an abnormal heart rhythm when heartbeats are too slow, too rapid, too irregular, or too early, and this can lead to cardiac arrest. The two leading causes of death among people with eating disorders are heart attack and suicide. Since I was continuing to train and was also still using symptoms, my blood pressure and EKG tests became important measuring devices.

One day in late October, I trained hard and then used symptoms before I went into The Emily Program for my daily session. I had my doctor's appointment, and they did blood work, took my blood pressure, and did an EKG. Later that day, when I was home, I received a phone call from the medical doctor.

"Are you OK?" she asked urgently.

"Uh, yeah," I said surprised. "What do you mean?"

"Your blood sugar is so low you should be on the floor right now," the doctor said, aghast. "There's no way you should be standing or walking or talking. Obviously, just telling you to eat is not going to be helpful. But maybe get off your feet for a little while, and make sure you hydrate."

The doctor told me that my glucose level was at 35 milligrams. For most people without diabetes, blood sugar levels before meals are around 70 to 80 milligrams. Normally, my blood sugar count was between 90 and 100. The doctor from The Emily Program knew things were out of whack just from this simple test. And she was right. I had used symptoms before I went to The Emily Program that day and had also trained, so my blood sugar was all off. I had thrown up and had not eaten again in a long while.

I sat down on the couch. The whole time I was using symptoms, I'd never had any sort of health scare up until that point. Yes, I had burst blood vessels in my eyes and minor stuff. But I hadn't experienced anything really serious yet. I never lost my period, and losing a menstrual cycle was always believed to be a major marker of being in a "female athlete triad," an interrelationship of menstrual dysfunction, low energy availability (with or without an eating disorder), and decreased bone density. As long as I had my period, I mistakenly thought I was doing just fine. But the phone call was a warning that I wasn't doing nearly as well as I thought I was. Those test results were a clear sign that I was trending in the wrong direction.

I was still headed toward the edge.

• • •

What nearly pushed me over the edge was a hamburger and fries. Which was funny because at that point I knew my eating disorder wasn't truly about the food. But this particular time it totally was about the food. A hamburger bun pushed me to the breaking point.

One day for lunch it was the dreaded "hamburgers and french fry day." My middle-school celebration of this meal had turned into a sickening feeling of dread. This was a big challenge for everyone. But the other girls, who had been at The Emily Program longer, were being beautifully stoic about it.

"This is really fucking hard for me," one of the girls said as we sat down with our trays of food. She stayed positive and said, "I'm gonna eat the french fries and burger and live with it. Life will go on."

But I fell apart.

It was a normal-size burger, a quarter-pounder, and just a handful of fries. That was the serving size that I needed for my dietary needs and caloric requirements. The problem wasn't the calories or even so much about the fat. It was the white-bread bun and french fries. I had an extremely big problem with the meal because I knew that athletes weren't supposed to eat white bread. We weren't supposed to eat fried food either. So, my brain was screaming at me in an all-or-nothing scenario.

Oh my God! I can't eat this, because I need more sustainable food! I just can't eat this! I'm in training! I can't!

"I can't eat this," I told Rasa, the dietician that served me the food.

"Well, you need to eat this," Rasa said. "That's part of the program. You signed on for it."

"Do I have to eat it *all*?"

"Yes, that's your caloric requirements, Jessie. We're not asking you to eat something that will make you fat. We're asking you to eat exactly what your body needs," Rasa said kindly. "This has been calculated for you. You should feel good about it."

I trusted her. But I broke down right there in the meal line. She gave me the hamburger and fries and set it down on my tray.

"I can't eat this." I repeated, and started to sob as I sat down. The other girls were very supportive.

"No, you can do it. You can do it."

"It's gonna be OK."

"You're a great athlete. This won't affect that."

I was absolutely beside myself because I simply couldn't eat the burger and french fries. Even now, this moment makes me so sad. It's hard to explain to people what it feels like for a person suffering from an eating disorder to "just eat normally," and it's even harder to believe that for that person, in the moment, those fears are real. But in that moment, I had no appetite whatsoever, and I could no more have thrown myself off the top of a building than I could have picked up one of those "death fries." Here I was, a nineteen-year-old girl who couldn't eat a hamburger and french fries, which was such a normal lunch for so many people. But my brain had been completely hijacked. It convinced me that I could not eat the white bread. I could not have a white bun with simple carbohydrates. I needed complex carbohydrates.

My brain was on fire.

You need bread that's going stick with you! Take longer to digest! Make you feel fuller longer! This will allow you to do a better workout. The white bun and french fries on your plate will ruin your skiing career!

The other girls sat with me for an hour, their own meals long since finished. I still couldn't eat it. I just sat there sobbing.

"We really want to support you," they said. "But we have to get to our next session."

"No, it's OK. Go," I said.

"But you can't leave until you eat this," Rasa gently reminded me.

"I know."

The girls each gave me a pat on the back. They were my teammates in every way.

"All right, you can do this."

"We believe in you."

It took me two hours to summon the courage to eat the small hamburger and french fries. I took a few bites, and the hamburger and fries were gross, soggy, and cold. Rasa stayed with me the whole time. I finally ate it and was somehow still hydrated enough to keep crying.

"Well, how do you feel?" Rasa asked. "Because it's really not about the food."

A simple white bun and french fries created so much guilt. I felt like I'd eaten rat poison or worse. I really thought my world was going to end. I could barely live with the bad athlete food inside me and felt such incredible self-loathing from eating white bread. In that moment, nothing in the world mattered except for the fact that I had just eaten rat poison and I was going to die.

It felt like the end of everything.

But I got through it. I survived. I realized I didn't instantly gain twenty pounds. I didn't instantly derail my ski career. The world didn't end. I was fine.

"Oh my God," I said through a stream of tears. "I did it."

"Yes!" Rasa said. "You did it! You made it through. You should feel a sense of accomplishment!"

My eyes were so raw and red from crying for two hours that Rasa even let me break the thirty-minute bathroom rule. She went into the bathroom with me so I could splash cold water on my puffy eyes.

Immediately afterward, I walked into my group session. When I opened the door, the room erupted in applause!

"Jessie did it!" Everyone cheered. "She did it!"

And, of course, I broke down again and cried, but this time from the overwhelming feeling of support.

"Thanks, guys! This was really, really hard, and I feel so stupid and embarrassed for crying about it," I told them.

"No, don't feel stupid or embarrassed," a fellow patient said. "We've all done it."

I quickly learned that each patient at The Emily Program had a definitive breakdown moment over food like the one I had. For one girl, it was a milkshake. For another, it was pizza day. Everyone had gone through what I had just gone through and recognized what a big deal it was. We finished out the day together as a group, as teammates.

• • •

In the end, my grandpa Bill Diggins was the one who saved my life. While I was in treatment, my grandpa learned that he had lung cancer. He was known by his patients as Dr. Bill, and my grandma Lois was a nurse, and they were the sweetest couple you've ever seen. They had met in ninth grade and were sweethearts their whole lives! They lived in Thunder Bay, Ontario, and moved to the United States when my dad was in high school. When they retired, they spent every summer in Thunder Bay at the camp and every winter in Texas.

My Grandpa Diggins was so incredibly smart and patient, and he loved to putter around the camp, tinkering with things, making improvements to the buildings, and taking machinery apart and putting it back together again for fun. He figured if someone else was smart enough to put it together, he could take it apart and rebuild it too. And he always could. I'll never forget when he sat me down on the camp porch to give me stick-shift driving lessons in the family's twenty-five-year-old rusty orange Toyota, Nellie. I was so impatient to get in the car and drive! But first, Grandpa made sure I understood what the clutch was and how it worked, and made sure I was able to recite it back to him before I was allowed to get into the car. That's the kind of man he was—sweet, caring, thoughtful, and a man who wanted to understand every angle of how things worked.

I had also never, ever, heard him complain about anything. If I burned the cookies I was making, he'd happily take one and say, "They're nice and crisp! Thank you for making these!" If he cut his thumb while building something, he'd say, "Dang!" then slap a band-aid on it and keep motoring along.

But one day, he told my dad he was having some back pain. We were all surprised to hear him voice something like that because he was so physically fit and he was so tough. He didn't really notice the pain the cancerous tumor in his lung was causing until it was quite advanced. Grandpa Diggins was given weeks to live, and he was admitted to a hospital in the Twin Cities area. My whole family flew in, and we would all go and visit him every day.

The first day I went to the hospital to see him, my parents told me what was going on and what to expect when I went into the room. I was determined to see him as much as possible, and I thought I had braced myself for the moment when it all became real, when he was actually in the hospital.

I went into his room, and it crushed me. I felt the air whoosh out of my lungs, and I was speechless. He looked like a different person because he had lost so much weight. He was still himself, staying positive and never saying a word of complaint, but obviously in tremendous pain. I couldn't handle the reality of what was going on. I told my family that I needed to use the bathroom, and I ran down the hallway, desperate to get out of the room before anyone saw me cry. I wanted to stay positive, to decorate his room with photos and sparkly posters, and crying was not part of that plan. Feeling emotions and processing them weren't part of the plan. But my mom found me huddled in a corner of a hallway, and she crouched down to fold me in a hug.

"I-I-I d-didn't think it would be this b-bad." I sobbed, and she just held me, letting me know it was OK to cry.

I would go to The Emily Program during the day and visit my grandpa in the hospital right afterwards. I felt such heavy guilt and shame during this time. It felt like I was the worst granddaughter ever. I was at The Emily Program because I was voluntarily killing myself, and here was my grandpa dying from cancer. I didn't ever want my family, especially my grandpa, to know that I was in The Emily Program with an eating disorder because I didn't want them to be sad or disappointed or focus any energy on me when making my grandpa's last days as happy as possible was all that mattered.

Family members would often ask, "Where is Jessie all day?" My mom would tell them I was training or running errands. My grandma eventually started to figure things out and privately asked my mom if I was OK. My mom told her the truth because she didn't want to lie in that situation. Even in that moment, in all that pain, in all that sadness, my grandma was so loving to me. She was always supportive of me, and my eating disorder didn't change that. She never once made me feel like a fool or blamed me.

While my grandpa was in the hospital, I found it really hard to see what this pain and cancer were doing to my family. The whole family had come together to support one another and grieve for the lost time we all should have had. Specifically, I saw up close and personal what it did to my dad. My dad is strong, patient, kind, and thoughtful in tough emotional situations. He's my hero. But he was gutted by this. Anytime you lose someone you love, it's obviously really hard. But the parent-child relationship is unlike any other. I saw my dad and grandpa in those quiet moments in the hospital, and it was heartbreaking. All of their love, all of the joy—their life together was coming to an end.

I was in the hospital room when I realized that I could never voluntarily put anyone in my family through that much pain. But I was. I was doing exactly that with my bulimia. In life, a person can't control things like getting cancer or other illnesses. People get sick. People have accidents. There are times when a person can't avoid death.

But I was putting my parents through so much pain, fear, and worry with my bulimia. For the first time, I finally saw the whole picture of what I was putting my family through with my eating disorder. I had always known how wrong it was, but now I was on the other end of watching someone I adored and loved with all my heart in the process of dying, and it felt like the world was ending. How could I do this on purpose to the people who cared about me? And as a big sister who had always tried to set a good example, how could I let Mackenzie see this path that I was on?

Because of my eating disorder, my mom was having nightmares that I had died in my sleep. Earlier in my treatment, we had learned that eating disorders could cause arrhythmia and that it was the leading cause of death for people with eating disorders. The truth that I had to face was that my mom was waking up in the middle of the night to check on me. She would come into my room and check my pulse to see if I was still alive. She was so worried about me having a heart attack because that really could happen. I could've died at any moment. It doesn't really matter how long you've been using symptoms with an eating disorder. It was that dangerous.

The realization that my mom was waking up at night to see if I was still alive was a new low. It broke my heart to think about her and my dad being so worried and in so much pain over my eating disorder. I came face-to-face with this reality as I sat with my family and we made my grandpa as comfortable as possible.

I could no longer put my family through so much pain. I now knew what it felt like to watch someone you love die, and I now knew what my parents were going through as they watched me slowly kill myself. It took my grandpa's death to save my life. Which is horrible. But he saved me, because sitting in his hospital room grieving with my parents was when I realized that I really, truly needed to get better. Up until that point, I was going through the motions. I was saying that I wanted get better. But I wasn't really ready to do the hard and painful emotional work of letting go of using symptoms. I wasn't ready to divorce ED (the bastard).

Near the end, my grandpa was never alone, not for one second. He was always surrounded by family. One of us would stay with him every night, sleeping in the little cot in his room. It was in those moments sitting alone with my grandpa at night when I finally decided to fully commit to getting better. As he slept, I looked out the window into the darkness and stared at the city lights. I told myself that I couldn't live with an eating disorder anymore. I couldn't continue to put my parents through the pain of watching their daughter slowly killing herself. I committed to my recovery and went after each day with a fresh determination.

I went back to the group sessions every day. But this time with a new purpose—to not just sit there and get through it but to truly recover from the inside out. I cut down my symptom use even further, from once a day to once a week, and with every day I felt victorious. Eventually, I felt that I was actually going to be OK and that I had the tools I needed to keep fighting off my eating disorder. So, I checked out of group therapy but still stayed in touch with Angie, checking in with her periodically.

Recovery from an eating disorder doesn't happen overnight, in a few weeks, or even in a few months. It's a slow process of using symptoms less and less frequently over time while fighting ED's voice in your head. I knew realistically I'd still have some battling ahead of me. But my recovery had been kick-started by The Emily Program. When I walked out the doors from my final group session, I felt strong, hopeful, and I knew I could always go back if I needed to. With that hope, I packed my bags to head west.

CHAPTER 12

BLOOD, SWEAT, AND TEARS

For more than forty years, the cross-country racing season in North America has started at the West Yellowstone Ski Festival in Montana. Over Thanksgiving weekend, thousands of skiers from the North American ski community flock to this special festival in search of early-season snow. After I left The Emily Program, I went west to begin a new season. But the change of scenery was also going to give me a fresh start, a chance to reconnect with my love of cross-country skiing.

During my recovery, learning to live out in the real world with my eating disorder was somewhat akin to an alcoholic leaving treatment and learning to live a life of sobriety. Except you can't just give up food for life (that was kind of the problem), so it was like an alcoholic learning to have only one shot of whisky per day and be OK with it. It wasn't always pretty, and I took it day by day. It wasn't as simple as putting all of my problems in a box and then punting that box into a ditch. When I left The Emily Program, I wasn't totally whole and intact, and I had relapses during times of stress. But because of the help I had received, I was in a much higher and better place. I had an intense desire to be healthy now for the right reasons. I was able to keep fighting my eating disorder anytime it would rear up, and remember why the fight was so important. I was able to say, *No. I really don't need you. I'm better off without you.* And I wasn't alone—I could still meet with Angie, my therapist.

I had previously gone to the West Yellowstone Ski Festival when I was on the Stillwater High School team, and I'd always thought the festival was amazing and exciting. To see skiers of all abilities and ages together and participating in races and lessons was so inspirational. Now, I was there as one of the big kids on a club team. I finished in fifth place in the sprint and was eventually ranked as the top junior skier. At the end of the festival, with a new lease on life and help from The Emily Program, I began to get myself back on track.

• • •

I had deferred my acceptance to Northern Michigan University to spend a year racing with the Central Cross Country Skiing team (or CXC), an elite club team for the central region of the United States. I was the youngest person on the team by several years. At times, I felt incredibly alone because I was on my own and far from home. But I was laser focused on my ultimate goal: joining the U.S. Ski Team. I joined the CXC team because it would allow me to live at home between training camps and continue treatment for my eating disorder, and to stay close to my parents should I need to reach out for help. I also wanted to join those amazing female athletes on the team and learn everything I could from them!

The head coach of CXC at the time was Bryan Fish, an awesome guy who has been a longtime development coach for the U.S. national team after a few years spent coaching CXC. He is smart, analytical, and incredibly passionate about helping develop young skiers in the sport. The assistant coach for CXC was Jason Cork. I had met Cork during my senior year at Stillwater because I had done some workouts with CXC before officially joining the team. At the time, I had a pet duck for my AP biology class (a project on imprinting), named "Corkie." When I first met Jason, our encounter went something like this:

"Oh cool, your last name is Cork? I have a pet duck named Corkie! Can I call you Corkie?"

"No. You can call me Cork."

"OK, cool. That's cool."

This was the unlikely but solid beginning of our coaching relationship, one that still exists today. There's nobody in the entire world I trust with my training, well-being, and preparation for World Cups more than him. He's quite possibly the smartest person I've ever met, and that's really saying something, because I know some genuinely awesome nerds. A real student of the sport, Cork will spend hours reading the latest research papers on cross-country skiing and coming up with new technique drill ideas, creatively working to keep my training plan fun, fresh, and, above all, the right one for my body. He knows when I need a hug, and he knows when I'm cranky and tired and he should probably just hand me a candy bar and slowly back away. He's become a sort of "ski dad" for me, and because he's shy, I know he's blushing an astonishing shade of red as he's reading this right now, but dude, you're really one of the most important people in my life.

I was traveling around North America with CXC that winter and was having fun as I started to fuel myself once again with positive affirmation and food, getting stronger and faster both emotionally and physically. It was so exciting to be racing the SuperTour—the U.S. Ski and Snowboard Team's premier race series for prize money. If I won prize money, I did not accept it so as to preserve my college eligibility, but I was there as a real participant, and as someone who wanted to perform well to get on the radar of the U.S. national team.

I learned how to live on the road that year too, which became a skill in its own weird functional way. We had a lot of long, crazy van rides and were on an extremely tight budget. We took turns cooking dinners for the team, and I discovered that I had a lot to learn about budgeting time and resources in the kitchen. There were a lot of times where we just fell asleep in the van and woke up in the middle of the night to check into a sketchy hotel with dust bunnies in the corners and strands of hair on the pillow. Throughout it all, I was still actively recovering from my eating disorder and felt that I really couldn't talk about it to anybody. It wasn't always ideal, but we made the best of each unpredictable situation, and I continued to fight through emotional struggles because I was curious about where the path of ski racing might ultimately lead.

. . .

During the fall of my 2010–11 CXC season, the team was a national powerhouse for a while. I had some amazing teammates, who were like older brothers and sisters to me. They really looked out for me and supported me. I have fond and positive memories of CXC, but a few things really tarnished my memories of my first years as a competitive ski racer. There was one teammate who treated me like a little sister until I started beating her in races. Once I started to become a podium threat, our relationship became toxic.

This CXC teammate found out about my eating disorder and started using it against me. During team meals, she would say awful things to me about the food that I ate, and make comments about the food that I didn't eat. She announced that I had fabricated my lactose intolerance (I actually do have some lactose intolerance, which makes pizza night complicated), and she would purposely drink all the soy milk so I had none. I was also subject to frequent pointed comments about my naturally sunny personality, as she was convinced that I was fake and couldn't really be such a happy person. This psychological sabotage and bullying were all an attempt to chip away at my confidence and self-esteem.

There never is a good time to get bullied. But being bullied when I was fresh out of treatment and at my most emotionally vulnerable absolutely gutted me, especially when it came from someone I had looked up to and who I believed liked me back. I had left The Emily Program in a good but vulnerable place and had been working really hard on coming to terms with just being who I was as an athlete and as a woman. I was learning to accept myself, accept my body shape, accept the fact that I was a girl who was naturally spunky, and an athlete who was full of grit and glitter. This teammate tried to take all of that away—and left some deep and lasting psychological scars.

This teammate began to tell me lies that were clever and extremely manipulative. At the time, I was racing really well and had begun to attend camps with the national team. She knew that the one thing I wanted more than anything was to be part of the national team and to be accepted by the national team skiers, and that I didn't have great self-confidence while recovering from my eating disorder. When I would return to the CXC team after spending time with the national team, she would tell me that the national coaches called to talk about me. The coaches supposedly told her that they didn't know how to deal with me because of my eating disorder. She told me the coaches thought my eating disorder made me hard to handle. Worse still, I was told that my eating disorder made me a burden to the national team, that none of my hopefully someday teammates wanted me around because they didn't know what to do with me. I was told that they couldn't stand my bubbly personality. This CXC teammate really dug into my psyche, routinely telling me that the national team members thought I was just a fake and that there was no way I was this naturally happy.

These lies were devastating. I wanted nothing more than to be accepted, to be part of the group. I was only nineteen years old. I was torn apart by the bullying, inclined to believe the lies. My mom was scared for me when I called her and told her what was going on. She called up the CXC coaches and asked them, "Have you ever heard the name Tonya Harding?" But they were unable to stop the bullying.

I still vividly remember one day when this teammate yelled at me, telling me I was a liar, that I was a fake person who only pretended to be happy, that I was a pathetic, bad person. It was as if she embodied the voice my eating disorder had used, making me feel less than, making me believe I was unworthy of love because I was a terrible person. I cried for hours, locking myself in my room in our team rental house. One of my teammates came to find me when I didn't show up for dinner, wrapped me up in a big-brother hug and whispered in my ear, "Jessie, you are a *good person*. We love you for who you are. Don't believe those lies she told you." But I wasn't sure what to believe anymore. I had been emotionally turned upside down.

When I finally earned the opportunity to race the World Cup with the U.S. national team, I was scared of what the team members would think of me. But during my time in Europe with the national team, the entire group was completely welcoming and accepting of me. There was no drama. I felt loved for who I was. I was a part of the group. It was the exact opposite of what my CXC teammate had told me.

One day, I pulled aside national team coach Matt Whitcomb to talk

about the bullying. I summoned the courage to ask him some hard questions. I needed to know, just *had* to confirm, that the coaches thought
my eating disorder made me a burden to the team.

"What? I would *never* say that," Matt said, aghast. "I'm really sorry
you thought that you were a burden to the team. But that never happened. I never called your CXC teammate asking to talk about your
eating disorder. I would never do that, that was a complete fabrication."

Finally, the truth was revealed. It gave me an overwhelming feeling
of relief. I finally felt safe. With Matt's kind words, I escaped the bullying and destructive things this teammate was doing to me. I eventually
left the CXC team and joined the Stratton Mountain School (SMS)
T2 team in Stratton, Vermont, where I once again found a supportive,
loving, and accepting team. I lived for the summer with Sophie Caldwell and Erika Flowers, two of the nicest skiers on the planet, and I
finally felt like I was where I belonged. After the support and guidance
I received from my teammates and coaches on the SMS team, I had the
distance and ability to look back at my time with the CXC team.

I had never been bullied before my time with CXC. The bullying was
based on my teammate's own insecurity. I was winning races that she
used to win. I was training with the national team. I was young, and
everything in my life seemed perfect (which it wasn't). So this teammate went for my Achilles heel: my eating disorder and fragile confidence. It was brutal, low.

Worse still, I would be haunted years down the road by the memory of feeling less than nothing. I had severe anxiety whenever I knew
that I'd have to see her again. I would feel my heartbeat pick up and my
palms get sweaty, terrified that I might be once again leveled by this
person who had reduced me to nothing so many years ago. Even with
good people all around me and a World Championship medal in my
sock drawer, I was still scared to face this former teammate.

But the dynamics had changed. The coaches and athletes on the
national team dug a line in the snow and said that bullying behavior
was unacceptable. I had a supportive team at my back, my confidence
was back to where it belonged, and I knew without a shred of doubt that
I was a good person and fine the way I was. Still, the power of these old
psychological scars scared me and made me realize how far-reaching

the effects of bullying could be. I vowed to never, ever let something like that happen to another athlete on the same team as I was.

• • •

My journey to get to the national team wasn't a straight, linear path. Nothing ever is! There were a lot of ups and downs. There was nothing but work and dedication, nothing more than long hours of competing and traveling from race to race, but I thought that it was the coolest job ever and had a lot of fun with it.

One of the reasons I was so excited to make the national team was the people. For me, it wasn't about the national team status or the sick jacket (although, let's be real, that's pretty sweet). It wasn't for the glory. I wanted to be surrounded by these amazing, kick-ass women who were all driven just like me but in their own fierce way. Before I became a permanent member of the national team, I had two moments with U.S. national skier Liz Stephen when I was younger that fired me up, fueled my spirit, and had a long-lasting positive impact on me.

I already knew that the national team had athletes who were caring, outgoing, and welcoming, none more so than Liz. She is the kind of person who knows what you need before you yourself even know what you need. She somehow always had a finger on the pulse of the team, and it was only years later that I realized she not only was a naturally caring individual but also worked hard to hold the team together in times of stress, prioritizing the team. She knew how people were doing, how to help them, and how to get people out of their shell. Liz always makes people feel welcomed, and that is a really amazing, special quality. You don't often meet someone so in tune with each member of a team, or someone who cares enough to truly welcome each newcomer.

I first met Liz when I was in high school and was invited to attend a camp at the Olympic Training Center in Lake Placid, New York. It was my first time at the Olympic Training Center. There were bobsledders everywhere who looked like Greek gods and goddesses. Some of the men had legs the size of my entire torso. There were lugers, skeleton athletes, rhythmic gymnasts, moguls athletes, freeskiers, and all sorts of athletes from all over the country. There were Olympic medalists everywhere I looked. I felt as though I had been let into some sort of secret world.

One day, I was told by the coaches that Liz was about to do some interval training on roller skis at below-race-pace intensity and that we could join her if we wanted to try and hang with her. Liz greeted a small group of us before she began her workout.

"Hi, guys!" She said and proceeded to high-five each of us. "Feel free to jump in right behind me!"

Liz took off, and I hung on to her like a barnacle on the side of a ship. As Liz skied, she was in total control with a perfect stride. And me? I was inches away from what felt like imminent death, just trying to stay right behind her. I was skiing outside myself in one of the hardest work-outs of my life. I was in race pace the whole time and crawled my way up the Whiteface Mountain Road behind her.

At the end of the workout, I was hanging on to my poles just trying to stay upright. But that's when the most awesome thing happened. Instead of being annoyed that I, this little nobody, was on her heels the whole time, breathing like a Basset hound with asthma, Liz turned back toward me and said, "Hey, thanks for joining me. That was super fun. You did a great job! I'm proud of you."

I felt this surge of confidence, admiration, and love toward Liz. For me, it was the equivalent of a high school basketball player being invited to play with Michael Jordan. And then at the end of the epic ass-kicking game, Jordan thanking you for playing with him. *I mean, what the heck? What kind of professional athlete is this open, welcoming, and kind?* Her encouragement was all the motivation that I needed. I held on to her words for the longest time. For the next year, whenever I was doing intervals, I pretended Liz was in front of me. I visualized it and could see her skiing with amazing technique. I trained so hard for so long because someday I wanted to be on the team with her and those other amazing women.

The second time I met Liz was . . . a total disaster. Not because of her, understand, but because of me and, specifically, my lack of self-confidence. I was once again selected to attend a national camp in Sun Valley, Idaho, as a guest, where I would be living and training with the team for two weeks. This time around, I was drowning in the depths of my eating disorder, and all my previous self-confidence from my early high school days had melted away.

It was my first workout on my first day, and we were doing speed drills. I was warming up and just stoked—trying to be chill, but on the inside, I was freaking out. *I'm at the national camp. Oh my god. Here are all my heroes. They're so fast!* Don't worry, my facade cracked within ten minutes. During our warm-up on the bike path, I got a stick stuck between my wheel and the fender of my roller ski. My ski stopped dead, and I got a physics lesson, flying into a pile of gravel on the side of the trail. My upper thigh and butt cheek got completely torn apart. It looked like I had taken a cheese grater to my leg, cutting a bloody mess a foot high and half a foot wide. The scar on the side of my butt and leg is still so defined that even now people at the beach will ask me about it.

"I'm fine, I'm fine, I'm fine," I repeated, as I sat in a pile of roadside gravel completely mortified.

I didn't want to cause a disruption, so I sprang up. I was in a lot of pain, perhaps because there were still rocks stuck in my butt. But I kept skiing. We started doing speed drills, and suddenly Liz looked over at me in shock.

"Jessie! Did you fall?" she asked.

"What? Nope! Well, maybe. I don't know . . . does it look like I did?"

Surrounded by my heroes and completely embarrassed, I realized that my shorts were plastered to the side of my leg and stuck in a bunch of blood. There was blood dripping out from under the edge of my shorts, down past my knees, and into my boots. There was a little puddle of blood on the asphalt beneath my skis. It looked like a bear had reached out from the bushes and taken a casual swipe at my leg.

Liz sprang into what I later learned was her instinctive "team mom mode" and said, "Oh my god, come here, let me see your leg."

"No, no. I'm fine. I can finish the workout."

"OK, but afterward, I'm fixing that," Liz said.

So, after our workout, Liz Stephen—one of the best American cross-country skiers ever—took me back to the condo and picked tiny rocks out of my leg and butt cheek with tweezers.

We both laughed at the ridiculousness of it all, and with our giggling, my real personality started to peek out. I had been so scared to show who I really was because my eating disorder had convinced me that nobody would like me for *me*. I still didn't have great self-confidence, although I was working hard on it. It took a handful of rocks in my butt to wake me up. I realized that one of the worst things that could've happened—an embarrassing training accident—had happened, and I wasn't sent home. No one kicked me out. They still looked at me the same way and accepted me for my klutzy self.

• • •

The winter after leaving The Emily Program and racing SuperTours with CXC, I was nineteen years old and one of the top junior skiers in the country. I was having a lot of success for a young racer, but I wasn't dominating the senior field. With healthy fuel now in my system, I became steady in my training and in my race preparation, and my momentum kept building. I went to the national races in Rumford, Maine, with the CXC team, excited to race as a pro for the first time and see where I stacked up.

The U.S. Cross-Country Ski Championships in January is where all the best American skiers—minus those who are currently racing World Cup and Tour de Ski—come together and duke it out. It's comprised of four races: two sprints (both classic and skate), a 20K mass start for the women, and a 10K individual start. These races are for all the peanuts, the vaunted national title. Just as important, though, a good performance at nationals helps earn that skier one of the highly coveted starter spots for the World Cup races. If that skier has also raced well in the fall SuperTours, she or he could potentially lock in a starter spot and race in the next period of World Cup races. This is a really big deal because the whole goal, in the end, is to race and eventually win on the World Cup circuit.

It was in the skate sprint at nationals where I had my first big break. I had an OK qualifier, and my tactics were a little on the, let's say, improvisational side, but the day was coming together for me, and I realized I had a serious shot at the podium. The course went out flat with a little dip under a bridge before climbing up, with a winding, gradual downhill toward the finish line. That last downhill stretch was less than half a kilometer. I went out in the skate sprint final, and things were going well, as I was out front for most of the race.

I was a half kilometer away from winning my first national title when I tripped and fell with the finish line nearly in sight. All of the skiers behind me blew right past as I was struggling back to my feet. For a brief second, I was in shock. How could I let this happen? How could I possibly win *now*?

With nothing left to lose, I sprang back into action as fast as I could, furiously pushing with my arms and legs as fast as I could move them. My whole body was so far into the pain cave that my limbs started to go numb. The good thing about getting passed by the entire heat was that with five girls ahead of me on the last downhill, I got a *very* good draft. I miraculously caught up before scooting through a little gap, picked my finishing lane, and skied with all my heart to win my very first national title.

It was a monumental win for me, not only for the title and the start in the 2011 World Championships skate sprint that I earned with it, but for my mental strength. I learned a valuable lesson about the power of never, ever giving up. Even when there seems to be no possible way forward, you won't know for sure until you try with everything you have.

•   •   •

Shortly after nationals, I flew to the World Junior Ski Championships and then met up with the World Cup team. My first World Cup race was a skate sprint in Drammen, Norway, in the weeks leading up to the 2011 World Championships in Oslo. This was the big leagues. You never forget your first World Cup: the lights, the crowds, the exhilarating feeling of seeing the biggest stage of the sport you've been living and breathing your entire life. I was blown away and, honestly, totally distracted by the glory of it all. I was right in the heart of the sport, the hardest place to score World Cup points. The host country of a World Cup gets extra start spots, which meant the field was loaded with Norwegian skiers. And—news flash—they are very, very good.

A sprint race starts with a qualifying round, where each skier starts individually, spaced fifteen seconds apart, and races the 1.2-ish kilometer course. The top thirty fastest skiers qualify for the heats and are placed in five heats of six athletes each. In each heat of six, the top two automatically advance, and then out of all the heats, the two next fastest times are lucky-loser spots, and those skiers also advance. There's the quarterfinal, semifinal, and then the final round, which ultimately determines who is on the podium.

I was a long way from the Minnesota state high school finals on a golf course! At the World Cup, I was dazzled by everything: the media, the fans, the cameras, and the noise. It was like cross-country skiing inside an outdoor rock and roll festival. The fans were everywhere along the course and loud, and they had clearly been enjoying a few brewskis. The Scandinavian fans know everything about skiing too. There was a massive screen on a semitruck that showed the race and results for fans.

The pageantry of it all made me feel like I was racing incredibly fast as I completed my qualifier lap. Back on earth, I got my butt kicked. I was so far from qualifying that it was comical. When I wheezily asked Grover, the U.S. national coach, what place I finished in, he said, "Yeah, let me look it up for you!" He started scrolling down the results on his phone. "You did great! Was it fun?" Still scrolling. "Yeah, it was super cool!" Scroll, scroll scroll . . . "You got sixty-fifth."

It would've been easy to give up and think that I would never make it at the World Cup races. But instead of wallowing, I used my defeat as motivation. For the first time, I saw what it was going to take to get to the next level.

At the 2011 World Championships, I finally qualified for the heats in the skate sprint (but to be fair, this isn't as hard as it sounds, because each country can start only four athletes at World Championships and Olympics). Although I finished twenty-ninth in the sprint (what the heck, I somehow beat somebody!) and twenty-eighth in the pursuit, my biggest happy moment was yet to come.

I had been scheduled to fly home to compete at junior nationals the following week, but my results, effort, and potential kept me on the World Championships team, and I was given the chance to anchor the 4 × 5K relay. This was huge for me, because it was the first time that I got the opportunity to draw face paint on everybody! I felt like part of the crew! The team was made up of Kikkan Randall, Holly Brooks, Liz

Stephen, and then me as the anchor. We finished in ninth place, but it was the best relay finish for the U.S. women's team in thirty years. It also marked the first time that I anchored a relay team for the United States. Since that race, I've anchored every relay over the past nine years, with the exception of being sick once. Even though they put me last simply because the older women could keep us in the race longer, that was the day I began to learn what it meant to carry pressure and take the team across the finish line. It became a valuable learning experience for me.

Back in the United States, I skied in the 2011 junior national races close to home in Minneapolis, Minnesota. I swept the series, gaining confidence race by race, experimenting with strategy and tactics. It was the perfect complement to racing in the big leagues in Europe. The highlight was winning the relay with my teammates and having so much fun living with this group of skiers.

That spring, I traveled to Sun Valley, the place of my epic rocks-in-the-butt wipeout, for "spring series," the second part of the U.S. national races, which included a few SuperTour races and the 30K mass start distance national title. It was a classic race, not my strong suit, and my first time racing 30 kilometers. I was in so much pain that I started to cry during the race but refused to give up or back off the pace. Sadie Bjornsen remembers me passing her and that in between gasping, wheezing breaths, I was sobbing. I mean, what the hell? Who cries in a race? I cried the whole way up the final steep hill, somehow powering to the finish line and the podium. Shortly thereafter, I got a call from the national team, and they offered me a spot.

I had made the national team literally through blood, sweat, and tears.

• • •

I still had a college acceptance waiting for me, and I had some lingering doubts about stepping off the traditional path. I called the NMU head coach, Sten Fjeldheim, and hesitantly told him I had been offered a spot on the national team. His reaction stays with me to this day, because of how incredible it was. Instead of trying to persuade me to come race for him and make him look brilliant by winning NCAA titles, he said, "Don't come here. You have an amazing opportunity to go out and chase down your dreams. You've really got something here, and I think you need to see it through. If you ever change your mind, we'll be here waiting for you, but I don't think college is the right path for you." His words really freed me, cutting through any last worries I had and relieving any stress I felt about letting him down by not showing up on his doorstep in September. So I put college indefinitely on hold and dedicated my life to racing for the U.S. national team.

CHAPTER 13

THE NATIONAL TEAM

In May 2011, I went to my first U.S. national team camp as an official member. It was in Bend, Oregon, where the spring camp is traditionally held. I was so excited. I roomed with Sadie Bjornsen, who was also new to the team. For the next seven years, whenever we stayed in that house at camp, Sadie and I would room together, share a bed, and sleep on the same sides, like Bert and Ernie.

Around this time, the U.S. national women's ski team was beginning to assemble a team that would compete in Europe in a major way. Kikkan Randall, a giant in the ski world, was there to share everything she'd learned and inspire us. It was the first year for Ida Sargent on the team too. Holly Brooks and Liz Stephen were our team moms, and as you might expect, they were incredible. Our team chemistry was coming together, and things were looking good.

I was the youngest member on the team, however, and was experiencing some growing pains. After a tough day, coach Matt Whitcomb sat me down. I was in tears because I was worried that I wasn't doing the right things. I was worried that I wasn't fitting in. I was still having some body image issues and wasn't totally over my eating disorder. And I was terrified to show that I was suffering in front of my new teammates, worried that I would bum them out or bring them down with my struggles.

"Who you are is good enough," Matt said to me. "You can just be yourself, because that's who we want to see. We don't want you to feel like you have to hide anything."

At times, I was being overly cheerful because I was insecure and nervous. I was forcing it because I didn't want anyone to see me upset. My low self-esteem still lingered. I thought maybe it wasn't OK for me to share my burdens with other people. I thought it wasn't OK for me to be sad and for other people to have to deal with my sadness or the remnants of my eating disorder issues.

"No, that's what we want. We want the authentic Jessie," Matt said. "However you're actually feeling, it's OK. We accept you. You need to trust us that we're going to love the real you. Warts and all. *Especially* the warts."

In the year after I left The Emily Program, I had faced bullying, self-doubt, embarrassing wipeouts and accidents, the intensity of my first World Cup, and a tough path to the national team. But I had eventually arrived.

"Who you are is good enough," Matt said. I believed him.

•   •   •

Later that year, I started to really find my mojo. I was much healthier and still working hard on my recovery from my eating disorder, but as it turns out . . . when you let yourself digest the food you eat, you race fast! Who knew, right? The fall of 2011, I won thirteen races on the SuperTour in five weeks, then swept the 2012 U.S. nationals. I went from winning one race the year before to being the top American in every race. This ended up being key as those points allowed me to lock down a start for the rest of the World Cup season, which was really important because now I felt no pressure. I wasn't competing against anyone else on the U.S. team for start rights.

I flew right from U.S. nationals to Milan, Italy, for my first full World Cup weekend. Up until that point, I'd done only one World Cup race outside of World Championships. The race was in a park right in the middle of the city. The snow was packed up above the green grass. There was a long finishing stretch filled with people in the stands, and the Italians were going nuts. There were flares, wild noisemakers, even a guy revving a chain saw. There were hundreds of people in colored wigs. I was jet-lagged and hadn't really slept at all. But I was game.

Because I had been the second American finisher in the individual sprint, I was chosen to be leg one of the team sprint with Kikkan, one of my biggest heroes. The only problem was that I had no idea how a team sprint worked! I had never done one. I'd seen it once before at World Championships, so I knew that each skier needed to do three laps. But that was about it. I had to learn how to do everything else: how to tag off, how to strategize, and how to pace myself.

Luckily, I got to learn from the best. Kikkan was already a major ass kicker on the World Cup circuit, which made her a superstar. But what I really loved the most about Kikkan was how dedicated she was to the team and how willing she was to share everything she had learned. There are so many pros in sports who say, "I figured this out on my own, I don't owe it to anyone to share what I've learned," but Kikkan was the exact opposite of that! She set the most incredible example anyone could hope for. She would patiently answer any questions we younger athletes had about racing, training, and tactics. At the World Championships the year before, she'd invited me into her room to watch episodes of *Glee* on her laptop between races to wind down. She was approachable and friendly and always made me feel welcomed to the team.

All of this came in handy when we were rooming together in Milan. She was so calm and nonjudgmental about the fact that she was paired with me—a hyper and total nobody who didn't know what she was doing. I was bouncing off the walls like a teenage racquetball, jittery with adrenaline and nerves. Meanwhile, Kikkan was as cool as ever.

"Hey, you're going to do great. Just relax," Kikkan told me. "Let's go have fun!"

Kikkan set the right tone for welcoming this young kid who was getting her feet in the water. I think that was really beautiful. She showed me how she warmed up. She showed me how she prepped for a big race. I just took it all in.

I was not used to how rough the World Cup races were. In the United States, when people wanted to pass, they just said, "track," and then you moved over and let them pass. If you were really lucky and racing in the Midwest, you might even get "Excuse me, please, I'd really like to pass you if that's OK?"

The World Cup circuit was an exciting, harsh reality.

As I went to tag Kikkan in the semifinals, a Swedish skier cut right over the tips of my skis. It caused me to somersault, and I crashed hard to the ground, letting out a surprised squeak. Luckily, Kikkan heard it, backpedaled to me, and reached down for the tag off.

In between the semifinals and the finals, I was mortified.

"Oh my god. I'm so sorry. I don't even know what happened! I'm so sorry!"

"It's OK. Let's just focus on being smart and staying out of trouble in the final," Kikkan said calmly.

Apparently, I did neither. In the team sprint finals, I wiped out again. No, seriously, I did. Two races. Two wipeouts in the tag zone. Despite my epic cartwheels, Kikkan closed with a fantastic last lap, and we still stepped up to the podium in second place.

Is this what it's going to be like every *weekend on the World Cup?* I wondered to myself.

No, it was not.

• • •

In November 2012, I embarked on my first full World Cup season. That year, we opened in Gällivare, Sweden, a town formed in the seventeenth century and a place that was always cold and dark during the winter. Perfect for racing.

The selection for the 4 × 5K relay team on Sunday was based on the results of the top four skiers in the 10K skate the day before. Holly Brooks, Kikkan Randall, and Liz Stephen were selected, and I was selected to anchor the team, which meant that Ida Sargent was picked as the alternate. We were starting the first year of many years to come where one or more skiers were going to have to sit out. It was a great problem to have, but it was also really tough on the skier who couldn't race. But how Ida handled the disappointment of not being picked would become one of the greatest moments in the history of the U.S. women's cross-country ski team.

I think a lot of athletes on a lot of other teams would have reacted negatively to not being selected as a starter. She had every right to be disappointed. But that wasn't Ida. She took the high road, and her relentless spirit and positivity became a bedrock moment for our team. It was the start of what we called the "fifth leg of the relay" because it was our way of saying that the alternate was our most important leg. It was the alternate's attitude and her approach to that day and to the race that could make or break the team. The alternate was just as much a part of the race as any skier with a bib on.

Ida wore pink sparkly suspenders and was out on the course cheering like nobody's business. She was yelling at me with so much passion while I was racing that I honestly didn't even recognize her. We all thought it was just some crazy woman in a weird outfit. But it wasn't. It was our beloved teammate! Ida stood on a hill for over an hour and screamed until she went hoarse. Her cheers lifted me up and sent me flying down the course, determined not to let her down.

Ever since Ida's performance in Sweden, every fifth leg has been amazing. I think that is one of the big secrets of why our team finally found success: putting the team above individuals. Over the years every athlete on the team has contributed in many ways, but Ida's selfless attitude really set a precedent.

As for the actual race? Holly, Kikkan, and Liz were amazing. I was the weakest link for sure, and it didn't help that as anchor I was up against the giants of the sport: Marit Bjørgen and Charlotte Kalla. They both flew right by me, and I was suddenly in danger of losing us a podium position. I dug in with everything I had in that final kilometer, doggedly clinging to Norway's second team, and just managed to outsprint them in a head-to-head drag race over the final hundred meters.

When I crossed the finish line, I let out an ear-splitting scream that came all the way from my toes and out of my mouth. People thought it was a celebratory cry of emotion, because I knew we had gotten third place, our first relay medal in U.S. women's history. But I actually screamed because I was in agony.

I collapsed on the ground. I couldn't breathe. I was seeing stars. My teammates all rushed over, and they were patting my back.

"Don't touch! . . . Can't breathe!" I screamed, and with it came the start of a new team tradition called "When Jessie's on the ground, don't touch anywhere near her rib cage, don't touch her back, don't touch her chest. Just . . . don't touch her."

Our celebrating was so loud that people thought we had won! We had so much joy because we had accomplished something that no one thought possible: the United States stepping on the podium in a team relay. In recent years, the United States had never been taken seriously on relay day—we were just not a skiing nation with the depth to pull it off.

But suddenly, we were in the medals. I look back on that picture I have of the five of us—Ida in her suspenders, and all of us at the finish line in this huddle—and it brings tears to my eyes. The pride and ownership of that moment were the start of something. It took everyone buying in and racing their hearts out to make it happen.

In that moment at the finish line, we started to really believe. It was a building block, a cornerstone of the team we were building together.

● ● ●

I inherited many wonderful things from my dad, but feet were not one of them. I have the worst feet ever. They're incredibly flat with almost no arch, and are prone to injuries. Although my spirits were high after our team relay finish in Gällivare, I was starting to develop a serious injury in my heels. Because of the way my feet are shaped, my heels were rubbing up and down in my beloved Salomon ski boots, and bursitis soon developed. By the time I realized what was happening, it was too late, and the injuries progressed into bone spurs. When I skied, every time I kicked my foot back, it felt like I was slamming my foot into a concrete wall. It was an all-consuming pain that I hadn't experienced before. Sometimes in training, I'd go down on my knees because I couldn't stand on my feet. I was often in tears behind my sunglasses, and I had no idea what to do about my wrecked feet. The team physical therapist stepped in to provide treatment: e-stim, where they put an electric stimulus on the heel to reduce the swelling; a topical ibuprofen patch; and lots of ice sessions.

To compound the pressure, we were flying to Quebec soon for the last World Cup weekend of period one, and my whole family was coming from Minnesota. My high school coach Kris and her family were coming. I wanted so badly to race well in front of them. I did everything I could to take care of my feet. Every single moment I was not in my ski boots, nothing could touch my heels. In an act of desperation, I bought a pair of pink Crocs. They were the wrong shade of pink. Not even a cute shade of pink. A bad shade of pink!

Two days out from the race, I needed to train but couldn't do anything to damage my feet. So I went to the gym in my scary pink Crocs and rode a spin bike to get in a one-hour, easy workout. Spinning was so boring for me when I had no one to talk to, so I brought my computer with me so I could watch *Gossip Girl*. I was in ragged shorts, a mismatched tank top and pink Crocs, spinning while watching Blair and Serena fight it out on the bike handlebars.

I was so involved in watching *Gossip Girl* that I didn't notice the gym slowly filling in around me. With a shock, I realized I was surrounded by the entire Norwegian men's sprint team. They were doing intervals on the treadmills, and every one of them looked like a Norse god. I was surrounded by an entire room of men that looked like Thor. They were so intimidatingly gorgeous. And me? I was in my Crocs, spinning and watching *Gossip Girl*. I wanted to die in that moment. These weren't just guests of the hotel, people that I would never see again. These were men whom I would see every winter for the next eight years. Whoops! My cover was blown, so with a bright-red face, I owned it. I went back to watching and spinning because I thought, well . . . what the hell, the damage has been done.

• • •

On the day of the team sprint, I was still in a lot of pain. The bone spurs never went away, and I was left with these pokey little spurs that still look slightly more purple than the rest of my foot. The Salomon ski reps saved me by drilling a hole in the back of my boots before the race to relieve the pressure, and covered the hole up with a waterproof patch. To be safe, I decided to not put my boots on until it was absolutely necessary. As I walked to the course, my feet were soaked as I punched through the icy, ankle-deep slop in my pink Crocs.

Thousands of American cross-country fans filled the streets and lined the course. Hundreds of high schoolers, ski club members, and students from colleges along the East Coast had come to Quebec. There were more Americans in the crowd than Canadians, and we felt like it was our World Cup too. It was so inspiring that I was able to mostly ignore the white-hot pokers that my heels had become!

I was once again selected to the team sprint with Kikkan. We ended up winning (because Kikkan was so amazing!), and it marked the first team sprint win in our history. In those early years on the team, we had a lot of "firsts" that we got to punch through! And I had a few life lesson firsts too.

On the podium, they handed us big bottles of champagne that were clearly meant for us to shake and spray on people. But having missed my college phase, I had never opened a bottle of champagne before, and I couldn't get the damn thing open! Kikkan, the Germans, and the Norwegians were spraying everyone, and nobody had access to laundry, so our jackets stunk like alcohol for weeks afterwards, fermenting in our suitcases. It was worth it.

Afterwards, Kikkan came up to me with a jokingly serious face.

"We need to give you a champagne-opening lesson."

• • •

We arrived like a buzz saw in La Clusaz, France, for another World Cup 4 × 5K relay. The U.S. women's team was full of confidence, moxie, and excitement, ready to take on the best in the world once again.

Then the race started, and everything went sideways. In the end, it would be the worst race we ever had. We fell apart in every way. There were a few big crashes, some broken poles. We didn't really nail the wax. We were not pacing it right, and all of us were blowing up in the altitude. By the time I joined the race as the anchor leg, we were over a kilometer behind.

As I raced, I remember seeing the techs and coaches for all the other countries leaving the course because all of their skiers were already finished. I was still out there giving it my heart and soul. It's an interesting mix, being the anchor leg. Sometimes there is a ton of pressure. If you're lucky, you get a little bit of the glory of being the one who gets to cross the finish line. But then you get times like this one where the spectators were flocking away from the course as I was racing. The entire crowd had literally turned their backs on me. It was so hard to be out there all alone.

But what was really interesting was what happened after the race, as we all went on a cool-down ski together.

"Wow, that . . . really sucked."

We all started laughing because that was the only thing we could do. We could laugh or we could cry. Even though we finished in last place by a mile (literally), it was a huge team-bonding moment. I was even more proud of how we handled the shittiest relay ever than I was about how we handled our first podium three months earlier. We came together as a team. Nobody pointed fingers. Nobody blamed anybody else. Nobody was angry. It was awesome.

• • •

Fast-forward a few weeks, and we were at the 2013 World Championships in Val di Fiemme, Italy. For the third time in my life, I was quaking in my boots and pee-my-pants nervous, as I was leg one to Kikkan's leg two in the team sprint. As leg one, it was my job to keep in contact with the lead pack. I didn't have to be a hero. Heck, I didn't even have to lead! All I had to do was stay close to the leaders.

The morning of the race, Kikkan and I got together. We noticed that it had snowed lightly overnight. Some skiers would've found the new snow to be an obstacle because it would make the course soft. But it was to be our advantage.

"This is great because it will slow the track down," Kikkan said.

"It will make it less of a pure sprint," I added. "More of a guts race." Thank God, because the sprint gene had really skipped a generation with me.

We had positive attitudes and were so supportive of one another. We were not the favorites. We just wanted to put together a great day.

We breezed through the semifinals, conserving some of our energy, which set us up perfectly for the finals. I had so much belief and confidence in Kikkan that I didn't even watch her laps as I jogged around between my laps. I just *knew* she was out there kicking ass.

When I went out for my last leg—lap five—of the race, I shot to the front of the pack, thinking, *I have a lot of energy, so I'll push the pace and try to tire everybody else out.* I wanted to give Kikkan the best position I could for the final lap. I kept a crazy pace up the first big hill and started dropping people. A Finnish skier got a little too close and stepped on my pole basket, and it ripped out of my hand (it was an accident, and she apologized after the race). The pole didn't even break. It just slid right off my skinny wrist, the strap still fastened in a loop.

I didn't even stop to think. I just kept going, turning the tempo up, skiing with my legs.

"Pole!" I yelled, and kept skiing.

Erik Flora, a U.S. coach from Alaska, was two hundred meters up the hill and saw the whole thing happen. He came sprinting down the hill to hand me a pole. But this part of the course wasn't one of our pre-identified conflict zones, so my spare poles were in another part of the course. All Flora had to give me was a giant men's classic pole. It was taller than I was, but I grabbed this monstrous pole anyway. I didn't even have time to put my hand in the strap.

Finland and Sweden had both passed me, but I had a lot of adrenaline, and thought I could still make it happen. On the downhill, I drafted them in a tiny bullet tuck and shot past them. With all the energy I had, I scampered around the top corner with my ridiculous big pole and came roaring into the stadium in first place. I tagged Kikkan with a lead. It was barely a lead, but I felt that I had finally, *finally* been a real contributing member to our relay team.

Most important, I hadn't been dropped. I was so stoked. In that moment, I felt that I was no longer just a young upstart, a kid with a lot of energy and nothing else. I was really proud of my effort and use of strategy. I did my part. We all knew Kikkan was going to be amazing in leg two, but nobody really had any expectations for me as leg one.

Kikkan took off, and I didn't even look at the screen because I knew in my heart that she was going to cross that line first, and I was too busy sprinting to the finish zone to look up! Kikkan kicked so much ass that

she increased the lead to a whopping *nine* seconds. She crossed the finish line, and I jumped right on top of her. I was crying, she was laughing, and we were both so emotional because the U.S. women's team had
never won a World Championship gold medal.

I was twenty-one years old. For the first time, I learned that I do not
crack under pressure with the world watching. I didn't panic. I didn't
give up. I just put my head down and worked.

All with a giant pole.

• • •

I was flying high that next summer, training hard and looking forward
to the 2014 Olympics in Sochi, Russia. I figured if I trained well and
raced similarly to the year before, I would definitely make the team.
What a naive thought! Nothing is ever guaranteed.

While training at a team camp at the Lake Placid Olympic Training
Center in New York, I suddenly stopped short on an easy afternoon
run, sudden and sharp pain shooting through my foot. I hadn't rolled
it, hadn't stumbled, but suddenly I could no longer push off my foot
without intense discomfort. Cork stayed with me as I hobbled back to
the car on one foot and one heel, a feat that took an hour. After an X-ray
and an afternoon spent with the awesome PTs at the training center,
we still didn't know exactly what was wrong, but a big purple bruise
mottled the top of my foot near my toes. I was put in a walking boot
and crutches. I was furious. We were five months out from the Olympics, and I couldn't even walk down the hallway without a boot. Cross-
country skiing is a sport where you don't take a lot of rest days, so I was
panicked about losing my fitness.

I found ways to train around it. I learned what "smizing" meant (it
means smile with your eyes, duh) from Tyra Banks as I gritted my teeth
and rode the spin bike with one leg for two and a half hours, alone in
the hot hallway of the training center. *America's Next Top Model* was the
only show that was on, so I got pretty seriously invested. I did strength
in my boot, doing pull-ups, dips, push-ups, and one-legged squats. I was
determined not to lose a drop of fitness while we figured out what was
wrong with my leg.

I needed more help, so I flew to Park City, Utah. Once there, I got an MRI and learned that somehow, miraculously, I'd managed to pull a muscle in between my toes, which was why I couldn't push off from the ball of my foot. I didn't even know you *could* pull those muscles! I healed up quickly and soon enough was back to training in full force, but it was a shocking reminder of how fragile my job was, and how quickly a freak injury might derail months and years of hard work.

CHAPTER 14

PLANES, TRAINS, AND AUTOMOBILES

By the time I was twelve, I had already amassed enough posters of professional cross-country skiers to wallpaper my room. I had all the heavy hitters, the big names in the sport, and they decorated the basement room where we waxed our skis. But my favorite poster was the one I snitched from my mom, and it was the only one I put up in my bedroom. I would lie awake at night and stare up at my poster of Bill Koch, America's only Olympic medalist, and dream about how rad his life was as an American skier. That poster was the first thing I saw when I woke up, and it was last thing I looked at before I went to bed. I was inspired by my Koch poster, but not for the reasons you might think.

I wasn't motivated by the poster because he was a medalist (although that was undeniably badass). I was motivated because in the poster he was sand skiing the surf in Hawaii. I mean, seriously, Koch looks like some sort of Greek god mixed with a skiing superhero. Instead of showing him off as a serious medal winner, the poster showed him cross-country skiing on a beach, clearly having a blast! He was tan and ripped and just howling down the sand with a wall of surf crashing behind him. I thought this poster was the absolute coolest thing in the world because it showed me that skiing could take you around the world to train and compete in amazing places. In fact, I still think that! That poster is still hanging up above my childhood bed, and it will come down when I die . . . or when my parents sell the house, whichever comes first.

I was motivated by the desire to become one of the national team members because it meant I, too, would get to travel and train in those places. I could be on a team with other people who were just as stoked as I was to ski and train and do weird things like cross-country ski in the surf! Was I motivated by the idea of winning a medal? Yes, of course. What kid isn't? But mostly I desperately wanted to make the U.S. national team so I could do kick-ass stuff like Bill Koch.

It was humbling to realize I was beginning to live out my childhood dreams. The U.S. cross-country ski team travels to the most remote corners of the world in search of snow. We're the "reverse surfers." Instead of traveling the world in an endless summer looking for waves, we are in a forever winter chasing snowflakes. I was beginning to roam the world with a ski bag, duffel, and backpack in year-long nomadic adventures that were equal parts a Griswold family vacation, an absurd *Planes, Trains, and Automobiles* fiasco, and an epic quest straight out of *Lord of the Rings*. If you will permit me to jump around in time and space, I'll show you what it feels like to be training and traveling as a professional skier; the good, the bad, and the straight-up ugly parts.

• • •

Training and conditioning season is from May through early November, and it occurs all over the world. Historically the first stop is at the U.S. ski team camp in Bend, Oregon. There's snow on Mount Bachelor typically all the way through the end of May, and getting back on skis to reconnect with good technique habits is a great way to kick off the training year. This is where the U.S. cross-country ski team reconnects with each other as well, after our April hiatus.

You can really learn a lot about someone when you travel with them. When you're far from home, tired, sometimes homesick, sometimes *actually* sick, your true colors come out. A lot of my teammates have been right beside me when I've been at my absolute worst. They've been there when there was no hint of a gold medal or glitter to be found. The biggest example of this was the time I traveled to Bend to begin a training camp, and within days of my arrival, my teammates had to lift me off the bathroom floor because I was so sick. To my stoic roommate Hannah Halvorsen, in her first camp as a new member of the U.S. development team . . . thanks for pretending this was not shocking and disgusting, and I'm so sorry you had to see that.

I got food poisoning so bad it had hollowed me clean out. Every drop of my typical hyper energy flushed down the drain (literally and figuratively). All of my teammates checked on me, bringing me Pedialyte and Ritz crackers. They were comforting even though I turned our condo bathroom into a no-go zone! The head women's team coach, Matt Whitcomb, came in to bring me Pedialyte and saw me wrecked on the bathroom floor. I had fallen asleep on the bath mat. My clothes were disheveled, and my hair was wild and tangled. Matt is such a chill dude, with a cool, laid-back surfer's vibe. He has a way of looking at you that makes you feel seen, and listening to you that makes you feel genuinely heard. He sat down on the toilet lid, looked down at me, and just said, "Whoa."

The next day, my body recovered. I felt fine and was determined to start training with the team . . . because that was why we were there! I wanted to do my part in building the squad into a kick-ass team of American skiers. Again, my teammates were supportive even though I still looked like Beetlejuice. But my coaches didn't want me to jump back into training too hard because my tendency is to just push and push and push, even when I should probably be resting.

The coaches made me ski alone in five layers of jackets. This was to ensure that I would ski nice and slow. I overheat quickly, and I *hate* being really hot. Since the harder I'd work, the hotter I'd get, the pile of jackets were meant to slow my pace down to a walk. So, there I was, skiing down a trail all alone, wearing five jackets like a circus clown.

Four days later, my energy had fully recovered, and I went out for a long, three-and-a-half-hour ski. At the halfway point of my long-distance ski, I stopped to eat a snack. I ate some more of a test batch of sports gummies that I had eaten earlier. I didn't know it then, but this was the original source of my food poisoning. I hadn't realized the first time that it was this innocent-looking little sports snack that had nearly killed me (and I'm being only a tiny bit dramatic here).

After my snack, I continued skiing, and within a short time the food poisoning came roaring back. Unfortunately for me, I realized I was in trouble when I was at the very bottom of the mountain trail system, a good forty-five-minute climb away from the parking lot. I puked so much on the trail that my retching became a countdown: every ten minutes, every eight minutes, every six minutes. I had already been skiing for three hours, so I was getting weaker and weaker. I dropped to my knees and started crawling the rest of the way back to the lodge.

Matt rescued me again. He found me crawling through the snow on my hands and knees, desperate for help, and alternately crying and vomiting as I crawled. I looked like Gollum, only significantly more disgusting. In the end, I couldn't make it to the lodge. My body had nothing left, and I felt like a shell of a human. They had to call a snowmobile to carry me off the mountain. Matt put me into his car and drove me down the mountain to our condo. It was a thirty-five-minute drive down a twisty mountain road, and I was still emptying out every part of my stomach. Matt had one hand on the wheel and one hand patting my head in a "believe it or not, you're actually going to live through this" gesture. He handed me our team's large Gatorade jug from his back seat.

"But Matt, people need to drink out of this," I said to him meekly. Then I retched into it.

"Not anymore," he replied.

• • •

In July, we sometimes head to Alaska to ski on Eagle Glacier, flying out of Girdwood, located outside of Anchorage. We are helicoptered up to the glacier, and it is quite possibly the coolest thing ever. The helicopters pack our skis and equipment into a giant sling, and our food and supplies into another sling. Then they drop them both off on top of the glacier, where we live and train for an entire week.

On the ten-minute ride up to the ridge, we fly over this gorgeous, lush forest that is tropical green in color. It's almost techno-colored, like when *The Wizard of Oz* suddenly goes into full color and dazzles you. It's electric and eye-popping. But when we leave the neon forest and fly into the mountains near the glacier, the reverse happens. Suddenly, we're in a world completely void of color. All we see can for miles on end is the dark rock of the mountains and huge fields of blinding white snow. It's gorgeous, in a classical, awe-inspiring, humbling manner. It seems like it is the end of the world. But high up at the edge of the mountain, surrounded by glacial snow and dark black rock, there is a small building that has been created out of Conex shipping boxes. This is our home for a week as we ski circles around Eagle Glacier.

Erik Flora, the coach at Alaska Pacific University and man in charge of this awesome operation, has a team of workers alongside him that have created this completely sustainable environment up there at the end of the world. They have a snow pond where they melt snow, then filter it for the water we use all week. There are bunk rooms and a kitchen for the athletes and crew. The athletes are paired into groups for meal prep, cooking, and cleaning duties. Every day, we'll ski for two to three hours in the morning and two hours in the afternoon. Any time that's not spent skiing, cooking, or cleaning is spent sound asleep in a bunk bed. It's an epic yet wonderfully simple time in this stark black and white landscape.

But if we're being honest (and this is my book, so we are), my favorite part of our Alaskan hideaway has nothing to do with skiing. The Alaskan Air helicopters that fly us to and from glacier camp sometimes do a push over the edge of the cliff. They'll fly up and hover over where the house sits, near the ledge of the cliff, and then nosedive over the edge. Both one's stomach and the helicopter drop like a roller coaster, and then the helicopter pulls out of its descent to swoop over the valley below. It is an insane ride! This helicopter amusement ride in Alaska gave me a taste of the thrill that I would soon receive on the opposite side of the world.

• • •

In late summer, we go on an epic quest to New Zealand to a place called the Snow Farm, one of my favorite places in the world. What makes it feel even more epic is that it's near some of the filming locations for scenes from *Lord of the Rings*, so just picture some of those landscapes in your head for a minute while the theme song plays in the background. I'll wait.

Now that we're in the right mind-set, realize that New Zealand's seasons are flip-flopped from North America because it is in the Southern Hemisphere. This makes it the ideal place to escape the heat and humidity and find some snowy winter wonderland to ski in during the long summer-training push. A fourteen-hour flight is no joke, but to me, it seems absolutely worth it in search of the best snow in one of the most remote corners of the world.

After we land, we load all our ski bags into vans and drive across this rugged and magical landscape. New Zealand is a geological wonder. There are huge crystal-clear blue skies, towering snowcapped mountains so picture perfect the horizon looks photoshopped, massive forests, ocean views, glacial lakes with islands, and volcanic rocks. We drive to the Snow Farm, located high in the mountains between the towns of Queenstown and Wanaka, on mountain roads so winding they're the worst nightmare for someone who gets carsick (as I do). Still . . . totally worth it.

The Snow Farm is a massive recreation area and retreat dedicated to sledding, snowshoeing, and cross-country skiing. It has 70 kilometers of groomed trails and accommodations for us to stay on-site. Perhaps best of all, the food is simply incredible with fresh fruit and veggies and delicious choices every day. It has an elevation of 1,600 meters, so the training is at some mild elevation. Technically, the Snow Farm is part of a larger operation called the Southern Hemisphere Proving Grounds. It's such a winter wonderland that it is used by car companies as the ultimate testing ground for their vehicles on snow, ice, and rough winter terrain. So as we're driving up to the farm, we will sometimes see some pretty fancy cars ripping around a snowy sort of racetrack!

The Snow Farm got its name from the practice of putting fences on the windblown corners of the mountains to trap the snow, which drifts in giant waves. Then they farm the snow from these huge drifts and spread it to preserve the course. They literally harvest the snow! The trails are like nothing you've ever seen. Winding along the rolling top of the Pisa Mountain area, I'm never bored on a long training session.

There is the most gorgeous sunrise every morning. The light hits the Snow Farm, and all the colors of the rainbow wash over the mountains. When I'm sitting in the lodge with my teammates drinking hot coffee, it makes me feel like I'm swimming in a sunrise. Then I'll take one step out the door, and I'm standing on the groomed ski track. I click into my bindings and boom! I'm gone! It's an incredible way to start the day.

My aerial thrill ride in Alaska was only a warm-up for what happened in New Zealand. I'd been dying to do this every year, and one year I finally talked some of my coaches and teammates into coming with me. On our one day off from training, we went bungee jumping at one of the world's highest jumps, the AJ Hackett Nevis Bungy near Queenstown. It's 134 meters of free fall, which takes 8.5 seconds. That's a *lot* of time to contemplate your life.

The jump took place from a little cabin with a glass floor, suspended on wires over a massive gorge. We put on a harness, hooked ourselves to a line on the rickety little trolley, and slowly creaked our way out to the center of the gorge, hundreds of feet above the valley floor.

They were blasting music so loud it both terrified me and pumped me up. I wanted to either run away or run through a brick wall, or maybe both. The worker tied my feet to the bungee cord, then I very carefully scooted my way to the edge of a plank suspended out over the endless open space. Everyone counted down "3 . . . 2 . . . 1!" and I swan-dived off the diving board launchpad out into the open air above the gorge. For a kid that grew up swinging upside down from a zip line and swinging from a rope trying to reach the treetops, the bungee jump was pure adrenaline bliss.

I loved it so much that I jumped twice . . . and couldn't wipe the grin off my face for a week.

• • •

If you think bungee jumping over a river gorge is New Zealand is crazy, then listen to this: there is a town in Canada that buries all of their snow in a pit. I'm not kidding. The ski center in Canmore, Alberta, pushes all of its snow at the end of the year into a pit and covers it with wood chips. The good people of Canmore have calculated that they'll lose 30 percent or so of the snow, but they keep the rest because it's so well packed and insulated. In the fall, they spread the snow around a 1.2-kilometer loop, and suddenly you're cross-country skiing in October before the natural snowfall starts! They call it Frozen Thunder.

Weirdly enough, they're not the only town that does this, although they have the most creative name for it. Talk about the impact of climate change across a sport worldwide . . . many race venues now have pits where they store snow in case the worst should happen and they don't receive any natural snow during the winter months before their planned hosting of a World Cup race. Davos, Switzerland, has become known for their snow-farming abilities, and every year now they spend the winter blowing snow into a deep pit to save for the season ahead. You can't even put in a bid to host a World Cup race if you don't have a backup man-made snow plan these days.

But enough gloom and doom . . . if you're not worried about our planet by now, I'm probably not going to be able to convince you by telling you how many times I've raced with green grass and mud on either side of the man-made strip of snow in January! Back to skiing, darn it!

I've traveled to Canmore many times in the fall over the years. It is a picturesque town with awe-inspiring mountains wrapped around it. The place is straight out of a postcard, and it's one of the places I'd most like to live in this world. It's a mountain town with endless adventures to be had, and the coolest people to meet. But the coolest thing they have for a Nordic junkie is their incredible ski trail system and their early-season skiing. Well, that and the gigantic muffins at Beamer's Coffee Bar.

• • •

My last Christmas at home with my family was when I was nineteen years old. After that, the Tour de Ski would always start too close to the holidays for me to be home December 26 and fly to Europe and adjust to the jet lag before racing on December 28. At first, this was pretty hard. I was OK with missing Thanksgiving, because it has less traditions attached to it, but at Christmas time I knew my place was with my family, opening stockings together in front of a cozy fire in our pajamas, going for a wintery hike through the woods together, and eating my dad's homemade hot cross buns. I could never truly escape the feelings of loneliness and sadness that come only when you've been on the road a little too long.

But they say when one door closes, another opens, and I can't tell you how amazing it was to grow closer to my teammates through spending months at a time traveling together. We would band up around the holiday break, renting little apartments and living together, usually in Davos, Switzerland, or Seefeld, Austria. My first year of doing the Tour de Ski, I roomed with Holly Brooks, and she pulled me right out of my sad little funk by pulling a bag of whole cloves out of her suitcase, buying oranges and twine from the grocery store in Oberhof, Germany, and insisting that we all have "arts and crafts" time together (this may have served a dual purpose of masking the odor of drying boots in our room). It was the first of many low snow years, and instead of snow we enjoyed rain while skiing on slushy, man-made snow in loops through trail systems that sported brown dirt and rocks on either side of the trail. I wish I could say this was the only time this happened in the middle of winter, but it actually became the norm. We started picking our holiday break locations based solely upon the availability of man-made ski tracks.

The next year I lived in Davos with Liz Stephen and Noah Hoffman, and I have the best memories of cooking to loud music, sharing meals together, and hosting a ridiculous "white elephant" gift exchange party with all the skiers living in town. I was having a hard time that year though, as it was my first full year of being on the road for five months straight. I'd been really, really looking forward to going out and picking a tree together, and Noah, who doesn't celebrate Christmas, very graciously said, "Whatever makes you happy, Diggs! We'll do it." One day I had a long ski, and in a very thoughtful gesture meant to surprise me and cheer me up, Noah skied home early, walked to town in his ski boots, and clomped all the way home, a perfectly shaped tree slung over his shoulder. I walked in the door and stopped, totally stunned.

"But . . . I thought we were going to pick it out together?" I said as tears welled up in my eyes.

I am ashamed to admit to how upset I was, but I was in a bad place, OK? I was super bummed because the act of going to pick the tree as a ski family was what I was after, not the actual tree itself. I rushed to the bathroom and took a long shower, during which I worked on adjusting my attitude. I heard Liz come in and Noah say, "Liz! I think I screwed up . . . but I have no idea what I did!" I apologized for my bizarre reaction, and we high-fived and laughed about it for years.

This same year, my mom had shipped me a "box of happy" with a Christmas card, stockings for all my fellow athletes in Europe, and some handy traveling presents, like new hair scrunchies and a fresh, cute T-shirt. I took the public bus to the Kulm hotel, where we'd been staying as a full team and where they'd graciously hold mail for us, and sat perched on the edge of my seat the whole ride back, clutching my precious box. An hour later, Liz found me sitting in the living room in a pile of packing peanuts, clutching the card from my mom and dad to my chest, tears rolling down my face.

"I can't do this! I can't be on the road for five months at a time!"

"Oh honey, it gets easier, I promise." Liz hugged me tight. She always knew how to give the very best hugs and make us feel absolutely, positively loved and supported.

And she was right. It never got *easy*, but it did get easier to be away from family. Better internet in Europe and Skype really helped, and I'm lucky that my family travels to Europe for a week almost every winter now so we can share this crazy journey together.

• • •

When I was nineteen and Sadie was twenty, we made the 2011 World Championships team in Oslo. We were the youngest members on the team and always up for adventure. We were bonding a lot over the experience of it being our first time . . . and also over watching everything Petter Northug did. We'd never raced at this level before, and it was awe inspiring! We'd never seen this many men in full spandex one-piece suits before, and *that* was also awe-inspiring!

We had been living and training at a hotel called Olympiatoppen Sportshotel in Oslo, which was near a popular subway line. The entire hotel was Olympic themed, and their website opens with "Eat, sleep, and train like an Olympic athlete," so obviously we, desperate to someday become Olympic athletes, were soaking it all in. During a two-week break before World Championships, Sadie and I decided to use the great public transportation and go to the city center to experience some Norwegian culture and visit the national museum.

We were so proud of ourselves and felt so grown-up and sophisticated. How fabulous were we? Traveling by subway in Europe by ourselves to see some art! Up until that point, neither of us had much experience with city transportation systems, because where I come from, Afton, is not a city, and Sadie is from Winthrop, Washington, also not a city.

We went to downtown Oslo, and everything was so fabulous. Our stop was right at the National Mall, a major entryway and tourist port. We made our way out by the water, and it was gorgeous. We were dazzled by one of the greatest cities in Scandinavia. We were slightly less dazzled to see a McDonald's tucked between cute restaurants and shops, but I guess you can't have it all!

When it was time to go home, we walked to the subway station and got on the subway back to the Olympiatoppen outside Oslo. As we waited for the subway to leave the station, Sadie started looking around and noticed something was off.

"All of these people have suitcases," Sadie said. "Why would they have suitcases on a subway?"

"Wait a minute . . ." I looked up for the sign above the door.

The doors snapped shut, and the subway left the station, with Sadie and me pounding on the doors, because it wasn't a subway, it was a train. And it was headed for Trondheim.

Shit. We are so screwed.

"Oh, no," Sadie mumbled. "Trondheim is *really* far from here."

It's seven hours and forty minutes by train, in case you'd like to know.

We failed to understand a lot of things but mainly the fact that the rail station at the National Mall was both a subway station and a train station. Fortunately, this wasn't a nonstop train. We got out at the next stop and started running around in this foreign train station, looking for help. We found a woman in ski boots. Of course we did. It's Norway!

"Excuse me! Excuse me!" I exclaimed as I ran up to her. "We're staying at the Olympia Toppen, Olympatopp . . . Olympic Top?" Honestly, we didn't even know how to say it. We didn't know how to pronounce where we'd come from or where we were trying to go.

The woman in ski boots finally figured it out. "Oh, honey, you're at the train station," she said in near perfect English. "You need to exit here. Go up to street level. Look for the T sign. That is the symbol for the subway station. And that's what you need to take to get to *Olympi-atoppen*."

I'd like to say that we never got lost in Europe again during the next eight years, but that just isn't true.

Recently, we had a travel day from Ulricehamn, Sweden, to Davos, Switzerland. After flying to Zürich, I was with a group of athletes (the coaches were driving rental vehicles a day behind us), and we were taking the trains all the way to our hotel. This was awesome, except that I'd never traveled by train before in a group with six ski bags, eight duffels, eight backpacks, and very tight connection times! We ended up making an assembly line, throwing ski bags to one another, sweat dripping off us as we worked as fast as possible to not piss off the locals. It was incredibly glamorous, and the locals just laughed at us anyway.

• • •

We often started our ski season in Rovaniemi, a city right on the edge of the Arctic Circle in northern Finland. Its great claim to fame is hosting the official airport of Santa Claus (which, to be honest, I feel is a misnomer . . . everyone knows that reindeer fly his sleigh) and an extremely cute Santa Claus Village. Even in mid-November, there was always plenty of snow and frosty cold temperatures that preserved the man-made loop of snow laid down early in the season for athletes to train on. It was the safest bet for early-season training in the world.

We weren't lost the last year we trained there, but we may as well have been. It felt like a completely different place from what we were used to, as it was one of the many places feeling the effects of climate change. We were shocked to see the ski tracks melting out, with flowers blooming between the green spongy moss and grass on the side of the trail. The running trails were quite excellent, but we shouldn't have been able to find that out.

Santa's village now sat in a puddle. Elves were sweating their asses off in their wool coats. Everything about it seemed so sad and so wrong. The organizers of the training facility were doing the best they could, but there's not much they can do when it's forty degrees Fahrenheit and raining on the Arctic Circle. But hey, at least we got to pet the reindeer.

• • •

In Sjusjøen, Norway, cross-country skiing is the lifeblood that flows through the town and countryside during the winter. For a ski-loving dork like me, it's absolute paradise in the form of cozy wood cabins (where you can eat brown cheese and cardamom-spiced waffles) dotted along perfectly groomed tracks. Sjusjøen is 20 kilometers east of Lillehammer and has close to 350 kilometers of cross-country trails. The trails wind through the mountains and fairy-tale forests, running all the way to Lillehammer, and then hooking up with the Olympic tracks at the Birkebeineren Ski Stadium (um, is this place heaven?).

In this remote, snowed-in countryside, we ski from one little town to the next along the trails. People actually use the trails to commute to work. There are loops that lead you past coffee shops and restaurants, where you can get the best waffle you've ever eaten in your life. Unless, of course, Anne Hart has ever cooked you a waffle, in which case it will be the second-best waffle you've eaten in your life. When we are out training on the trails, we'll see all these little grandmas and grandpas out skiing too. They slowly and peacefully trudge down the winding path through sparkling snowdrifts, a sandwich wrapped up in their backpack. They are simply out there enjoying their beautiful corner of the frozen wintery world. They hear our freight train skiing coming down the trail behind them and simply pull off to the side, amused at our huffing and puffing. They look around, appreciating how wonderful everything is while we buzz by and apologize for ruining their beautiful day. We see couples all the time who are sitting on a bench and eating their lunch. Cutest. Ever. I aspire to be one of these grandmas one day . . . so I can ski all day and laugh at the silly young things out torturing themselves by skiing so hard and so fast.

In Sjusjøen, skiing is woven into the fabric of their culture. You could say it's their thing. On Sunday mornings, we'll be out training and pass a church. In the parking lot of the church, there will be a ski rack full of skis. Then there will be a smaller rack for the little baby skis.

People ski to church! They ski to school! There are ski racks next to the grocery stores too! What is this place?

In Seefeld, Austria, there is also a similar vibe, albeit with more beer and schnapps involved. The extensive trail system will lead you to bars and shops and restaurants tucked up into the hills or in neighboring towns. I had a memorable experience with my family one winter while they were visiting me, in which a warm pretzel from a ski-up-to-the-window wooden hut saved us from impending disaster after three hours of skiing up and down the valley.

Sometimes, in training camp between World Cups, we'll go for a short night ski in search of beer and apple strudel. We'll switch on headlamps and ski out from town to the "alm" in the woods across the dark, moonlit landscape and enjoy the wonderful ski culture in Austria. But my travel adventures aren't always full of warm pretzels and skiing through fairy-tale forests. Sometimes they are a horror movie set in Russia.

• • •

One of my most enlightening travel experiences ever was when I was twenty years old and staying in a hotel attached to a casino in Moscow, Russia, for a city sprint. For breakfast on the day of the race, the only food available was pickled fish, pickled beets, and brightly colored Jell-Os. All sorts of strange pickled things. And bulgur wheat. Contrary to popular belief (and Dwight Schrute) beets aren't exactly great for breakfast immediately before an intense cross-country sprint in subzero temperatures. Just saying. But I needed to eat something. The only thing I saw that seemed remotely edible and recognizable was a dense chocolate cake. Hardly perfect athlete food right before a race, but luckily my training in The Emily Program had allowed me to relax my rigid thinking of "good food versus bad food" enough to simply eat what I had to in order to race. And you know what? That chocolate cake ended up saving the day.

The temperature at the racecourse was hovering right at the legal racing temperature. It was near minus fourteen degrees Celsius but felt way colder with the humidity. It was so cold that skiers had to use masks to help warm up the air before it went into their lungs. When you're breathing really hard in extremely cold air, you'll usually get a temporary, yet terrible phlegm-filled cough known as race hack. Sometimes, you'll get race hack just from the effort of pushing your body so hard, even when the air isn't ridiculously cold. Although cross-country skiing is maybe the world's healthiest sport, it's pretty brutal on your body when you do it for a living. Life is full of these little ironies. The inflammation in your lungs is one of the most annoying things to have when you're a cross-country skier.

These air warmers aren't exactly the sexiest things either. They look like really wide cigarettes. They are oval-shaped and about the length of a cigarette, and they have metal coiled up in them. Your breath out warms the metal, which in turn warms the air on the way in. Which sounds great and all . . . until you end up with this string of frozen drool on the other end of it. The other option is a mask that looks like a doctor's mask, only it's stiff and sticks out from your face. We call them pig snouts, and they have a little circular disk that helps warm the air on the way in. But then you get all that condensation, sweat, and snot inside the mask. Neither one is perfect. Did I mention how sexy this sport is?

I was getting ready for the sprint, surrounded by all these skiers wielding their poles and skis while sporting pig snouts and cigarette plugs in their mouths. We looked like some sort of weird tribe from *Mad Max*. But I got into the race and remarkably . . . won the qualifier. I imagine that at the time you're reading this page, it will still be the only qualifier I've won in my life. Everyone thought the timing system had broken, because I was this little nobody wearing a big pink hat overtop a crooked headband, who flailed around too much when she skied and didn't look nearly fast enough to win a qualifier. I was not a regular on the World Cup yet, for goodness sake. Yet somehow, I won the qualifier, and everyone, especially me, was shocked. The normal response to winning a qualifier and then being the only American to reach the finals isn't usually "but are you *sure*?" . . . but that was my reaction to my coaches that day. It was an amazing experience, even though I got last place in the final heat. This still put me in sixth on the day, and it was, at the time, the absolute best race of my life. Everyone was so happy for me, and to think! The whole day was fueled by a Hannibal Lecter mask and chocolate cake!

The night after the race, the buzz ended.

Sadly, there wasn't time to celebrate with more of that cake. We were loaded onto a bus that night and driven from Moscow to the town of Rybinsk. It was an eight-hour bus ride, and we were scheduled to arrive in this tiny, frozen town at 3:00 a.m. The bus was packed with skiers from all different countries, so at least we were all in this together. The bus was old and kind of rickety, and it felt kind of like a bus *The Muppets* might ride in.

I got on the bus and sat with Kikkan.

"Hey, I downloaded a new movie. Do you want to watch it?" Kikkan asked me.

"Great. I'd love to watch literally anything," I replied.

"It's a new one, with Gwyneth Paltrow . . ." Kikkan said.

"Cool!"

". . . and Matt Damon."

"Even better."

It was a miserable, bumpy bus ride over the back roads of Russia. We were in the middle of nowhere. It was pitch black outside. The movie was *Contagion,* a horror movie about a worldwide pandemic that began with an infectious cough. The cough spreads from person to person, and then anarchy ensues and the world ends. Let me tell you, this was a big departure from our usual *Glee*-watching escapades together. As I watched the movie, my life slowly became the horror movie that I was watching.

We drove through the dark Russian countryside, and the entire bus became an orchestra of coughing and hacking stuff up. Everyone had a race hack because we had all pushed our bodies hard in the subzero temperatures.

But I wasn't thinking about a race hack. My mind leaped straight to the anarchy and to the world-ending scenario. Kikkan and I huddled together and watched *Contagion* as people all around us were constantly coughing. Then, to our horror, Kikkan and I both started coughing too. We both tried to hold it back. But the cough kept coming. Soon, we were both coughing while simultaneously watching a movie about the world ending from people coughing.

"We're going to die," Kikkan said jokingly. "This is it."

We were joking, of course. Kind of.

Then the bus fell eerily silent. The race hack had died down because everyone had fallen asleep. But I didn't trust it. My first thought was that my fellow skiers weren't coughing because they had died and were now, obviously, transitioning into zombies. I started going through all of this apocalypse logic: *How long after someone's death do they become a zombie? If the person who died was a super-fit Nordic skier when they were a human, does that make them a super-fit and fast zombie? If I'm being chased by a zombie, do I run in a zigzag away from them like they tell you to do when being chased by an alligator? If I turn into a zombie tonight, does that mean the last thing I ate on this earth was Russian chocolate cake?*

Around midnight, everyone woke up, and the chorus of coughing erupted again. Which was OK because I now knew for sure they hadn't transitioned yet. Now, everyone had to pee. But there was no bathroom on the bus, even though it was an eight-hour ride. Because, well, it's Russia. Things don't always make sense. After several requests for a bathroom break, the bus driver simply pulled over in the middle of nowhere.

"OK," the bus driver grunted. He opened the bus door and said in rough English, "Out."

"Well, I guess that's it," Kikkan said.

"We're all going to die, aren't we?" I only half-jokingly said. "He's going to leave us here because we asked for a bathroom break."

Everyone filed off the bus. All the guys lined up on the right side of the road, all the girls lined up to the left. The bus driver stood there, smoking a cigarette in the middle of the road. It was minus twenty. *Just remember, you asked for this,* I told myself. *You wanted to race at the highest level of sport in the world, so here you are, living the dream!* I just didn't realize that part of living the dream included peeing in front of strangers on the side of the road in the middle of Siberia.

We arrived in Rybinsk at 3:00 a.m. The bus driver pulled over on the outskirts of the town and opened the bus door.

"Out," he said again.

We had to drag our bags from the bus to the town with the cabins where we were staying, because there was so much snow that the bus wouldn't go farther. It was a half a mile to Rybinsk, and we dragged our bags and gear behind us, snow catching in the wheels, the bags bumping into our legs and tripping us up. We finally got to our cabins and collapsed into bed, shivering.

But the nightmare wasn't over yet. One more horrible thing happened.

The next day, we were all sitting silently in the dining hall eating bulgur wheat and boiled beets when there was a big commotion outside. We looked out the windows and watched as the police pulled a dead man out of the frozen river. Welcome to Rybinsk.

CHAPTER 15

FROM SOCHI, WITH LOVE

The ski chalet in the Olympic village in Sochi, Russia, was brand-new. They had just finished building a few of the chalets and the hotel as we arrived, and most of the athlete village was still under construction. This was 2013, one year before the Sochi Winter Olympics. Before every Olympics, the venue is required to hold a test event in the form of a World Cup the year before. The Olympic officials and host country want to make sure everything is going to work, that the venue is running smoothly, and that the accommodations are going to work out. Which is why I had spent hours getting a visa with my teammates the summer before, and flying to Sochi on a chartered flight crammed full of racers from a few different countries, with the back fifteen rows of the plane piled high with duffel bags from around the world.

Upon arrival, the entire German team's ski bags had somehow gone missing. I hadn't realized that was even possible on a chartered flight! Don't worry, they showed up in time for the races. After we had our visas checked, we drove for two hours from the coastal village of Sochi, site of the biggest of the three athlete villages, up to the base of the mountains. From there, we took a long gondola up the mountain, to the aptly named Endurance Village, which would house the cross-country and biathlon athletes.

The roads weren't completed yet and were so bumpy and wild we thought we were driving into Jurassic Park. As the Russian driver launched the van over huge ruts in the road, we went airborne off the seats like crash-test dummies. Noah Hoffman had his camera out for his blog, a grin spreading across his face. We were all thinking the same thing: *Nobody is ever going to believe this.* We arrived at our chalet with vertigo, nausea, and a new fondness for asphalt. All the racers were living together, with the men upstairs and the women downstairs.

One morning after training, the team was getting ready to walk to lunch at the huge cafeteria a half mile up the bunny slope that bordered the edge of the athletes' village. One of the guys was showering in the room directly above the bedroom Holly Brooks and I were sharing. Suddenly, water started pouring down through the ceiling. I'm not sure I've ever moved faster in my life than that sprint upstairs to yell at the guys to turn the water off. Water kept raining down through the ceiling, and all of us scrambled around, putting out every bucket we could find to catch the drips. The brand-new chalet was a soggy mess.

We told the managers at the main hotel and our coaches about the flooding. One of these two parties found it quite hilarious, the other less so. An hour later, a succession of Russian men paraded through our chalet to "fix" the plumbing problem. Except none of the men was a plumber. Not a single one. I was sitting in my room (wearing clothes, luckily), and without a courteous knock or a simple warning, a Russian guy just walked in. He looked at me sitting there and didn't say a word. He was holding a hammer. He turned his eyes away from me and stared at the ceiling. Then he hit the ceiling with his hammer. Wap, wap, wap. He looked up at the ceiling and paused. Then hit it again. Wap, wap, wap. Pause. Then the man shrugged and walked out of my room. Ten minutes later, another Russian man arrived and did the same exact thing. Hammer. Ceiling. Wap, wap, wap. Seven different guys came to the chalet. We never used the upstairs shower again.

A year later at the Olympics, we were in a different chalet, built in the same style, also at the Olympic Endurance Village. The same thing happened. Someone used the upstairs shower, and water came raining down through the ceiling, also on top of me and Holly. We didn't even run this time, just looked at each other and went, "Again?!" A parade of men showed up unannounced to repair the problem. With a hammer, of course.

Welcome to the Russian Olympics.

• • •

People often ask what it's like to travel and compete in the Olympics. I tell them it's a lot like going to Disney World in Florida. You see the magic of Disney, but you're not really experiencing the true Florida. Everything is a carefully curated image. When you see pictures from the Olympics, you don't know what's on either side of that frame, just barely cropped out of the shot.

In Russia, the TV cameras were specifically angled and set up to show exactly the perfect shot. Essentially, the Olympics are like a very popular Instagram influencer . . . you're not seeing anything other than what they want you to see. Well, I saw what was outside the frame. In Sochi, there was most likely a barbwire fence, army men in the woods holding machine guns, unused land, or a half-constructed job site. Immediately outside the frame of the most beautiful ski chalet you've ever seen were construction workers up on the roof of some half-framed building, and they weren't roped in. They were smoking cigarettes and barking at each other. There was no safety. If they fell, they might die. But gee, that shot of the village looked great on TV.

• • •

I was twenty-two years old, and the 2014 Sochi Winter Olympics were my first go at the Games. In a lot of ways, Sochi was wonderful because it was a zero-pressure environment for me. It was kind of a testing ground, where I got to go and experience all the bright lights and hype without the external pressure of having to produce a medal. Obviously, I was still nervous, but I knew the world wasn't watching my every move, and I felt free to go after my races without the fear of making mistakes. On the international stage, I was still somewhat unknown, so I flew under the radar, and although I didn't fully appreciate it at the time, being an unknown was truly kick-ass.

The race trails themselves were awesome. They were really hard, but they were wide, and they'd done a good job grooming. We were lucky that there was a lot of natural snow and the trails were well covered. The competitions themselves were very, very fair. I can't say the same about the cleanness of the athletes competing in them, but you can read the McLaren Report for the World Anti-Doping Agency (WADA) if you want to learn more about that. If you don't know how I feel about doping in sport, it's this: don't do it. Ever. Never, ever.

While the actual competitions from my perspective were fair and impartial, there were a lot of shenanigans off the course, and one of them landed right at my doorstep.

Within ten minutes of arriving at the Olympic Village in Sochi, I was notified by a WADA chaperone that I had to go with them to give a sample. I hadn't even unpacked yet and was excited to go walk around the village with my teammates. Then WADA knocked on the door and called for me. Which was fine! I get tested all the time. The entire idea behind random testing is that it's supposed to be, well, *at random*. You're never supposed to be able to guess when you'll get tested.

So this is where I'm left still scratching my head: Liz Stephen and I would get selected three times in a row to be tested at the same time, the only ones on our team to get pulled those first few times. The odds of that happening are in line with winning the lottery or getting struck by lightning. Our team doctor told us that he'd been at multiple Olympics and had never seen the WADA protocol happen like that before.

It was the very definition of not random.

Along with urine samples, I also had to give blood samples. Again, this was totally fine. I'm scared of needles, but as long as I don't look, I won't pass out. And anyway, it wasn't like I had any choice in the matter: you give the sample, or you get banned from sport for refusing to give a sample. The problem was that the Russian nurse who administered the blood draw was bruising people. She was epically bad at drawing blood, and she was hurting athletes. Our team doctor, Larry Gaul, accompanied me when I got pulled, and saw it all happen. The Russian nurse was eventually removed. But the next time I got pulled again by WADA, she was back. They threw her out, and she just returned and was back bruising people again. It was so weird and messed up. Larry stepped in and wouldn't allow her to take our blood anymore, insisting on a different phlebotomist.

One of the times I got pulled by WADA was the night before my sprint race. I was already in my pajamas, in bed, preparing for a day that I'd been training years for. I was nervous and excited, ready to go sprint as hard as I could. It was 10:00 p.m. Technically, WADA can come anytime. But I'd never seen them come that late at night, and *never* the night before an athlete's race. I was the only person racing the next day to get tested. There were other athletes that got pulled at that weird late hour, but none of them were racing the next day. I was the only one that had to compete.

According to WADA protocol, athletes can get tested any time, any place. We have a preset sixty-minute window that we have to provide for testing every day, when the WADA officer knows where to find us. I always set my window from six to seven in the morning (because I know I'll always be at home then). They've never come the morning of a race, as they know it's unfair to do that to an athlete because it screws up their rhythm and their process of race preparation. They can't single one racer out the morning of a race, because then instead of keeping the playing field level, they've suddenly made it unfair for the person they're testing.

In training camps, the entire off-season, and in April when I'm not even training, I have to be available any time from six to seven in the morning to be tested. I have to be where I say I'm going to be. And I'm always happy to do it because I believe in clean sport, and I know that testing is an important way to keep sport pure.

The testers are always respectful and don't want to disrupt your life and performance. Sometimes they do by accident, and I've had to cancel a first date because of testing, be late to parties, and have family dinners interrupted. But that's just part of being a pro athlete! Many of the testers are incredibly nice, and if they happen to come while I'm finishing up a workout, they'll cheer me on! The idea is that the officials come and test when you would least expect it. Obviously, you don't know they're coming. But it's usually not a disruption of your life or preparation for a race. In Russia, it was the biggest disruption at the biggest moment.

I wasn't allowed to return until after midnight the night before my Olympic race.

• • •

There was a big, aggressive barbed-wire fence around the perimeter of the Olympic village. To get in, we had to show our credentials. Once inside, we proceeded to get our credentials checked about twenty thousand more times, and that's only a slight exaggeration. Every hundred meters, my identity was checked over and over again. We had to show our IDs when we exited the village, when we entered the village, when we were within the village, when we were going to the race venue, and when we were going to different parts of the race venue. Security was tight, and in the end, we appreciated that.

The crazy thing, though, was that in our part of the village there were only cross-country skiers and biathletes. There just weren't that many of us. The same guards were always in their same spots at the same checkpoints. They would see us every single day, multiple times a day, and check the same credentials every day. They got to recognize us, but they acted like they didn't recognize us at all. We would pass through their checkpoint, then a hundred meters down the road we would get stopped again. Obviously, our credentials were valid because we had just passed a checkpoint a hundred meters back. The same guards at the same checkpoints would watch us walk up to them from the other checkpoint. It made me laugh every time. The dramatic part of my brain really wanted to see what would happen to someone who tried to sneak in. They never smiled, and they stood like stone soldiers. They all had guns.

"Credentials." That was all they ever said to us.

During our time spent in the village for the 2013 World Cup test event, we made a team music video to Taylor Swift's song "I Knew You Were Trouble." These same guards were at the same posts, practicing just like we were for the big leagues that were to come in twelve months. Someone decided that it might be kind of funny if we tried to get one of the Russian guards to dance with us. And by "someone," I mean it was highly likely that this was my dumb idea. The girls got together one day after training and went up to one of the younger guards. We had seen this guard multiple times a day all week, so he knew us. We were playing Taylor Swift out of speakers, jumping around him, smiling and trying to get him to dance. He never even looked at us. He never moved. He never smiled.

We kept singing and dancing around him. Finally, he raised a single eyebrow. He cracked the tiniest smile you've ever seen. And it was clear that he was in fact amused. He'd been standing in the snow all day. He was probably bored out of his mind. And here were all of these girls just trying to dance with him!

When he cracked a smile, we all cheered super loud. I think I might have even hugged him.

We went back the next day to say hello to him, and he was gone. A new guard was in his place. I felt an immense wave of guilt, wondering if I'd gotten the guard in trouble for hugging him or for making him smile. I was just trying to get the man to live a little! This was a test event, nobody but skiers were up in the mountains! But I lay awake that night worrying about the imagined fate of the guard who dared to smile.

We never saw that young guard again.

• • •

All of these strange experiences kind of threw me off, which is pretty much par for the course for a first Olympics. But then I started racing, and that settled my nerves a lot. I was competing in the 15K skiathlon and the skate sprint, anchoring the 4 × 5K relay, and racing the 30K skate. I finished in fortieth place in the 30K skate, our relay team finished below our hopes and dreams in ninth place, and I came in twelfth in the sprint. But in the 15K skiathlon, I tied the best distance result ever (eighth place) for an American woman at the Olympics. At the time, it was one of my best distance results competing at that level, and one I certainly hadn't expected to have. What made this extra special was that my mom, dad, sister, grandma, and Ken and Barb Larson— our family friends who also own Slumberland Furniture, which was my headgear sponsor—were all there cheering on the side of the trail. I heard my mom's and dad's voices loud and clear, and it felt like a warm, happy boost of energy going through me. Even at the Olympics—no, *especially* at the Olympics—I needed Mom's and Dad's emotional support!

The final climb of that race was a grinder of a hill that took six straight minutes of climbing. Frankly, that thing was absolutely brutal. But while I was grinding up the hill, I heard my parents on the side of the trail, and it fired me up. I dug deep and had my best finishing kick of the entire year, outsprinting the pack I was skiing with. It was my first race at my first Olympics, and I tied the best result we've ever had in distance. For me, a twenty-two-year-old, getting eighth in the Olympics was huge, beyond what I could have ever imagined.

• • •

But Russia wasn't done with me yet. I had the worst going-away party ever! We were traveling to Europe from the Sochi Olympics to finish the World Cup season, driving to the makeshift Olympic airport at 1:00 a.m. for a 4:00 a.m. flight. The airport was literally a tent. It was pitched in a field, and it was absolutely freezing cold, because it was Russia in winter, of course!

There wasn't enough space for all the athletes, so we were all piled on top of one another. There was a runway somewhere outside, I do know that much. It must have been some sort of a converted military base or something, but I will probably never know the full story. We were all huddled on the floor, and our flight was delayed, of course. We were just trying to sleep, tired beyond belief and shivering in the cold, curled up like puppies on top of each other, trying to stay warm. People started crawling inside these large garment bags they got from the opening ceremonies. They zipped them up and tried to make them into sleeping bags. There we were—America's best winter athletes—all puppy piled on top of each other, shivering and shaking in a tent in the middle of a field.

Despite the influenza that I got two days after leaving Russia that tanked the rest of my World Cup season, I walked away from the Olympics feeling elated. I had one amazing race, one good race, one OK race, and one poor race. I had experienced the whole range, and it left me really excited for the future and hungry for more.

• • •

After the Olympics, all of the American Winter Olympians and Paralympians were invited to the White House—a *big deal* for this girl. I was so excited to see the White House and even more excited to potentially meet President Obama. I had heard that not every American president took the time to shake every athlete's hand, so I tried to tamp down my expectations.

But President Obama, he shook our hands. And not just the ones that held medals in them. He shook *all* the hands! He stood for hours and hours, having a short visit with each winter athlete. Which was kind of amazing when you think about all the other things he could have been doing. It meant so much to all of us that he carved out that time.

I stood in the long reception line, and as I inched toward President Obama, I got nervous and excited. Mostly nervous that he would be grossed out and flinch at my uncontrollably sweating palms. By the time I finally reached him, I was beyond frazzled. He reached out his hand. I almost passed out, I was so overwhelmed and starstruck. *I didn't realize he was so tall.*

"And where are you from?" he kindly asked me.

I froze. I forgot. I remembered just in time.

"M-Minnesota." *Since when did I have a stutter? Oh my god, get it together, Jessie.*

"Oh, you're from Minnesota? That's so cool," President Obama said to me. "They have great winters there."

"Uh-huh," I said, as I spastically nodded. Then I lost my mind and blurted, "Can I hug you?"

Up until that point, President Obama had shaken every athlete's hand. He had given zero hugs. Nobody had asked.

"Yeah, sure!" President Obama replied with a cool shrug of his shoulders.

"Thanks!"

Sadie was right behind me in line. As I went in for the hug, Sadie shook her head and tried hard to keep from laughing, "I can't believe it! Of course Jessie's going in for the hug."

I was so overcome with joy that I just had to hug him.

So, there I was, hugging the most powerful man on the planet. My emotions were screaming in celebration. *That's it. I've peaked. Nothing I do will ever be cooler.*

When I was released from the presidential hug, my eyes instantly welled up. This happens sometimes when I'm feeling a strong emotion, and it's never once failed to embarrass me. I was so overcome with joy and deliriously tired from the whirlwind of the past few days touring D.C. that my poor eyeballs couldn't take it anymore and betrayed me by filling up with tears. I was quickly becoming a hot mess.

Totally embarrassed, I took two steps to my right to get away. But there was the First Lady Michelle Obama. That's when the waterworks really started. I was blinking fast, desperately trying to contain my tears. The First Lady saw that I was emotional. She instantly went into mom mode, reached out, and wrapped me in a hug.

"We are so proud of you," the First Lady said to me. "Thank you for representing our country."

I lost it. Dang it, why did she have to be so *nice*? If she was cold or uncaring, I might have been able to reel back my tears!

Michelle Obama was as sweet and genuine as you could ever imagine. After she hugged me, I really melted down. Meeting President Obama and the First Lady at the end of a long, tiring season was a perfect storm of emotion. Her motherly hug and kind words unleashed the dam.

"Thanks," I said, bursting into tears.

I was mortified and desperately tried to wipe away the tears. My nose was running now too. *Why can't I just be cool like everyone else?*

"Oh, sweetie, it's OK," the First Lady said, as she reached out and held my hands.

"*Thanks!* Thank you so much!" I blurted out, knowing I had to run away or risk a full cry fest in front of the President and First Lady of the United States.

Then I booked it out of the room. But then I checked myself and stopped running because I realized security was everywhere, and they might take me down. I was just looking around and waiting for Nicolas Cage from *National Treasure* to open a trapdoor for me to escape or something. I was absolutely mortified.

I found a bathroom and furiously wiped my eyes. I splashed cold water on my face, trying so hard to erase the evidence that I had just broken down. I wanted a do-over! I was under the impression that Sadie was the only one that saw me break down. But apparently everyone saw me do it. Which was even more embarrassing. I thought I'd be labeled from that point on as "The Crying Skier" or something worse. As the day went on, though, all these Olympians that I didn't know, who had been to the White House before, came to me and offered, "It's OK. I cried my first time too. Well, actually that's a lie, I didn't, but I sort of wanted to." *Great, thanks.*

It was one of those moments that I'm sure President Obama and the First Lady will never remember. But I'm never going to forget.

• • •

Later on in the day, the entire Winter Olympics and Paralympics crew were gathered in a ballroom in the White House because President Obama was going to address the team. We were outfitted in official team gear: a nice, smart-looking white jacket with the flag on it. The men were in black pants, and the female athletes were given black athletic tights. They needed something that everyone could wear. But the tights were a new item from the clothing supplier, and they had this tummy-control wrap that stretched up above the waistline. Well, I'm short. So the wrap on my official Olympic tights stretched from my waist up to the bottom of my rib cage. I'm not kidding. They were like wearing Spanx for a pregnant woman. Because apparently, you are not allowed to meet the president with a poochy tummy. You got to tuck it all in!

The official Olympic tights were so uncomfortable they gave me a massive stomachache. They were pressing so hard into my stomach and waist I could barely sit down. I finally got up and casually walked around the room in the White House . . . the *White House!* . . . and nonchalantly reached under my USA jacket to discreetly roll the stomach flap down at my hips just so I could breathe.

Stay classy, Jessie!

After I had fixed the Spanx cummerbund in my tights, I found a place at the back of the room. President Obama made his way to the podium. As he spoke, I felt that he genuinely cared about us and appreciated all of our hard work that went into training and competing for the United States. It went beyond politics. I believed that he recognized that most of us had been training our whole lives to compete in the Olympics. It was awesome.

"Enjoy the house," President Obama said in closing. "Just don't trash the place."

• • •

Fast-forward momentarily to the next Olympic cycle, when I was offered the same trip back to the White House, this time to meet the newly appointed president number forty-five. As it was an invitation, not a summoning, I realized I couldn't bring myself to stand next to someone who bragged about sexually assaulting women, who doesn't believe that my friends who are LGBTQ deserve exactly the same rights to love and marry as anyone else, and who doesn't protect the rights of everyone in this country regardless of race, background, or gender identity. I don't have a lot of free time anymore, and if I was going to D.C., I wanted my time to count, to make a difference for something I cared deeply about.

I was warned that there might be backlash for not going; as one of the medalists, I was now somewhat in the eye of the media. I was cautioned about taking a stance because I might lose fans, I might lose sponsors. I said I'd rather sleep well at night, because at the end of the day, I have to look at myself in the mirror and live with who I am.

I decided to spend my day on Capitol Hill with Protect Our Winters, talking to senators and representatives about the impact I've seen climate change have on our sport and on our planet through my travels. I didn't know it at the time, but our visit had a positive impact, as two weeks later a Minnesota representative joined the Climate Solutions Caucus. As I drove past the White House, I imagined Barack and Michelle Obama hugging me all over again.

CHAPTER 16

GIVE IT ALL YOU GOT

The spring after competing in my first Olympic Games, I should have been full of confidence. I was an Olympian and in the best shape of my life. With a solid off-season training schedule in place, I set big personal and team goals and was excited to get out there and work hard to achieve them.

But one event that spring rattled me, and I lost faith in myself. At the time, I should've had unbreakable confidence in myself and pride in my abilities and in the muscles that I had spent hundreds of hours sweating to build. In an instant I was once again leveled by the power of my eating disorder.

My family had a bonfire party at our house in Afton to celebrate the end of the cross-country season. We had invited a bunch of friends over, and one of the many awesome volunteer coaches for my high school team came over to wish me well. After talking for a few minutes, this person nonchalantly made a remark about my body shape.

"Wow, you look a lot bigger than you did in high school!" this person said. "Have you gained weight?"

The casual comment about my size and shape was an unintentional cruelty. In fact, when I look back on it, this person may have even intended the remark as a compliment! But whatever the intention was that evening, I slid back into my eating disordered habits, relapsing for the first time in well over a year. For three days, I threw up everything I ate.

I was no longer the reigning team sprint World Champion, the Olympic athlete, the confident woman who had carried her body onto World Cup podiums. I was nothing. I wanted to *feel* nothing. I wanted to *be* nothing.

I was so ashamed of myself, embarrassed and furious at my lack of willpower. I blamed myself. Why couldn't I just be stronger, more confident? Why didn't I have thicker skin? How could I let one person's words destroy me like this? But eating disorders are tricky little monsters, and their long gremlin fingers are always reaching back out for you when you least expect it.

Eventually, I asked for help and recommitted to taking care of myself. I got my life back on track after my little derailment.

I didn't reach out to or talk to the person who made the comment for three years. Even now, when I think about this person, that comment is the first thing that comes to mind, which is honestly really sad. Clearly, this person didn't have any idea that the comment caused me harm. But those words caused me such physical distress that I was one unlucky day away from a serious trip to the hospital.

That an off-hand comment from someone who wasn't even extremely close to me could have such a destructive impact on my mental and physical well-being seemed crazy and alarming. I had relapsed into my eating disorder because I no longer felt fast, powerful, or confident. I only felt "too big."

If one sentence can spiral an Olympic athlete back into an eating disorder, take a moment and imagine what a parent or coach could cause by telling a young athlete directly under their mentorship something along the lines of "you'd be much faster if you lost weight" or "you could jump higher . . . if only you dropped ten pounds." Or my personal favorite zinger, "you need to work on your 'endurance athlete' body."

What we say to the people who look up to us—especially as coaches and parents—can have a huge impact on young athletes. You can't directly cause an eating disorder with your words—eating disorders are complicated, and multiple factors contribute to their development. But the words we say can be significant contributors to a person developing an eating disorder.

What we say and how we say it does matter. I've seen this first-hand, with coaches telling athletes things that either build up their self-confidence or shatter it. Words matter.

•　•　•

The time period after the Sochi Olympics was a blend of the moment I had at the bonfire. It was a time of celebration and adversity, of raw emotional and physical pain but also of joy, and, ultimately, of resilience. I made huge strides both professionally and personally. I began to win races on the world stage and felt comfortable in my own style of leadership with the national team. I met my boyfriend and fell in love, and this relationship nourished me like no other. In the years after my first Olympics, my personal life and athletic career began to build and gained momentum toward a promising future, one full of love and new-found self-confidence.

Off on the horizon, in the furthest reaches of my brain, in the outer margins of my rigid training and competition calendar, was the next Olympics, the 2018 Winter Games in PyeongChang, South Korea. I was now focused more than ever before on continuing to build a team of women who could compete with the giants of the sport in the World Cup and the next Olympics. But my determination came with a price.

I was so fired up to train hard to achieve my goals that my body began to break down a little bit. I suffered multiple low-key injuries and sheer exhaustion due to the rigorous demands of cross-country skiing. I learned firsthand the importance of distinguishing between training smart and training hard. They are not mutually exclusive. You can't just burn yourself to the ground and expect to get back up again. If you're not taking the appropriate amount of time to recover and rest, you'll start to get injured or sick. You have to figure out how many hours and intensity sessions your body can handle at this moment in your life and recognize that different bodies accept different amounts of volume. This is hard, because in an age when everyone looks on social media to be training incredibly hard, it's easy to get caught up in thinking you have to work even harder . . . until you overtrain and can't even run around the block, much less race.

Athletes tend to focus a little too much on the numbers and the volume of workouts. For me, training one thousand hours is not impressive. Any athlete who wants to can do that, although he or she may not race very fast. Training exactly the right amount of hours for *your* body is way more impressive! Pushing your limits, pushing your comfort zone, and then recognizing when it's right at the edge and pulling back are crucial. The sweet spot for me is finding the moment to ease off the gas pedal in training, so that I recover and ensure that my next workout is high quality. When it's time to train easy, I make sure I'm actually training easy and that my heart rate stays at the right level. I do this not because I don't want to work hard but because it allows me to work *even harder* when it's time to push my body in intervals. If I tire myself out by always skiing faster than I'm supposed to, how can I truly expect to be fast when I'm purposefully trying to shift gears?

This training philosophy is a lot easier said than done, though. The summer and fall after the 2014 Sochi Winter Olympics, I definitely got caught in a cycle of overtraining. It happened so slowly that I didn't notice it. I had been training a lot, and I thought it was going well, but slowly over the summer I hadn't been fully recovering between big blocks of training. I was getting more and more tired and slowing down over time. I wasn't fully in tune with my body and definitely wasn't listening to it telling me, "Hey! I'm still tired here!" It can be hard to notice the first signs of overtraining, because hard training blocks are *supposed* to make you tired and sore! The trick is knowing when you're recovered and rested enough after them to start the next one, and I had just blown through the signs, eager to train harder and longer than the summer before.

I went to fall camp, and my coaches Matt Whitcomb and Jason Cork both instantly noticed that I wasn't quite myself. It was like someone had muted my entire personality.

"You're not in a good place. You are really tired right now," Matt said, pulling me aside, "Also, you're really pretty sad, and you're never this sad."

He was right. When I get too tired, I get unreasonably sad, for no reason whatsoever.

"Yeah, this is not working," Cork confessed. "We've got to change this up."

So we did the only thing you can really do: stop training and let your body finally rest. I was told to take two weeks off, and I was instructed to do nothing. Zip. Zero. Nada. Which was terrifying to hear, because in the fall I would normally be training hard with a lot of intensity and starting to get my World Cup season ready to go. I was incredibly anxious about being on an emergency rest . . . but I also knew how badly I needed it. Somewhere deep down, I felt an incredible sense of relief. I could finally put up my tired feet and just sleep for ten to twelve hours a day.

Matt saw my anxiety and self-doubt and took me aside. In the way that only Matt can do, he made me laugh by telling me, "Nothing is fucked. You can still have a good season here, but you have to rest first. Nothing is fucked, OK?" It became our inside joke, a tagline for times when things looked pretty bad, but we hoped we could still pull out of it. "Nothing Is Fucked!"

I started the balancing act of putting my mind and body back together. I did yoga, watched Netflix, and slept. Then I started training again, and slowly, luckily, my body started to come around. I wasn't so overtrained that I couldn't bounce back. I finally got my fitness back just in time for the 2015 World Championships. I really learned a lesson during my hiatus: I had to train smart, not just train hard. You can train hard and train smart, but you can't train hard *without* training smart.

• • •

The U.S. national team still wasn't an elite powerhouse in cross-country skiing. Norway, Sweden, Russia, and Finland continued to dominate the World Cup and take podium spots in almost all of the Olympic competitions. But the U.S. national team had been making great strides and splashing onto the scene here and there with hard-earned victories and moxie.

We've become known for our team chemistry, the way we've created a positive and uplifting culture where individuals can support one another and thrive as one unit in the world of individual sports. Media can speculate and write all the stories they want, but I'll let you in on a little secret. We don't succeed because we have a team leader or a team captain. In fact, we succeed because we purposefully don't have one. We don't place the burden of leadership on one set of shoulders alone, because it is *everyone's* job to contribute to the team in his or her own way and style of leadership.

Not all acts of bravery are flashy, and not all forms of leadership are obvious, but it truly takes every piece to make the puzzle come together. Some lead by taking their communication and organizational skills to meetings as athlete reps, the way Kikkan Randall and Rosie Brennan have done. Some lead by caregiving and being nurturing, as Liz Stephen and Sadie Bjornsen do. Some lead by quietly observing and noticing details, then being the helpful listening ear and guiding hand that steers you in the right direction, as Sophie Caldwell and Caitlin Patterson do. Some rally the team and create excitement, as Holly Brooks and I do. Some have some serious creative and artistic talents, like Julia Kern. Some know how to pull a teammate out of a funk and make a training session joyful, as Hailey Swirbul, Hannah Halvorsen, and Katharine Ogden do, especially when they're paired together. And some skills shine in the dark, such as Ida Sargent's innate sense of how to comfort someone in a time of grief.

Though the women's team has received a lot of attention for our collective spirit, we succeed because we're one large team unit, and I believe we succeed because we train and travel with the men as well. Simi Hamilton has rad guide skills for any outdoor adventure we dare to embark on. Scott Patterson bakes the best cookies in the world, I promise. One talk with Paddy Caldwell will set your brain straight when you're feeling confused and need a friend to talk it out with. Andy Newell has literally saved my life in the team van with his catlike reflexes, and he's cracked me up with funny cat videos. Erik Bjornsen and Noah Hoffman always know how to make me laugh, and Kevin Bolger is a really fun running buddy. We function so well because of the balance of funny and serious, of hard work and meaningful downtime, of the men and women on the national team helping one another to greater heights.

Every day we go to practice on the national team, it is partly our responsibility to make sure that the day goes well. It's our job to find a way to lift up our teammates, to take and to give, to openly communicate with them, to learn and push them, and to let them push us to be better than we were the day before. In my years on the team, that's the real attitude that I've seen create lasting friendships, strong bonds, and a whole lot of success on a professional and emotional level.

My role on the team was made up of pure energy, and although it's evolved and grown up a little over the years (as I have, I hope!), it's still best defined in a phrase synonymous with sparkles, smiles, and "rah-rah" energy: team cheerleader. Sometimes that means rallying the troops for team dance class, where I teach everyone on the team a silly and fun hip-hop dance for a team music video (or just because). We end up giggling and laughing and not taking ourselves seriously at all, which in the end is exactly what we need during a competitive season filled with high pressure and nervous energy. Sometimes being team cheerleader simply means being myself and bringing a happy smile and some extra hugs and high fives to practice, especially when it's the second workout and people need a boost to get out the door. And sometimes when I can tell someone is troubled by self-doubt, it's pulling that person aside for a pep talk and letting my teammate know I really believe that she or he has what it takes. I love my role on the team, and I take great pride in knowing that I can be part of the reason someone else has a good training session or gets through a stretch of homesickness on the road.

Our collective fight and the bond between all the men and women on the national team have helped me grow as a human being, not just as a ski racer. And as with most things in life, the more you put into it, the more you get back! Our amazing team culture helped me grow during a critical moment of anxiety and self-doubt.

At the 2015 World Championships in Falun, Sweden, I was chosen to race the team sprint with Sophie, and we were both extremely excited but also so nervous that we were both about ready to puke our guts up. You see, for the first time ever, our team was the defending champs. Instead of a normal race bib, we were given snow-white bibs that proudly proclaimed "World Champion" on them. Yikes. Even

though it was Kikkan and I who had won the last World Championships team sprint, the bib follows the team, not the individuals, in a
team event. It was two years later, a different team of girls, but all eyes
were on us to do something special with those damn bibs. Talk about
a target on your back! We went in with the spotlight on us for the first
time in our lives.

We raced well, and we turned ourselves inside out for the team,
doing everything we could that day to put together a good performance.
In the end, that's all you can ever do, but still . . . finishing eighth, I
think we both felt like we had perhaps let the team down a little bit. We
had wanted, worked, and hoped for so much more! This was the first
time I had to really deal with the pressure of the World Championships
and the pressure of feeling like people were counting on me to perform.
I suddenly felt that the thin nylon champions bib weighed about a thousand pounds, and I thought it was too heavy for me to carry.

Alone in my hotel room that night, I finally cracked, and all the
emotions I'd held back during the media zone came flooding out. I
didn't feel like I was good enough to wear the U.S. racing suit. I didn't
want to go race in two days. I just wanted to go home. As I sat curled in
a ball on my bed having my mini meltdown, my phone rang. Liz has a
sixth sense like that.

All of my nerves, pressure, disappointments, and homesickness
came out in great big sobs on the phone. In a flash, Liz was there, and
she wrapped her arms around me and just held me for a while. She
didn't judge me for my emotional breakdown, just told me with her hug
that she loved me and was there for me and understood that sometimes
ski racing at the highest level isn't all it's cracked up to be. Then she said
something that single-handedly screwed my head on right and allowed
me to remember why I was there in the first place.

"OK, Diggie, this is what I want you to do. Tomorrow I want you to
just go out there and ski around that course as fast as you can. Go have
fun. Ski like you know how to ski," Liz said, her voice full of compassion. "Don't worry about anyone else. Don't worry about results. Just go
do this one thing. Go ski as fast as you can." That World Championships
bib had been indescribably heavy, but Liz helped me take it off.

I then called up my sports psychologist, Lauren Loberg, who has been behind the scenes, yet at my side, through my entire World Cup career. She helped me formulate a game plan for the 10K race: a pacing goal, technique goal, and mantra that I would repeat to myself when in the pain cave. I finally felt ready to put on a bib again.

Two days later, I was out testing skis with Cork before the 10K individual-start skate race. The Salomon ski reps had given us a new pair of skis the night before, and these skis created a different sound against the snow, almost a whooshing noise. These were new, clear-base carbon skis, and both Cork and I were looking at each other like we had just won the lottery.

I skied the best race of my year that day and won a silver medal. There was a crazy snowstorm that started early on in the race, and since I was bib number 26 and the exact middle starter of the race, I had some of the extreme slowing effect from the sloppy, wet fresh snowflakes . . . but not as much as the race favorites, who started at the back of the field. I wasn't naive or stupid enough to assume that my second-place finish was solely because I was one of the fastest skiers, and in fact I felt a lot of guilt over having better race conditions than the people who were "supposed" to beat me! But I also recognized that I had no control over the weather and had to simply accept what I was given. I also still had to beat the twenty-five people in front of me, who had better conditions than I did. It was one of those days when I was fiercely determined to ski free and as fast as I could. I harnessed that feeling I had as a child when all I wanted to do was go super speed. Our techs nailed the wax that day, Cork nailed the skis, and together as a team, we created an opportunity for me to ski the race of my year and step onto that medals platform.

Most important, I did what Liz told me to do. She had given me permission to let go of all of it: the pressure to medal, the media, and all of my internal anxiety. Without her hug, her love, and her words of wisdom, I wouldn't have been on that start line at all. On our team, we recognize that anytime one of us has a great race, it really belongs to all of us, because it took the team working together to make it happen. When I stepped onto that podium, I knew (and most important, my team knew) that I was only there because of my teammates pushing me in training and getting me emotionally in the right place; my sports psychologist, Lauren, helping me make a race plan; the coaches creating great training plans and camp environments; our strength coach, Tschana Schiller, helping me get strong; and the wax techs working day in and day out to nail the right combination. On any given race day, it takes at least a hundred people behind the scenes to make it all come together, and perhaps the greatest magic of our team is our ability to not only recognize but cherish the fact that nobody succeeds alone.

• • •

A year later, during the 2016 Tour de Ski, I came to the 5K individual race in Toblach, Italy, in an absolutely rockin' positive mood. I fell in love with the sport again. The joy was organic, clean, and pure, just like it was when I was a child skiing with my friends for the promise of Hershey's Kisses. This joy allowed me to push my body past it limits. Every athlete has a moment when everything clicks. A moment when the skills and the heart, the equipment and the strategy, the muscles and the brain are all in sync. My first individual World Cup win was that day for me.

That 5K skate marked one of the best races of my entire career. I have always loved individual-start races because there are no tactics, no games, no strategy other than just going out there and skiing your heart out. And my goal was to do just that—leave every ounce of energy I had out on that course and ski every inch of it as well as I possibly could. I knew it was a course designed for me because of all the gradual uphill sections and long, winding downhills, where I could either sit in a tuck or continue skating and working the downhill, looking for the best line around every corner. What also helped a ton was all the crazy cheering that was coming from the woods! Sophie, Ida, Simi, and Andy were all out there yelling and freaking out. The coaches were jumping up and down. It was such a boost of adrenaline every time I heard them!

For the U.S. cross-country women, distance skiing had remained a barrier that we hadn't yet broken down. In 1978, Alison Owen-Spencer won a World Cup distance skate race in Telemark, Wisconsin. Since that race, no American woman had won a distance World Cup event until Toblach. Kikkan had won a ton of sprint races, but in long distance we were still looking at a wall of Scandinavian dominance. We are always standing on the shoulders of the pioneers in the sport who worked so hard before us. And yes, while I was the one who skied the race and attacked every inch of the course, there was a huge support team of people who had attacked every other aspect of the race, making sure I had the best skis, the best training, the best teammates, and the opportunity to win. So this breakthrough brought tears, happy dances, and high fives all around the World Cup. I sat there in the snow, happy laughing and crying at the same time, in total disbelief that I was finally realizing one of my biggest dreams: to be the best in the world in a *distance event*. Other countries' skiers knew what this meant for us, and seeing their genuine happiness and receiving their congratulations meant a lot to us.

More important, though, my teammates found great success at this time too. Sophie won a World Cup classic sprint, the first American skier—male or female—to win that particular race. When she won, I was one of the first skiers on the scene to greet her with a hug. After I won my race in Toblach, I went straight over to the fence, and Sophie was right there with arms outstretched, a true teammate. I shared this incredible hug with her.

"I am so happy for you," Sophie said, as she wrapped me in a huge hug.

When Sophie says something to you, she genuinely means it, and you genuinely feel it. This moment really showed Sophie's character. She is so humble and so genuinely supportive and happy for other people. She was right there cheering for me in my moment, just as I was cheering for her. This momentum, this camaraderie, were definitely carried forward and propelled us to greater heights. We were able to take these amazing positive feelings and tuck them away.

It is natural to fear the success of others, to assume that for someone else to win, you must fail. By focusing on our happiness for one another and how we had each contributed to each other's success, we were able to blow through this hurdle that trips up many competitive teams. It's not that we don't each want to win—that's why we're there, competing! It's just that we're able to genuinely want to see each other succeed as well. And when it's not our day but happens to be our teammate's best day, we rally around and lift that person up. Obviously, this is easier said than done. It's human to hurt a little bit inside anytime you see someone else get the thing you really want, whether that's in sports, in work, or in love. But it's what we choose to do that counts, and setting in place a team culture that you're expected to be there for one another makes your next steps an easy choice when you're confronted with the situation of not being the one on top.

Teammates and the words they choose to use are a powerful thing. In Davos last year, after I was eliminated from the quarterfinals, I walked up to Sophie and gave her a huge hug. I told her that I thought she was skiing so incredibly well, and her performance that day had already been brilliant. "I want you to know, I think you can win today. Not that you have to! No pressure! But you're skiing so well, I just want you to know that you *can* win," I told her. She very nearly did, and stepped onto the podium in second place.

Later that year, Sophie returned my words to me. After being eliminated in Cogne, Italy, she slipped an arm around my neck and whispered in my ear, "You don't *have* to win today . . . but you can if you want to!" And then I did.

Words are a powerful thing, indeed. Confidence is a weapon, and so are powerful teammates.

• • •

We had a strong team on the national level that could withstand any storm, and on the club level we were also building a force that would become a source of strength, happiness, and sense of belonging for our Stratton Mountain School T2 team. Our team roster changed through the years, but the feeling of support and camaraderie through tough training, highs, and lows always remained the same.

When I moved to Stratton, Vermont, in spring 2012, I had never been to that part of the country before. I knew a few of my new teammates from racing trips, but I was largely taking a leap of faith, hoping that this new team and training location would be what I needed. I couldn't have been luckier. Sophie and Erika Flowers took me under their wings that summer, and we spent time between training sessions jumping in the water at the snowmaking pond, painting our toenails, starting a book club, and getting to know each other better. I would spend countless hours over the following years being a (probably slightly annoying) dedicated third wheel to their relationships, seeing Erika fall in love with Andy Newell, and Sophie fall in love with Simi Hamilton. Annie Pokorny and Anne Hart both joined the team, and Anne taught me everything I needed to know about cooking good food while we lived together. Annie opened my eyes to the art of the quick weekend adventure with trips to the White Mountains in New Hampshire and kayaking in Burlington, Vermont. Kelsey Phinney and Alayna Sonnesyn are incredibly hard workers but would also get us giggling after crushing intervals. I learned that nobody gets up earlier in the mornings (or drinks more coffee) than Paddy Caldwell, that Ben Saxton is the ultimate trivia partner and is always up for a game, and Ben Ogden can build or fix anything. Kyle Bratrud is quiet but possibly the funniest person I know, and Ian Torchia will get us fired up and out the door, no matter how hard the training plan is.

Sverre Caldwell (Sophie's dad, Paddy's uncle) is our club director, and aside from founding the team, he and his lovely wife, Lilly, often have the entire squad over for team dinners. Our club coach, Pat O'Brien, goes absolutely above and beyond, spending his spare time mapping out new running routes, scouting trails in his clogs at sunset so we can keep training loops interesting with new additions. After a few years, Cork also moved to Stratton to selflessly help everyone on the team with summer training, even though that's not in his job description between training camps. He's just so dedicated to making sure we have everything we need to find success! All in all, training was going well, life was good, and the team atmosphere kept everyone motivated and inspired.

• • •

Cross-country skiing is possibly the healthiest lifelong sport you can participate in. It's a full-body workout, you're moving under your own power, and it has an extremely low risk for injury. Whereas many of our U.S. Ski and Snowboard team teammates have suffered blown knees or broken bones, we simply aren't moving at speeds high enough to sustain crazy injuries. It's a healthy, wholesome sport, and yet . . . when you take it to this level and are pushing your body to extremes in pursuit of finding your training limits, it's perhaps not that healthy for your body anymore. The injuries we tend to suffer from are overuse problems, little things that, left unchecked, can blow out of proportion.

In summer 2015, I found myself with a foot injury that tested the levels of both my sanity and pain tolerance. For years, I'd had plantar warts on the bottom of my foot. They hadn't bothered me much, but I knew they could potentially hurt during race season since they were right under the ball of my foot, where we kick off from in classic striding. In an effort to prevent problems, I went to a dermatologist that spring to get them removed. I didn't have the option of repeat visits, so I decided to have them cut out. After the procedure, I had two rather gross, large holes in the bottom of my foot. They slowly healed, but what I didn't know was that while the top layer of skin grew over the hole, the cavity got infected. A dense mass of skin cells had formed over the hole and sealed the infection right in there. Gross.

Weeks later, I flew to New Zealand for a two-and-a-half-week training camp. It was a really key camp for me, and I had visited the dermatologist before leaving because I wanted to make sure my foot was good to go. He took a quick look and said I was fine, so I got on the plane, thinking the slight pain in my foot had to be because of something minor. But one week into camp, the pain in my foot was unbearable. I had an infection, and there was now a patch of hardened skin driving that infection into my foot with every step I took. It was excruciating. It felt like I was stepping on a nail every time I kicked my skis.

I had been given the green light at the dermatologist's office, so I blindly kept training, and the pain kept growing. I was desperate to relieve the pressure, so I would use a little blade to cut out some of the dead skin around the top of the corn (the hard patch of skin cells in my foot). Every night, I'd sit on the bathroom floor with this X-Acto blade, cutting out the bottom of my foot to relieve pressure, which sounds incredibly stupid, I know. But hey, I was young and dumb and full of great ideas! The pressure and pain would always come back a day later.

It got to the point where it was so painful that I was limping around during training and could no longer ski. We found a hospital in town that said they'd take a look at my foot, so Cork drove me down the winding ten-mile dirt road. I was pressed up against the windshield looking down, trying so hard not to get car sick.

A super friendly doctor met us in the emergency room. Ironically, the doctor was also an endurance athlete. He was a triathlete and had competed in a few Ironmans. So he knew what it felt like to be in pain and suffer during a training session. He diagnosed it as an infection, then told me he'd need to scrape it out and clean out my foot.

"All right, this is going to hurt. You can yell if it makes you feel better, but it won't stop me," the doctor said. *What the hell? Isn't he supposed to numb my foot first, or something? Is this the budget hospital experience?*

I didn't make a single sound as he took a scalpel to my foot and scraped out the infection. It hurt, but as soon as the doctor finished, there was instant relief. I could finally breathe again. My foot felt back to normal! Well, except for the fact that I was now back to square one with a large, bloody hole in the bottom of my foot. But even that felt one hundred times better than an infection!

"All right, coach, I want you to take a look at this now," the doctor said to Cork. I turned my head to look at Cork, and his face was chalk white. He does not like blood. *Grey's Anatomy* is not his favorite show.

"Really?" Cork said, trying not to puke.

"Jessie can't see the bottom of her foot super well so it's going to be your job. Before training every day, Jessie is going to put her foot up, and you have to take this syringe full of antibacterial ointment and fill the hole in her foot with it."

"I do?"

"You do."

Cork really does go above and beyond as a coach.

• • •

The feet that so often betrayed me and caused me pain finally healed up, and I moved on, forgetting it had ever happened . . . but learning my lesson for preventive foot care. I was soon preoccupied with greater things in life, however, no time to worry about injuries!

I met the love of my life over a game of Jenga at a wedding. More specifically, the wedding of a good friend and amazing skier, Chandra

Crawford, from Canada. When she married Jared Poplawski in September 2015, they threw an epic party. In lieu of clinking forks against wine glasses at the reception to get the bride and groom to kiss, they had a giant, oversized Jenga game set up near the dance floor. You'd go up with a partner, and if both of you could successfully remove and stack a block without knocking the whole tower down, Chandra and Jared would kiss. If you knocked it over, you'd be the one kissing your partner.

Long after the Jenga game was forgotten and everyone was breaking it down on the dance floor, this really cute guy asked me if I'd like to take out some Jenga blocks with him. I looked at the table. That thing was *rock solid*. Not going to fall anytime soon. Sure, why not?

Rob Whitney, my teammate Holly's husband, has a great sense of humor and had been trying all night to find someone for me to dance with (thanks, buddy). As this mystery man was placing his block on top of the tower after I'd successfully placed mine, Rob waltzed by and with a sly but mighty kick sent the whole tower crashing to the floor. The noise was deafening. The dancing stopped. Everyone turned and looked. This handsome guy had no choice but to grab me and kiss me in front of everyone, including his extended family, because his cousin had just married Chandra and his entire family was there.

That's how I met Wade Poplawski. He's my person! And although he wins every other kind of game against me, he's never beaten me in Jenga.

CHAPTER 17

BECAUSE 96 ISN'T 100

So what do you do in the years between Olympics? Sit around and wait? Nope! We have World Cup races nearly every weekend of every winter, and there are World Championship race series in the years before and after the Olympics. With that many races, we need to be training hard. The training never (OK, *almost* never) stops. While writing this book, I was repeatedly assured that skiers are totally nuts, our workouts are extreme, and nobody would believe me unless I wrote about it. So here we go . . . I'm writing about it.

It was a hot and sticky June morning in Stratton, Vermont, nearing eight o'clock and I had already been running for thirty minutes. I reached down in the dirt, lifted a volleyball-size boulder to my chest and started doing squat jumps with it. I was surrounded by my club teammates on the SMS T2 team and a group of junior skiers from the Stratton area, all doing the same thing. We had met at the base of Stratton Mountain near the gondola for our morning workout. This was only part of our warm-up before intervals, but we were already collectively dissolving into a sweaty mess. One at a time, we sprang up and heaved the rocks high into the soupy air like a shot put. No one marked the distance of our throws. No fans were cheering us on. We were simply grinding our way through a dryland training session worthy of a *Rocky* montage. We weren't hefting rocks because we wanted to look like Sylvester Stallone (although, honestly, who doesn't?) but because it was more practical to use the rocks that were already there than to haul medicine balls from the gym to the foot of the Alpine mountain.

First, we had gone through an easy jog on the flats for about thirty minutes. Then we started an active, dynamic warm-up, moving our bodies in different ways to prevent injuries while warming up different groups of muscles. We did jumps, running drills, squats, and sprints, culminating in the rock throws for a little extra resistance on our jumps. This was all just a warm-up for the main event.

Our training plan called for a hike up Stratton Mountain, which has an elevation of 3,940 feet. We might have done our warm-up by the gondola, but we were going to have to get to the summit the good old-fashioned way: straight up the Alpine runs, sweating our way to the top. We were walking or bounding (sometimes called "moose hoofing") with our ski poles to mimic the same motions and use of our muscles as cross-country skiing in the winter. Moose hoofing is not jumping, and it's not running. It's the beautifully awkward in-between. But you use your poles to help you have that split second where you're suspended weightless, gliding through the air up the hill, which mimics the glide phase after you kick a classic ski.

My intervals up Stratton Mountain weren't random; they were set by Cork and our training plan. When I train, I work in different levels that correspond to different heart rate zones. These heart rate zones correspond to training intensities or intensity zones. We simply call them Levels, with a capital "L" to indicate how badass it is.

I plodded my way up the mountain in Level Three (L3), which is an intense rate just below a race pace. You can use a heart rate monitor to help you figure out what level you're training in or you can go by feel. I usually do a little bit of both! In L3, it's hard work, and it would be hard to have a conversation, but if I had to do it for an hour straight, I could (just barely). Sometimes, we *do* go for an hour straight in L3. This morning, I hiked up the mountain alongside my teammates for seven minutes at a really hard pace, then turned around and jogged back downhill for three minutes. The running downhill was our "recovery," the only break we'd get before starting uphill again. We then repeated the interval—up for seven minutes, down for three—as we inched our way up the mountain.

Strangely, the goal had nothing to do with reaching the top. We knew we were going to get to the top. In fact, we did the interval in this sequence because we actually run out of mountain to climb! The seven up–three down intervals allowed us to, in essence, climb the mountain twice. The other fun part about inch-worming our way up was that the junior athletes who were joining our training session could jump in behind us, and when they fell behind on the seven-minute section, they would still get another chance to follow us "big kids" when we ran by them on our three-minute recovery to start our next interval slightly below them. When I was thirteen years old, I would have given *anything* to be able to follow a bunch of Olympians around during their weekday training sessions. For these kids, it's totally normal, because they do it a few times per week!

We ascended over the bunny-slope part of the mountain and made our way onto a service road that winds up the side of Stratton Mountain. The service road was made of loose gravel and at times made me feel like I was bounding uphill in sand. Each seven-minute trip up the mountain became more painful, as we began each interval less rested than the one before. My face blanked out into pure focus; I have a curiously blank look on my face (so I'm told) when I'm intensely focused on my technique and pushing myself as hard as I can. I don't even have the energy to spare to contort my face into a grimace! We held our pace and kept pushing forward up the mountain at a punishing speed. My breath grew ragged, but I did not give a single inch to the pain that was now rising in my sore muscles like a flood.

Up on Stratton Mountain, I was a world away from the FIS World Cup of Skiing and the Winter Olympics. But every cross-country skier will tell you that winter skiers are made in the summer.

• • •

Every athlete thinks that their sport is the hardest sport. And with good reason! Every sport brings its own mental and physical challenges. Some sports are skill based while others require brute strength. Some sports require technical tricks or tactics to win the most points. Some sports are entirely endurance based, while others require short shifts and sprints. Some require a solo effort, while others are team based with players relying on their teammates for success.

Cross-country skiing lies in the intersection of all of these attributes. It blends a need for endurance, power, speed, and technique in two different modes of racing (skate and classic). But it also requires extreme muscle endurance and smart tactical decisions that are made on the fly. And sometimes team tactics when it comes to relays! Some races are individual starts, with only our own willpower to push us along. We also race in mass start formats, which are similar to the start of a marathon. On the two-to-three-minute side, we have sprint heats where it's head-to-head racing with no lanes separating opponents. And we're doing this in every cold weather condition (we didn't have a race canceled even when there was thunder and lightning. What the heck?), and all we've got for battle armor is a thin spandex suit.

All things considered, in my *completely* biased opinion, cross-country skiing is the toughest sport out there. With all these different demands on us, we have to train extremely hard. Our warm-ups are many athlete's entire workouts. Heck, my recovery workout (which is our easiest feel-good workout used to get our bodies moving after a big workout) is an hour on a spin bike or over an hour of swimming.

But here's the coolest thing: while we train extremely hard at the top level, cross-country skiing is something that everybody can learn to do. At entry level, it's exactly as hard as you want it to be, like running. Not all runners want to pound out the Boston Marathon, but that doesn't mean they're not allowed to enjoy running! Skiing's kind of the same way.

For example, take a normal strength-training session I'll have in the late afternoon on a Tuesday. This is in addition to my morning interval workout that was around two hours, but after an easy afternoon filled with a lot of good food and some downtime. For my warm-up, I'll jog or be on a spin bike for thirty minutes. Then I will do a series of dynamic stretches. This includes 110 body squats while pulling on stretchy bands with my arms, to warm up all my muscles in a few different planes of motion. That's all just part of the warm-up, to prevent injury during the harder lifting. Then I'll put a band around my ankles and do a series of band walks and static holds that fire my glute muscles. It feels like I'm about to rip my muscles in half. This entire warm-up series will last forty-five to fifty minutes. Then the real workout begins, and I'll lift weights, do plyometric jumps, and do about fifteen minutes of core exercises. Many of our weight-lifting exercises cover multiple muscle groups, because cross-country skiing is full body.

Tschana Schiller, our badass strength coach, writes the lifting plan for me. She individualizes it for each of her athletes according to their body type and what they need to get strong and perform in their sport. So while not every skier's plan looks the same, a typical set of exercises for me might look like this: pull-ups, triceps dips, incline bench press, horizontal pull-ups on a bar with my feet on a Swiss ball. For legs, I'll do cleans, hex bar dead lifts, side-to-side jumps, broad jumps, and single leg jumps onto a box. This sounds like a lot, but it's fundamental strength training, the kind I used to do back in my high school days. It's just been taken up a notch or two or three!

• • •

In a normal nine-to-five job, people get to clock out at the end of the day. In some ways, when they go home, they get to leave their work behind. Having a beer after work, being on their feet all night at a party, or staying up late isn't, perhaps, something they think about. For me, though, I never clock out from my job. And that's not some sort of weird humble brag! It's just the truth.

As a professional cross-country skier, my job is to take care of my body. And believe me, it's a full-time job because my body can be really bossy! My job is an entire lifestyle, a delicate and measured balance of training, nutrition, competing, and rest. I get one rest day a week (usually Mondays, if you're curious), but it's not *really* a day off. This is because my body and mind need to recover from training sessions or competitions, so my day off is a maintenance day, with self-care like yoga, stretching, or foam rolling and without anything strenuous, even if going for a hike is what I'd like to be doing. It's also the day I try to get caught up on emails and life things. Being an adult (or at least, trying to be) is hard!

I hardly ever go to parties. I need around ten hours of sleep at night, and sometimes in big training weeks I'll also need to nap during the day. I can (and do!) eat some junk food, but I definitely can't eat only junk food. Plus, I prefer to bake my *own* cookies, thank you very much. I can't stay up late binge watching shows (even though I sometimes go on a *Vampire Diaries* watching spree). In case you haven't noticed the pattern here, it's not like I'm some inhuman robot. I still have fun, I still eat dessert, I still overdose on Netflix. I mean, come on, a girl's still gotta be happy, and if you told me I had to be the "perfect" athlete in every way for every day of my ten-to-fifteen-year career, I'd be retired at this very moment. It's all in the moderation and balance, and before I do anything, my first thought is, how will this affect my racing? But to be honest, I'm only slightly weirder than your average human.

The places I notice the differences most are in the amount of control I have over my schedule, the astonishingly high number of hours I sleep (nine to ten per night), and the astonishingly low number of alcoholic drinks I consume. Fun fact: if I had to guess, I probably drink under twenty drinks a year. I actually don't love the taste of alcohol. Maybe, perhaps, skipping college did have some long-lasting effects?

The place where it's the hardest for me and just about the only time I feel that I'm truly making a sacrifice for skiing is when I can't spend nearly as much time with my boyfriend, Wade, and our families. Being on the road so much is tough sometimes. In that normal nine-to-five job, you get weekends off, holidays off, and (I hope!) around four vacation weeks that you can choose to spend however you wish.

With skiing, I get thirty days annually that are truly off, all lumped together in April, where I can be where I want and do exactly what I want. So yes, April is a *very*, very sacred month! The rest of the year, I do have some flexibility in where I train. For example, it's easy for me to visit my parents and be in Minnesota because the training in Afton is so amazing. But our schedule is determined by team camps, on-snow training opportunities, and doing what's best for my ski racing. The people I love in my life are absolute rock stars for working with me around this crazy schedule of constant travel and also understanding that ski racing isn't forever . . . at some point, I'll retire and become a (slightly) more normal human being again! But for now, from May 1 through the end of the season in March, I commit my entire life to training and conditioning.

•   •   •

For everyone who wants to nerd out with me, let's jump into the nuts and bolts of my training.

The typical afternoon strength workout is almost always prefaced by an intense intervals workout in the morning. Intervals are a series of cardiovascular training sessions. When I'm training and doing intervals, Level One (L1) is the lowest intensity. I can run for five hours at L1. The pace is easy and casual, enough to carry on a conversation, and normally I do because (shocker) I like to talk to my teammates! My heart rate for L1 is 115 to 140. Anywhere in that zone, it's pretty easy.

Level Two (L2) is when my heart rate is 145 to low 150s. I don't train in that zone because it's not helpful to me. Enough said.

Level Three (L3) is the first of our intense interval zones. This is where things start to get uncomfortable. In L3 I'm producing lactic acid, but I'm flushing it out nearly as fast as I can produce it. I could do L3 for an hour straight if I had to (but it would suck). Sometimes I do, so I can practice pacing. In L3, my heart rate is in the low 150s to about 165 to 168. L3 is the zone where it can be really hard to talk while I'm doing it. It's still hard, but it's sub-race pace.

Level Four (L4) is race pace, and because our races are so varied in length, my coach and I break L4 into subsections: L4A and L4B.

L4A is a pace so hot that I can't do it for more than two to three minutes. Essentially, L4A is a sprint race pace. L4A is when my heart rate is 173 up to its max in the low 180s. L4B is when my heart rate is 168 to 172. It's race pace, but it's more like a 30K race pace (Conversion note: 30 kilometers = 18.5 miles). We do a lot of intervals that are four to six minutes in L4B. Mid-distance races like a 10K are a mix of both intensity zones, depending on where you are on the course.

Level Five (L5) is sprint zone intensity. It is an all-out ten-to-fifteen-second sprint, your maximum effort. It doesn't have a corresponding heart rate, because in that amount of time your heart rate can't get that high!

My first winter, and I'm already loving the tradition of skiing every weekend with Mom and Dad.

Eventually I gave the backpack spot to my sister, Mackenzie, and got my own skis.

"Go, Dad, go!" I always wanted to join in the fun and embraced my role of team cheer-leader early.

Reading *Snow White* to Mackenzie in our favorite position for reading time.

Family canoe trips way up in the middle of nowhere! We thrived on these fun family moments outdoors.

First roller ski . . . you can never have too many knee pads, although the fanny pack was an added bonus.

My amazing Stillwater team-mates—state champions in 2008! I am second from left in the top row, next to our incredible coach, Kris Hansen.

Going for team sprint gold at the 2013 World Championships in Val di Fiemme, Italy—moments after losing a pole. If you look closely, you'll see my missing pole in the snow.

Holding the flag with Kikkan Randall and the rest of the U.S. Ski Team after winning the team sprint in Italy in 2013, the first-ever World Championship gold for the United States. Photograph by Sarah Brunson/U.S. Ski & Snowboard.

My Olympic journey begins in Sochi, Russia, in 2014. Like anywhere else, you leave it all on the course. Photograph by Harry How/Getty Images.

Training in New Zealand, going off piste! Working on those 25 percent grade climbs . . . and taking a little break between laps. Photograph by Matt Whitcomb.

Getting nasty with the training in Soldier Hollow, Utah, during a team time trial. Photograph by Matt Whitcomb.

Jason Cork and I test skis before the Tour de Ski. Photograph copyright Nordic Focus.

Your teammates are the ones who scrape you up off the snow after you've given it everything you have. Ulricehamn, 4 × 5K women's relay in 2019. Photograph copyright Nordic Focus.

Lunging for Olympic history. Photograph by Dmitri Lovetsky/AP Images.

The moment I sat in the snow and started to understand what we had
accomplished in PyeongChang: a dream that took many generations
working together to fulfill. Photograph by Matthias Schrader/AP Images.

Kikkan and I celebrate with the team after winning gold. It truly takes a village, and this is just the tip of the iceberg. Photograph by Steve Fuller.

Our amazing coaches have been with us every step of the way. *Left to right:* Erik Flora, Jason Cork, Kikkan Randall, me, Chris Grover, Matt Whitcomb. Photograph by Reese Brown/U.S. Ski & Snowboard.

My support team at the PyeongChang Olympics. *Back row, left to right:* Aunt Holly Murdoch, Wade Poplawski, Uncle Blair Murdoch, Clay Diggins. *Front row, left to right:* me, Grandma Betty Santa, Deb Diggins, Mackenzie Diggins.

The hugs, tears, and outpouring of emotion from the team right after the Olympic victory remain the most precious memory to me: it meant everything to have them there. Photograph by Sarah Brunson/U.S. Ski & Snowboard.

Gold medal dishes! Three hours after receiving the gold medal at the awards plaza, I was in my happy place with Wade and my mom.

Stealing a moment with Mom after a stage of the Tour de Ski. Photograph copyright Nordic Focus.

Sometimes you train in wind and rain and mud . . . and sometimes you get this. Eagle Glacier skiing on a good day in Alaska. Photograph by Matt Whitcomb.

I spend as much time as I'm able with kids, encouraging them to be active and have fun. Photograph by Derek Montgomery/derekmontgomery.com.

Where it all started and continues: in the snow, with my family.

Many people ask me, "Why are your heart rate zones so small? Shouldn't the max heart rate for an elite athlete be higher?" Here's the thing: I have the max heart rate of a little old lady. Maybe it's genetics, maybe it's from years of training my body to become more and more efficient at pumping blood around, but for whatever reason, my heart rate just keeps getting lower and lower every year. I haven't seen a number over 188 in years! This makes my zones, such as L4 and L3, pretty narrow windows to hit. It's a finely tuned balance of listening to my body and its perceived exertion to know if it feels like "race pace" to me or not.

• • •

If you'd like to spend a week training like my teammates and I do, here's how we do it:

I will train six days a week. Most of those days, I'll have two training sessions per day. But sometimes the morning training session is very, very long, such as a four-hour run or three-hour roller ski. Then I will have the afternoon off, with time for stretching, yoga, or foam rolling.

Unlike runners, we don't count our miles. Cross-country skiers log their training in hours spent moving in each zone. That way, we are not worried about how many hundreds of miles we are covering but are instead focused on the quality of training within those miles: what the goal for each workout is, what level we want to train in, what technique goals we want to focus in on. My training log records the amount of hours I spend training in each level per week, and the amount of hours I spend doing various modes of training (roller skiing, skiing on snow, running, swimming, spin biking, weight lifting, and "other," which usually means I'm dancing). My training log also has a section where I rate my recovery so I can stay in tune with how my body is feeling and responding to training, and track it over time. I'll rank from one to ten how my body feels in the categories of tiredness, muscle soreness, and happiness (you'd be surprised to see how strongly this correlates to how hard I'm pushing my body). I also keep track of my sleep hours and quality of sleep. When you're pushing your body incredibly hard and walking the fine line between training a huge amount and not recovering from it, you have to be really careful not to step over the edge.

In an average week, I'll train around twenty to twenty-five hours. And that number fluctuates depending on what training cycle I'm in and what the focus is for the week (if I'm focused on intervals that week, the overall volume might be slightly lower, because intervals put more stress on the body than easy, slow distance training). But that is only time that I'm actually sweating. If I counted all the prep time and hours getting ready, it'd be more like a thirty-five-hour week! What I count as training time is only when I'm in L1 or more. Hours spent reviewing technique videos, planning training, stretching, foam rolling, doing yoga, visualizing, meeting with my sports psychologist—those are definitely a serious part of the job, but they're not counted in the training log.

I have Mondays off. God, Mondays are so boring. Wait, I take that back! Mondays are their own kind of workout: the mental kind. I'm usually working on a blog post, planning sponsor content, answering emails, and planning out meals for the week since it's a rather lengthy drive to the grocery store. The importance of a rest day cannot be stated enough, in my mind, because it took me so long to really learn it and believe it! But every time I go out and train, I'm really just breaking my body down. The hours spent resting and recovering are when I actually see fitness gains, because my muscles repair themselves and come back stronger. They can only do that, though, if I let them have the space they need to recover!

On Tuesday, I will have intervals in the morning and strength in the afternoon. The intervals will all be in L3, which means it will be tough, but it (probably) won't make me puke. The great news is that we're in this together as a team, so I'm still in for a suffer-sesh, but surrounded by my Stratton teammates, which somehow makes it feel significantly less painful. We'll warm up for about thirty to forty minutes, just easy roller skiing at L1. Then we'll start the intervals. An example of a typical course for us is up a winding, uphill mountain road, probably a little over two miles. It will take eleven minutes to skate up to the top of the hill, and then our recovery time is sitting in a tuck on the way back down. Obviously, it's not as hard as Alpine skiing, but our recovery is in a tuck because in cross-country skiing, you get to recover only while step turning or tucking your way down the hill you just climbed.

It takes three or four minutes of tucking to get back down to the bottom of the mountain road. Then we turn around and do it again. *Oh, joy!* I'll do this five times or more, accumulating about fifty-five minutes of time in L3. Then I'll cool down for another thirty minutes in L1 as I roller-ski home. As a whole, the workout will take between two and two and a half hours. And that was just the first session of the day!

Tuesday afternoon, I'll go the gym and do the forty-five-minute warm-up with jogging, active dynamic work, and bands, and then I lift weights. I'm in the gym for around two hours, but I have a lot of rest in between sets. All things being equal, I count it as about an hour and a half. Honestly, I also spend a lot of time messing around on the slackline with my teammate Julia Kern, coming up with new tricks to test our balance and coordination! Like everything else I do in training, I'm rarely alone. Sophie is usually my lifting buddy in the gym, since we're on the same strength plan, and her sense of humor and work ethic always make the time pass by quickly. My all-time favorite way to end a strength workout is by spending fifteen minutes on the super trampoline in Stratton's aerial awareness gym, flipping head over heels into the foam pit over and over.

On Wednesday morning, I'll meet up with my teammates for a two hour and fifteen minute roller ski with speed stations. We'll warm up with an easy classic (or skate, depending on the day) roll to a specific location, where the coaches have set up stations. A typical speed workout involves three "stations," with cones marking out a fifteen-second section of road with some feature we want to improve on. That might be a sharp corner, a mock starting gate, a steep uphill, or a drop in from a downhill to mock finishing lanes. Taking turns to push each other or doing them solo to focus on technique, we'll complete six to eight sets of all-out sprints for fifteen seconds at each station. Unless we're in the middle of an epic lightning storm, we'll do this in rain, in freezing winds, or under a baking sun. Then we will roller-ski back to where we started.

On Wednesday afternoon, I'll be on my own. I might run for an hour. I might spin for an hour, listening to a podcast (most likely *How I Built This* by NPR or *Peace Meal* by The Emily Program, in case you're wondering). If it's really hot out, I might go for a run and then swim. I'll keep it flexible, but it's usually a way to get some easy volume training in and an opportunity for non-weight-bearing exercise, like swimming, to give my body a break.

Thursday morning will bring another set of intervals, and this time they might be L4, which is race pace. As a team, all bets are off on the puking. There will be a warm-up for thirty to forty minutes, ending in a power dynamic warm-up with squats and jumps and running drills. And then I'll do six-by-four minutes at L4B. I will go epically hard for four minutes, rest for three minutes, and do it again and again. By the end, my lactic acid will be building up because in L4 I'm not clearing it as fast as I'm building it. No bones about it, it will be really hard and very painful. These L4 intervals are where I build my ability to be comfortable with the uncomfortable. This is where I learn how to waltz into the pain cave and still function. As a team, we help each other practice the art of suffering (the mosquitoes really add to the general discomfort).

The first time I enter this level of pain can't be in a race. The feeling needs to be hardwired into my mind and body. I learn how to cope in the summer so that when I'm in a race and suffering, I can still function and execute my skills and strategy. There's a lot of physiological reasons why I do those L4 intervals in the summer, but sometimes it feels as though the main reason is to teach both my body and mind how to operate while they are under attack.

Thursday afternoon, I'll go back to the gym and do the same forty-five-minute warm-up and strength training, with slightly different exercises. Because why wouldn't you?

Friday morning, I'll meet my teammates to go on a long-distance roller ski in the rolling Green Mountains of Vermont. In the afternoon, I will go on another distance roller ski or run. If this is starting to sound repetitive, that's because it is. Luckily for me, I have amazing teammates who are also good friends, and talking makes the time fly by quickly. That's one of the things I love most about training for skiing! It's very social, you get to mix it up with different modes of training, and you get to be outside.

Saturday morning, I will sometimes do more L3 intervals, depending on the week. Tragically, the afternoon is not for running errands and shopping at L.L. Bean. Instead of strength training, it'll be the active forty-five-minute warm-up, but then I'll do forty-five minutes of core work, with some balance training thrown in.

Sunday is the traditional day of rest for many people. I know this because we recently had a cooking fiasco at training camp when someone accidentally set the oven to "Sabbath" mode, and it wouldn't turn on to let us cook dinner. Breakers were flipped on and off, creative curse words were used . . . it was very exciting! But generally on Sundays, cross-country skiers do the opposite of rest; an overdistance workout (OD). I suppose you could also look at it as an overdose of ski training, when we will go much longer than we would normally go in a race. We might run a point-to-point in the mountains, and it might take four hours. We might roller-ski for two hours and run for an hour and a half. Or we might roller-ski for three and a half hours to four hours. Fun stuff, I say!

I get a lot of questions about why we train this way and with this much volume. The short answer is because the sport of cross-country skiing demands it. Any cross-country skier at the elite level is going to be training similarly to what I described in a typical training week. There are really no secrets. Most people lift two or three times a week, do intervals two or three times a week, and do a lot of distance work. Most people do speed training or pick-ups. The week I described was pretty average for all the skiers I know.

• • •

The sheer volume, intensity, and frequency of our workouts make our sport pretty extreme, but we don't see our training as a big deal. We're conditioned to not complain, although sometimes we do anyway, just to give the coaches grief. Joking complaints aside, no one ever seriously says, "It's too hard, I don't want to go run for ninety minutes in the afternoon after doing two and a half hours of skiing in the morning." We just get it done, because everyone's training that way. That's the job, and I appreciate it. I feel lucky to *get* to do this job! I don't see it as this big sacrifice or crazy set of workouts. Although I've been assured that it is crazy to love training this hard.

To survive any cross-country race, I think back on all of those hard hours that I put in during the summer in Stratton. The hay is in the barn, you know? I know that I did the work. I have the mental comfort of knowing that I emptied my tank all summer, and it fully prepared me for what was coming ahead in the winter. Every once in a while—not very often, just once a summer!—I do what I fondly call my Big Stupid Thing. It's a training day designed to push my comfort zone, push the limits of what I think I'm capable of doing, so that if I ever doubt myself the night before a big race, I can think back on it and know that I am made of tougher stuff. I'll switch it up year to year, sometimes focusing on distance, sometimes on pain tolerance in intervals. I only do it once a summer because, in terms of energy expenditure, it's a very expensive workout. Just like ridiculously expensive shoes, you need only one pair to make a statement.

• • •

I've roller-skied 100 kilometers in one day (that's sixty-two miles, to save you a quick trip to Google). This is a classic "Big Stupid," because I've done it a few times over the years. The most recent was the summer of 2018, when I did the first three hours with some of my SMST2 teammates because they used it as their overdistance workout. Then Cork and Wade joined me on their bikes for the second half. Luckily, Wade and I had been dating for a while, otherwise he might have decided to get rid of me once he saw how stubborn and ridiculous I became.

We mapped the 100 kilometers beforehand and parked my old, beat-up Subaru, whose name is Jasper the Second (go ask my sister what happened to Jasper the First) at the finish line. The entire time I roller-skied, I told myself that when I reached my car, I would be done. I believe I stashed a large bag of homemade cookies in the car, too, so I had a little extra incentive to not cave and call an Uber. While I was skiing, I had my Suunto watch tracking the kilometers, just for fun. This turned out to be a stupid idea, as my watch was more accurate than our plan.

At the end of my epic workout, I approached my car and was super stoked that I had finished 100 kilometers. I was *ready* for that cookie. Then Cork broke the news to me.

"So, um . . . you're actually only at 96 kilometers . . . ," Cork said sheepishly, as he rode his bike up next to me.

"What?!" I said with shock, as I approached the finish line. I looked down at my watch. *Well, I'll be damned!*

I could've just stopped and been done, because 96 kilometers was a huge accomplishment. But I could not ignore the simple, nagging fact that the math was wrong.

96 wasn't 100.

I blew past Jasper the Second and called over my shoulder, "I'm going four more kilometers!"

Cork and Wade just shook their heads. Then they pulled their bikes alongside the Subaru.

"All right, we'll pick you up!" Wade yelled after me.

I finished the last four kilometers just because I'm stubborn enough to do that sort of thing. It would have been so easy to give up, and nobody would have blamed me. After all the intervals and strength training that we normally do during the week, the 100K was the cap. Nobody would have even cared how many kilometers I had done. In fact, they would have preferred that I stop, as we'd been out there for over six hours, and everyone was hot, dusty, tired, and hangry (hangry is when you're so hungry, you start to get irrationally angry). But I cared. I needed to dig deep and finish it.

• • •

I've always wanted to run a marathon. I could never run one, though, because I don't have the time to train specifically for running, especially on pavement. It's too much pounding on my joints. But then I had an idea! We run on the Appalachian Trail all the time! It goes right past my condo and up and over the mountain. It's right there, in all its rocky, root-filled muddy glory. I was scheduled to do a long run at the end of a big week of training a few summers ago, so I decided to make this my Big Stupid and run a full marathon on the Appalachian Trail.

I set my GPS watch to its "most accurate" setting and got after it, starting out with my awesome SMST2 teammates. It was Anne Hart's birthday, so we made the four-hour run a huge celebration, telling our favorite "Goob stories" (that's her nickname) and taking funny photos as we went. The Appalachian Trail was full of rocks and roots. We were hopping over boulders and logs as our route took us up and over four different peaks. We ran slowly, as our OD workouts are set in a comfortable L1 pace. Which was helpful, as we were running up and over mountains! After a few hours, the group ended in a parking lot, I gave Anne one last sweaty birthday hug, and Wade joined me for the last few hours of my Big Stupid stubborn mission.

There aren't public maps of the Appalachian Trail mileage because you're supposed to buy the guidebook, right? So I had decided to just run until I hit 26.2 miles. The whole thing took me six hours and forty-five minutes. I thought that seemed really long, but then again, I am an extraordinarily slow runner. Anyway, it was fun so I didn't care how long it took! I was really sore but totally satisfied and happy. Later on, our club coach Pat O'Brien found me in the gym when I was stretching on a foam roller.

"Hey, Jessie, check this out," Pat said, holding out an old book. "I found an Appalachian Trail book in my parents' house the other day and tracked your run just for kicks. The GPS has a hard time getting the mileage correct because of all the cuts and jags in the trails. Apparently, you didn't run 26.2 miles. You went over 30!"

"Oh, that makes sense," I said and laughed. "I was out there forever."

•   •   •

Perhaps the best Big Stupid is the one I never picked for myself but got to do anyway. It's also one that athletes around the world share in common: VO_2 max testing. We used to do this twice a year at the U.S. Ski Team headquarters in Park City, Utah, called the Center of Excellence.

When we get the giant roller ski treadmill fired up, all the other athletes in the gym roll their eyes and thank their lucky stars that they were smart enough not to pick cross-country as a sport. The test is designed to measure the body's ability to process oxygen. It is so intense that I have to wear a harness because I will ski until I fall over or collapse, and I'd rather not add treadmill burn to the laundry list of discomforts that I have going on in that moment. It is the most brutal thing ever because, once again, it has to be completely self-motivated. I can quit whenever I want to.

I start at a predesigned speed, but every minute the incline of the treadmill goes up by 1 percent. It starts off with a ridiculously easy pace. I'm thinking, *I got this. I'm not even in Level 1!* It's like a casual walk, but it quickly becomes a nightmare. Most people don't last for more than twelve minutes.

By the end, I'm in an all-out sprint on my skis. But it keeps getting steeper and harder every minute. It is now my will to cling on versus the machine's goal to throw me off. The one saving grace is that I'm surrounded by my teammates and coaches, and they're all yelling like they're watching the running of the bulls. Even though I'm surrounded by support and I can practically feel the adrenaline in the air, it's still my choice to keep fighting. The battle is inside my head.

The VO_2 max test is basically the mental workout of a lifetime. In the end, I don't even care what I score on the test. I can't tell you what I've scored in the past. It doesn't matter to me, because I know it's just one tiny piece of the puzzle that makes me a good skier. When you are under severe distress and pushed to your absolute physical and mental limits, that is when you really learn something about yourself.

The question that matters the most to me is simple: How long am I going to keep fighting? I know that the treadmill is going to win. The treadmill *always* wins. That's why there's a harness.

But we keep fighting. Why? Because 96 isn't 100.

CHAPTER 18

KNOW WHEN TO FOLD 'EM

At the 2017 World Championships in Lahti, Finland, I dropped out of the skiathlon in the *middle* of the race. That year, one year out from the PyeongChang Olympics, I was trying to race five of the six races that were packed into about two weeks at World Championships. It was much more condensed than the Olympics schedule would be, and I was racing every other day with two of the competitions being back-to-back.

The skiathlon (2 × 7.5K) can be a successful race for me on the right day (hah! What a cop out. Isn't that always the case?). It combines both techniques, starting on classic skis and then switching to skate. If I get the classic portion right—my weaker technique—I can do really well. But when the gun went off and the mass start scramble began, I was about to learn quickly that if I got the classic portion wrong, it can make for a long day. Within minutes, the leaders were working together and pulling away from the pack, and it was extremely hard to regain ground.

The course in Lahti had some long and steep hills, especially on the classic side. I didn't ask for enough wax on my skis, and I own responsibility for that. I had to use so much energy in the classic half, bouncing up and down on my skis, trying to get them to kick, that I had lost well over thirty seconds to the lead pack before the transition to skating even happened. The wave of tiredness that came over me was something I just couldn't shake off.

As the race went on, I started asking myself some serious questions. It got to the point where I contemplated dropping out of the race, which I almost never do. Even at my worst, I have a reputation for not giving up. But this race was something else entirely, because it was placed back-to-back with the event I loved most of all, the team sprint. I asked myself midrace, *Do I kill myself and maybe get twentieth place, or do I drop out now and save all my energy for the sprint tomorrow?*

We had a solid chance for a medal at the team sprint the next day—and by that I mean absolutely *nobody* except Sadie and I thought we had a shot at the podium. But we figured everyone loves a good surprise, and we both dreamed of earning a medal together in the team sprint. Sadie was already confirmed by the U.S. coaches as the leg one of the team sprint. She told the coaches she wasn't going to start the skiathlon race if she was doing the team sprint, so they had to confirm with her so she could make her race plans. She wanted to conserve her energy, which was a smart, veteran move. I make absolutely no claims to be that smart.

Rightly or wrongly, I assumed I would be her teammate on the team sprint. The coaches hadn't officially picked the second racer yet, but because of the way I had been racing, I assumed I was a lock. I'd been the team's top scorer by earning points in every World Cup race I'd entered. Nine times out of ten, I was the first American across the line in every sprint and every distance race. The team sprint was a combination of sprinting and distance skiing, so logically, I was the best skier we had for the job. But technically, they hadn't picked it yet.

While planning out the championships with me, Cork had let me know that unless something went terribly wrong, I would be the logical choice for the team sprint. But there I was, skiing poorly in the skiathlon, growing more tired by the stride, and feeling the energy slowly drain out of me the day before our chance.

I was trying to process all of this in real time through a tired, foggy brain atop an increasingly tired body. To compound matters, I couldn't stop and talk to a coach. It sounds like a snobbish thing to say, but in 2017 I wasn't racing to get twenty-fifth place anymore. I was racing to where I knew I could be: the top six or, ideally, a medal. I knew realistically that I would have to really scoot just to earn a twenty-fifth-place finish in that skiathlon. And, most important, I knew that I was fit and fast, and that my current slogging predicament was because of the wax, not my capability as a racer.

Still, it was agonizing. Conflicting thoughts were perched on my shoulders and whispering in my ears:

I never drop out of races unless it's a serious problem. But there's nothing wrong with me. Being tired is not a serious problem. Keep racing!

Stop racing! I'm being really selfish. I'm putting my own individual race over our team race tomorrow. Drop out now!

No! Do not drop out! There's so many people who would kill to be in your spot right now, getting to race!

Drop out now! I'm not even in a position to medal or even realistically get top ten. If I kill myself now, I will ruin my chances of getting a medal with Sadie tomorrow! Then that's going to take away her dream too! Drop out now!

I dropped out.

• • •

In a moment of pure race-day coincidence, when I pulled over to the side of the course and stopped, it was right in front of Chris Grover, our U.S. head coach. I'm sure I've been responsible for many anxiety-producing moments over the years as an athlete under his coaching, but I felt especially sorry for this one.

"What are you doing?" Grover said, clearly shocked. I almost never drop. He had to have been wondering if I'd crashed out and gotten injured.

"Grover, I'm not having a good race," I said to him, as I tried to slow my breathing. "I need to save my energy for the team sprint tomorrow."

Then I took off my bib and turned it inside out before putting it back on—the official sign that a skier has dropped out of a race.

Grover looked at me with a surprised look on his face. "Well, we haven't even picked the team sprint yet."

"What?" I gasped.

"We haven't finalized the skiers for the team sprint," Grover repeated.

Well, shit.

My decision to drop out of the race was based solely on my assumption that I was going to be one of the two skiers selected for the team sprint. I dropped out so I could save my energy for a race I wasn't even entered in yet. All of a sudden, my whole plan blew up.

And I had put Grover in a stressful situation. He had just witnessed me—one of his main skiers—drop out of a race at the World Championships, and there was nothing medically wrong with me. Grover is a great coach. I have so much trust in him and so much respect for him. I think he was a little shocked that I had just uncharacteristically pulled the plug on my own race. He must have been worried (rightly so) about where my head was at. He might have wanted to encourage me to keep fighting and not give up. But in my head, I was doing everything for the team. I was giving up on my individual race so I could save energy for the team.

• • •

As if the shame and guilt of dropping out of a race wasn't enough, I still had to ski myself off the course. Which was horrible, because all the fans lined up along the course were now looking at me. The crowds in Lahti were amazing too. There were thousands of fans around the course waving flags, clanging cowbells, and cheering. I felt that I now had a scarlet letter on me: a giant red *L* for loser on my inside-out bib. As I skied back into the stadium, TV cameras followed my every move. A cameraman focused right on me and got in my face. I just turned from the camera, saying nothing, focused on getting dry clothes on and taking my "loser" bib off.

Our support staff in the finish pen rushed over, and the concerned questions started immediately.

"Are you hurt?" the doctors asked.

"Are you OK?" the massage ladies asked.

"Jessie, you never drop out of a race. Why now?" the print media journalists asked.

"Are you hurt? Are you hurt?" the TV camera reporters hounded me.

Everyone was taken aback by my decision to drop out. I told myself that I was not going to read any media of any kind because I knew they might tear me to pieces in the quest for a story. Little did they know that I dropped out of the race because I was going to win us a medal tomorrow! At least, that's what I kept telling myself. I was more motivated than ever because I had a specific reason why I saved my energy: for the team. Haters gonna hate. I know that all too well. But I was determined to show them that my reason for dropping out was valid.

That was the brave face I showed in public. But in private, I was in tears. The hardest part was that Grover hadn't picked the team yet, and I had put my placement on the team sprint squad in jeopardy by dropping out of the skiathlon. He was probably (logically!) worried that my head wasn't screwed on right, that my fitness had bombed, that I wasn't tough enough for the pressure of anchoring the relay. These self-doubts started swirling through my brain as tears slid down underneath my glasses.

I asked myself, *What have I just done?*

$$\bullet \quad \bullet \quad \bullet$$

I was now filled with doubt. Instead of going down a mental rabbit hole of negative thoughts, I tried to focus on the positive. I had faith in myself. I had complete faith in Sadie, and more important, she had faith in me too. Unbeknownst to me, Sadie told the coaches, "I know you're maybe confused right now about Jessie. But if you don't pick Diggs for the other leg in the team sprint, I think that's stupid. I don't want to do it without her."

In my moment of doubt, Sadie stuck up for me. My teammate had my back.

Cork found me while I was jogging up and down the hall that separated each nation's changing room. He had correctly guessed that I was getting really nervous.

"I know you're probably second-guessing right now," Cork said. He's kind of like a second ski dad for me. I needed a hug of reassurance from him. He gave me that hug. "I believe in you. I know you may be doubting yourself. But you know what? You did the right thing."

I went to meet with the other U.S. coaches, and I made my case for selection to the team sprint.

"What's going on?" Grover asked matter-of-factly.

"I dropped out because I didn't ask for enough kick wax and blew all my energy trying to get up those steep hills. But I'm still good for the team sprint. I know these tactics, and I know I'm in good shape. Trust me, and I will prove you right," I told him.

Then I doubled down on my confidence.

"I've never been this confident in my life about anything," I said. "I just feel like I'm in great shape. We can medal tomorrow."

In fact, I had already started to prepare for the team sprint the next day. I had cooled down and immediately changed into dry clothes. I had refueled and hydrated. I was already taking care of my body and making sure I was doing everything right.

"We're going to start you with Sadie. You're going to be the anchor," Grover said.

"I won't let this team down," I promised. "I will prove that this was the right call."

•   •   •

Luke Bodensteiner, our chief director of sports, was also at the World Championships. He is our boss's boss, and he just saw me drop out of the race. Uh-oh. When I saw him, I paused, not knowing how to handle it. Bodensteiner walked up to me with a big grin on his face. Then he high-fived me.

"Fucking *great* call. Genius," Bodensteiner said. I can't tell you the feeling of relief that washed over me in that moment, hearing his pure belief in my choice as a racer, but it felt like coming up for air after being crushed by ocean waves. "I knew exactly what happened when you pulled out. I knew that you were saving it for tomorrow. You're going to crush it."

"Thanks, Luke," I said. "That means so much to me."

Then Liz Arky, a huge fan of the team, big supporter, and one of the trustees, walked up and joined us.

"Girl . . . you are so *smart!*" Liz said, as she high-fived me.

They both walked off. I later realized that Luke and Liz didn't really know if I was going to pull it off. But they said the exact right thing. They were full of confidence, without even a shred of doubt. The coaches couldn't have been sure either, but they trusted me when I said I was ready to rock and roll. I carried that with me into the team sprint the next day.

• • •

The U.S. team had never won a medal in any classic team sprint. To be fair, we hadn't won a whole lot of team medals in *anything,* so this is sort of a pointless stat, but the lure of uncharted territory was definitely present. There were thousands of fans in attendance. The stadium was a madhouse, full of screaming fans. Even the snow that started to fall couldn't dampen their screams or their enthusiasm.

Sadie skied an amazing, world-class race as the leg-one racer. She held tight to the lead pack and put me in great position every time. As for me, I spent the first two of my three laps tucked into the group, making careful note of where my strengths were, when other countries were getting tired, how my skis stacked up. Every little detail that would help me go up against the best in the world. After the race, one of our team's media people would come up to me and say, "Wow, I didn't think you were even competitive, just hanging on there at the back, but I guess you found a second wind, huh?" I stared at him. It didn't seem worth it to explain tactics and drafting or even spend energy explaining that how I skied was on purpose. But since this is my book, I get to say that, yes, staying out of trouble and saving energy were on purpose!

On my third and final lap, I went all out and tried so hard to get us into medal position. Norway had a super team of Heidi Weng and Maiken Caspersen Falla, the number one sprinter in the world (she had won gold in the World Championships in the sprint days before). Falla was cruising into first place, and Russia was right behind her in second place. But third place was still up in the air. On the last brutal hill, I was in fifth place. Right where I wanted to be.

I dug and clawed and fought my way up that last hill. I awkwardly herringboned up the impossible-to-kick slope as though my life depended on it. Now, it was just me and Stina Nilsson—one of the best skiers in the history of the sport and easily one of the best sprinters in the world—battling for third place. As we came down the hill, I slotted into Stina's draft, then used a slingshot to pass her. This ended up being important, as I now had my choice of lanes on a snowy day when only one track had been skied in, thereby making it much faster. To my undying credit, I picked the wrong lane! It truly takes a special talent to miss the only lane that was skied in on a snowy day. If you're skiing in Lahti and you see part of my brain on the final corner, it's because I left it there that day.

The entire race came down to the final hundred meters. I scooted slightly ahead of Stina just as we left the last curve, and it became a classic drag race to the finish line. There were thousands of fans pressed up against the fence along the course, and they were all screaming.

Stina edged up to me, and now we were tied. In the last fifty meters, we were neck and neck, both of us grinding it out, furiously double poling as hard and fast as we could. Since I come from a long line of Hobbits and am fairly short, it must have looked comical, my double-pole tempo almost double time to Stina's powerful pushes. I did not hear a single sound. I did not see a single thing. I had only one thought, *Go! Go! Go!*

Then I lunged for the bronze medal, praying to the snow gods that my stupidly hyperflexible knees and legs would finally be useful for something.

· · ·

Sadie was right there at the finish line, screaming. I also screamed, then plowed headlong into her arms before collapsing onto the snow. My heart was pounding, and my lungs were screaming for air. Snowflakes showered down on me as I desperately tried to catch my breath.

Wrapped in a U.S. flag, we hugged our coaches and celebrated as a team. We had trusted each other every step of the way, and it was a total team effort. The coaches had trusted me, even after my dropout the day before. All of our teammates were so supportive. Cork gave me the hug that I needed when I needed it. The coaches, techs, our teammates all summer long, Sadie, and I had all worked our tails off, and we ended up with a medal to show for it.

At the end of the night, long after the podium celebration, I took a moment to think about what I had learned from the last few days of roller-coaster emotions. I had proved to myself that I knew my body. Even after all the abuse I had put it through with my eating disorder, I'd learned once more how to listen to what my body was telling me, and to be willing to hear instead of shutting it down or ignoring it. I proved to myself that after thousands of hours of training, after years of racing and training all over the world, my body and mind were in tune with each other, and because of that I could trust my gut instinct without a single doubt.

I also knew I could compete with the giants from Norway and Sweden, that it wasn't an impossible task (although still really freaking hard). I knew that my summer training schedule had put me in the best shape of my life, and the plan that Cork wrote for me was working year after year. I knew that I could make strategic decisions during a race in real time. Perhaps most unlikely but somehow true, I learned that I had a finishing kick to win a drag race against the best sprinters in the world on the right day. Once again, I proved to myself that if my teammate's career goals were on the line, I was going to absolutely kill myself before I'd give up. The skiathlon had been humbling in every possible way, and I knew that I wasn't going to feel like superwoman every time I showed up at the start line. But I now knew that that was OK, as long as I saw the big picture and showed up ready to fight.

I also proved to the coaches that I knew what I was doing. Not that they were real doubters in the first place, but it's one thing for them to say that they trust my knowledge of my body, my fitness, and tactics. It's a whole other thing to listen to an athlete make a call in real time like I did and then act on that trust and put me back in the race. That moment solidified our trust in each other and strengthened our coach-athlete relationship. The coaches now had solid proof that when I said I was ready to go, I wasn't kidding around. I don't always have the confidence to say that I'm ready to go. But when I do say it, I mean it.

But something else happened during those forty-eight hours in Lahti. We didn't know it at the time, but the adversity, unshakable trust, gutsy and scrappy racing style, dramatic sprint, and finish-line lunge that happened in Lahti would play out again exactly one year later in South Korea at the 2018 PyeongChang Winter Olympics.

CHAPTER 19

PYEONGCHANG

I sat in the back of the athletes' bus on the way to the racecourse at the Alpensia Cross-Country Centre and muttered German phrases to myself into my phone.

"Die Mädchen schwimmen. Die. Mädchen. Schwimmen," I said out loud like an awesome nerd. "The girls swim." I'd better not lose my day job, because becoming a language specialist isn't really in my future. The German skiers three rows ahead of me turned around, wondering who let the two-year-old just learning to talk on the bus.

It was two and a half hours before I was to compete in the 10K individual skate race at the 2018 PyeongChang Winter Olympics. I was trying to learn German because I needed something to distract my brain. My little language lab helped me to not obsess about my upcoming race and the pressure-packed feeling of competing at the Olympics.

The great paradox about being an Olympic athlete is that it is simultaneously the best time of your life and also one of the most stressful times of your life. When you get a chance to represent your country, to compete on the biggest stage against the best on the planet, it is a true honor. But that honor comes with a lot of pressure and expectations. At the 2018 Winter Olympics that pressure was even more intense for the men and women of the U.S. cross-country ski team, as we hadn't won a single medal in any Olympic competition in over four decades. That was a lot of pressure for a girl from Afton, Minnesota.

So, naturally, hours before the race I was trying (rather unsuccessfully) to learn German. Not exactly as cool as LeBron James strutting into the arena before a basketball game. Yes, I like to put on my Bose headphones and get pumped up with awesome dance beats, but not until right before it's time for me to warm up. This far out from the start, I was dorking out and using Duolingo. Because nothing gets you jacked up to race in the Olympics quite like spreckenzie Deutsch!

"Ein Fisch fährt ein Fahrrad," I muttered into my cell phone. "A fish rides a bicycle."

•   •   •

The Olympics are all about pageantry, ceremonies, medals, and athletic heroics. The media loves to shine a spotlight on the world-class skills, the victories, the upsets, the agony of defeat, and, of course, the miracles. But outside the spotlight, tucked into the shadows far away from the television cameras and reporters and fans are all of these tiny little moments that can truly define the Olympics for an athlete.

For me personally, one of these unnoticed, undocumented moments was when I went to test my skis before the 10K race. I was jittery with nerves, trying to remind myself that this was just another ski race, but not quite able to banish the thought lingering in the back of my mind. *This could be your shot. Make it count.*

I grabbed my poles and jogged from the rows of wax cabins stacked up like a little city, to the side of the course where Cork was waiting for me. He had six pairs of skate skis ready for me to test, the six singles laid neatly in a row in the snow with their matching mates tucked into the ski bags next to them. He had already narrowed my skis down from eight potential pairs based on the conditions and the testing the team had been doing all week. We would each click into a pair of singles, and that way, we could test four different pairs together in a short time. With cross-country skis, there is no right foot or left foot; the pair of skis are simply identified by the last three numbers of their serial number. So testing a different ski on each foot is an easy way to compare their speed and feeling. Through a series of mixing and matching, we would narrow it down to the fastest pair.

Throughout the course of a year, I probably spend more time with Cork than anyone else, and he is finely tuned in to my frequency. He could tell that the pressure was starting to get to me. But instead of giving me a raucous Herb Brooks type of speech to fire me up, Cork took the opposite approach. He knew exactly what I needed at that moment to help me have the best performance I could possibly have.

He started telling me dad jokes.

"I used to hate facial hair," Cork said. "Until it grew on me."

His jokes were so lame that I instantly started laughing, and it made me relax. Cork's jokes weren't just to keep things loose though. They had an actual tactical purpose. Sometimes when I'm nervous, it's really hard for me to feel the skis when I'm testing them, because I'm too tense. Once I loosened up a little, I was able to refocus on the feeling of the skis on each foot, gliding over the snow.

"Pair 889 feels faster to me, what do you think? " I asked Cork, as we swapped skis to balance our opinions. As we tested the skis, we also got a last-minute inspection of the course. After forty minutes of testing, we narrowed it down to the final pair of skis. Cork sprinted off to the wax room to prep them. The second-best pair of skis were now the official spares and were put aside to be on the side of the racecourse, should I break a ski and need a midrace replacement. I kept the third best pair of skis and began my warm-up on them.

It was thirty-five minutes out from my race start. I did a five-minute Level 3 pick-up, then I took my inhaler for my asthma. I ate some Pro-Bar sports gummies and drank more Nuun endurance sports drink. With twenty minutes to go, I did a two-minute Level 4 pick-up. Then I rested for a few more minutes, just skiing easy around the course. With seventeen minutes to go, I did one last pick-up, a one-minute effort at sprint pace. I was warmed up and ready to go.

I ran to the athlete changing cabin and changed out of my sweaty top and into my spandex onesie race suit. After running to the start pen, I swapped out my official warm-up bib (which doubled as course access) for a race bib. I jogged around one last time and got the timing chip Velcroed around my ankle. Then I entered the start area, and as one of the awesome Salomon reps knocked the snow from my boots and helped me click into my bindings, I was ready to start the race. I looked down at the palms of the gloves that I'd custom-designed with Swix. On one palm it read, "Your race," and on the other, "Your moment."

It was a reminder to me that I control the race. I was in charge of me. I could go as hard as I wanted to. And I was ready to empty my tank.

•　•　•

As the 10K started, I was focused on my technique. The roar of the crowd faded, the bright lights of the TV cameras were just course lighting to me, and I was locked in, thinking only about every single push. I was setting my pace deliberately because it's all too easy to go blasting out of the start gate and fall apart later. As I moved down the course, I followed my carefully mapped-out pacing plan. I was pushing absolutely as hard as I could go for each kilometer of the course, metering out my energy so that I'd be dead at the finish, being as efficient as I possibly could be. I had memorized my race plan: where the snow was fastest, when exactly I should change from V2 skate technique to V1 on each hill, when to start to use V2 to power over the top of the hill, when to tuck, when to pull out of my tuck, and how long to skate without poles. I was thinking so hard about all these things, while simultaneously pushing myself as hard as I could.

Early on in the race, the pain crept in for real, and my whole body started to feel ragged. My head started bobbing, my hearing went fuzzy, and I heard only certain things—particularly Cork's voice, chirping in from the sidelines as I passed him. Everything else got blocked out. The intense pace and the crushing physical discomfort made me slip into my own little world, only focusing on each push of my poles and skis, following my race plan. It was a dark and familiar place, and as I walked into the pain cave, I held my head up high and headed straight for the lawn chair in the back of it that had my name on it. I didn't avoid the pain of the race, I welcomed it, embraced it, because I knew it was coming.

My body began to shut down. The wheels were coming off . . . but I kept working. Frantic alarms enveloped my brain, screaming at my body to stop. A solid decade of professional racing under my belt, and I am still not the strongest skier. I'm not the quickest. I don't have fast-twitch muscles. I'm not a pure sprinter, and I'm not a pure distance skier either. I don't always know all the right tactics at the right moment. My technique is not beautiful, and it's not "pretty skiing." But I am really, really good at being in pain.

• • •

I knew I was in medal position from the splits I was hearing through my mental haze. Each time I passed one of our coaches on the sidelines, they would shout out an update.

"You're tied for third."

"You're two seconds up on fourth."

I knew the race was tight, and it was coming down to the wire. I couldn't push any harder than I already was: my lungs were on fire, my legs were getting stiff, my arms were tired and sore. But I was intensely motivated by the fact that I was having the race of my life.

I dropped the hammer and gave it my all.

On the final hill, I pushed my body so far past its limits that I felt my body actually start to seize up. I started to fold in half from the waist down as I couldn't get enough air. The pain was heavy and so suffocating that I was on the verge of passing out. I tripped up the hill. I was trying to beat the clock because I knew that my body was going to implode at any moment.

I emptied my tank on the last hill and was running on fumes, no longer efficient. But I miraculously made it down the S-shaped turns on the steep sprint hill into the final turn to the finish-line stretch. As I sprinted to the line, the finishing lane had a camera on a track that zoomed next to me. The camera followed along at the same exact speed that I was skiing. I had one thought running in my head.

Beat the camera, beat the camera, beat the camera.

I crossed the finish line. As I collapsed into the snow, scarcely able to breathe and in an incredible amount of pain, I knew I had laid down one of the best races of my career. I allowed myself to look up at the board.

I didn't get a medal.

There was an initial feeling of disbelief. Because I had gone so hard for so long, and I was in position for a medal.

But I had lost.

Over the course of 10 kilometers, I had lost winning the first-ever medal for the U.S. women by 3.3 seconds.

• • •

I had lost, and yet as I was gasping in a hazy, semiconscious heap in the snow after the finish line, I felt like I had won something. In the race against the course, against my own limits, against what my brain told me wasn't possible, I had won. I had pushed myself so hard that I almost passed out on course. I did absolutely everything that I could, and made every right decision in the *years* leading up to that race, always putting ski racing first. I knew in my heart that I never really lost; it just happened that four other racers were better than I was that day (four, because two athletes tied for third place). And I was truly happy for them because I respect, admire, and care about them as people as well as athletes. Their success didn't equate to me being a failure, it just meant that I wouldn't get a medal to show for it.

After the race, I found my family: my mom, dad, grandma, aunt, uncle, sister, and boyfriend. What can I say, I have a full entourage! It was amazing because in that moment, they all said the right things. There were no tears. There was no sorrow. There was no disappointment about missing by a hair. There was not a single discussion of the bronze that would've been the first Olympic medal for an American in cross-country skiing in four decades.

There were no tears, because I had given it my all. And that, in itself, was the ultimate victory.

"I went so hard, and I did everything I could," I said to my family. "Of course I'm really bummed, but I can't beat myself up about it, because I honestly don't know where I could have found those seconds."

"We saw you race," my dad reaffirmed. "You were so brave. You were so ferocious. The way you attacked that course and those hills was an amazing thing to witness."

"We're so proud of you," my mom said. "You are in such amazing shape, and it was a true pleasure to watch you race."

"Babe, you are fucking *amazing*," Wade told me, planting a big kiss on my cheek.

But my little bubble of positivity didn't last. When I went through the media zone, I had to face the weight of our historic medal drought at the Olympics. The media zone was hard because every person told me that I should be distraught, through their words, their body language, their pointed questions.

Over and over, they asked about how disappointed I must be, waiting for the inevitable breakdown.

Inside my head I replied, *Don't tell me how to feel. Don't you dare tell me how I'm supposed to feel about this, because I am proud of myself, and you cannot take that away from me. I gave that race my all, and I know that, and I'm at peace with that.*

I know the reporters were just doing their jobs and trying to get a story. Since I'm not a reporter, I have no idea what it's like for them, reporting on race after race, trying to make each one stand out somehow with a character story. But I didn't take the bait. I stood strong, faced the cameras, and spoke into every microphone.

"I went absolutely as hard as I could, and I'm proud of that," I said. "I have more races to go, and I'm already getting ready for the next one."

But inside, a tiny, vicious voice from years ago raised its ugly head. *Maybe you would have gotten that medal if only you were leaner, skinnier, lighter. Maybe recovering from your eating disorder actually hurt your chances. Maybe, maybe, maybe . . .*

But this time, I was stronger. I told that voice to go *straight* to hell. Then I went to get another hug from my family.

I went to work preparing for my next race. I changed into dry clothes, drank a huge shake to take in all the calories I would need. I drank more sports drink. I got pulled aside for an anti-doping test, peed, filled out the paperwork, and was out in twenty minutes. I did all the right things. I may not have gotten a medal, but at least I didn't let old ED win.

• • •

I went and found a spin bike to cool down on, to continue my preparation for the next race. The spin bike was under the stadium stands, below the finish-line area where the flower ceremony was taking place. I was totally alone. In a dark hallway underneath the Olympic stadium, I spun by myself.

There were no tears.

I did not cry.

But I screamed into my jacket.

It was a scream filled with pain and disappointment. It was a scream that said, "I wish that what I had was good enough."

I knew that I had truly given everything that I had. And yet, it still wasn't good enough to earn a medal. That stung. So, far away from the TV cameras and flashing lights, I let all of my emotions out right then and there. Spinning in the dark, I screamed my frustration and loss into a balled-up jacket.

Honestly, the pain of going through the media zone after the race was what did it. Because I had felt good about myself until I went through that zone. I had to dig deep to keep my self-worth when so many people were saying, "There's all these little kids looking up to you and you didn't win," and "Tell me, how does it feel to know your home-town was watching?"

Underneath the stands, I let out the roller coaster of emotions that come when you're in position for a medal, you push your body past its breaking point, and you still don't win that medal.

3.3 seconds.

Seriously!

I screamed into the jacket. I put all of my pain and frustration, hopes and dreams into that scream, so I could let it all go.

Then I started focusing on the next race.

• • •

I jogged back up to the wax cabin, and when I saw Cork, the tears finally came. I had wanted this for him as much as for me, to validate all the years and hours he had spent coaching me through ups and downs. He reached out and wrapped me up in a huge hug. He was still in it for the ups and downs, medal be damned.

"We worked so hard. I gave it everything I had. I just couldn't make it happen," I cried. "But we tried so hard."

"Even if it doesn't happen, that doesn't change how awesome you are as a skier and person," Cork said kindly. "You are so fit. You skied an amazing race. If you say that you gave it everything you had, then that's absolutely true. Because you're the toughest person I know."

I stood in front of Cork, my longtime coach and ski tech, and I dug deep once again.

"I am good to go for the next race," I told him as I put the tears away. I was done wasting emotions and energy over this. "If I don't make a medal happen in the team sprint, it won't be for lack of trying. People are going to have to kill themselves to outpace me, because I'm going to give this everything again. I'm so ready to make this go right for us."

I jogged out of the wax complex, got on the bus, and went back to the athletes' village.

In two days, I would get another chance.

CHAPTER 20

BRAVE HEARTS

One hour to go, and we're not talking about medals. We're only talking over our strategy.

Kikkan and I are about to compete in the final of the women's team sprint. Because we were in the second semifinal, we have twenty-five minutes less rest than our competitors from the first semifinal, but we don't worry about that. I don't worry about anything I can't control, because my mind is full of what I *can* do. The stands are beginning to fill. The flood lights illuminate everything, and the night air is starting to pulse with anticipation. My lungs are burning, and my legs feel a little heavy, but I know I can get through it and recover in time for the most important team sprint final of my life.

• • •

I chug an energy drink and shake out my legs in the holding pen at the finish line immediately after the semifinal round. Kikkan and I leave the course and are directed through the media zone but don't stop to talk to anyone—we'll talk to them when we're done for the day, and the media people respect that. We split up to cool down after our semifinal the best way we know how, a mix of jogging and spinning. I run back and forth along the boards separating the stands from the finishing stretch, constantly running through technique in my mind.

I jog to the athletes' room underneath the stands. I can hear the crowd and feel the energy throb through the floor. I feel like a gladiator getting ready to go fight, and in just under an hour I'll do just that.

Steph Mckeen Caverhill and Zuzana Rogers, two of our amazing volunteer massage and physical therapists, are ready to give us massages. They do a flush on our legs to get the lactic acid out and a little bit on our backs too.

"Can you do some squeezy things in my triceps?" I ask, and they laugh because obviously "squeezy things" is not a technical term. But I need it because I'd been having trouble with cramping earlier in the Games. I just want to be sure.

As they work on my arms, back, and legs, I close my eyes and run through every possible race scenario in my mind just like my sports psychologist has taught me to do. I've spent endless hours visualizing the course here in South Korea and how I want to ski it. I can visualize every inch of the snow, and I know how to race it to the best of my ability. I've imagined it down to the tip of my skis sliding over the man-made snow, the feeling of planting my poles, absorbing the impact in my arms and pushing through my core, lats, shoulders, and triceps to propel myself forward, the pain of pulling ragged breath into my bursting lungs.

I run through twenty different scenarios for how the finals can go down. In team sprinting, you have to be willing to adjust your strategy on the fly. When different situations randomly occur during the race, you want to react instantly, like a muscle reflex. In the heat of a cross-country race, a skier has to blend clear thinking and strategy while overcoming fatigue. Sounds easy, right? But when your muscles are screaming, lactic acid is burning your muscles down, alarm bells are going off in your brain, and everything is begging you to stop, you can succumb to some really poor judgment. You need to work through the pain, clear away the fog and noise, adjust to the course, and trust your instincts.

After our massages, Kikkan and I huddle together. I know that Stina Nilsson of Sweden is a world-class sprinter in top form, and she's bringing it. I also know that Marit Bjørgen from Norway is the most decorated Winter Olympian in Winter Olympics history, and she's peaking right into the finals. Maiken Casperson Falla is the reigning World Cup overall sprint winner, meaning the past year she's been the best sprinter in the world over the course of the whole season. Which means she wins, um, a lot! The odds are not in our favor, but here we are, sitting in the warming room below the stadium, about to try and do the impossible. Right now, though, we treat the facts about our medal-less history like Voldemort in *Harry Potter*. They shall not be named. The words never leave our mouths. Obsessing over our past and our opportunity to rewrite the history books could only make us more nervous, take away our focus. Kikkan and I simply huddle together and go over our strategy for the finals, determined to focus on everything we can control, and let go of the things we can't.

• • •

I'm completely stoked on how things played out for us earlier in the semifinal, and that I didn't have to sprint it out to secure a spot in the final. The whole name of the game was conserve, conserve, conserve. Save as much energy as possible for the finals.

Every lap in the semifinal was a test run because each of us was taking notes on everything. Kikkan and I go through all of it now: how our skis stacked up against the snow and our competitors, how the other skiers were taking the final downhill, when and where people were tiring out. I spotted areas on the course where you had to be careful, spots where the corners had ice opening up. I now know that the Russians aren't great on the big steep climb. I also saw places where we could take control. For instance, nobody wants to lead out of the gates. We can push the pace at specific spots on the course, and we'll tire the pack out, and people will drop off quickly.

Kikkan and I talk about which skier might try to break the pack on a certain climb. We talk about the parts of the course where we could be put under pressure or when others might attack. During our semifinal, one tiny detail caught my attention. I know that no one can get a good draft on another skier from the first downhill, but that a skier could get a huge draft from the second, big, winding downhill that leads into the home stretch. I store this nugget away, committing it to memory so I can unleash it later if the race comes down to the wire.

• • •

I go for a quick jog around the area near the bleachers to warm myself up again and keep my blood moving. As I jog, I hear the announcer say my name a couple times over the PA system. Which is weird and startling. My name shoots out of the speakers like an arrow and seems to arch in the air for a long time. It's simultaneously creepy and amazing to hear. I force myself to ignore this as much as possible though. The excitement in the air has changed from a steady pulse to a hearty drumming. There are lots of drunk fans. The joys of a night race!

Everyone is pumped up now. I can see fans above me, and they're all waving. I'm trying to zone out, but the crowd is buzzing, in every sense of the word. I don't really focus on the people in the crowd because I'm busy getting warmed up, but I do stop twice to try to find *my* people in the crowd. My family and Wade have traveled here to see me and cheer me on. And their cheers are undoubtedly the loudest! I know they will love me with full hearts whether I'm first, last, or anywhere in between, and I know they all believe that my team and I can do this.

• • •

We're inching closer to the start of the finals, and the sparkles on my cheeks glow in the stadium lights. I've been using glitter before my races since high school. In my early years on the ski team, I was given the nickname "Sparkle Chipmunk." The sparkles on my cheeks are a reminder to myself that I race because it is fun and because I love to ski. I used to get so nervous before races that I could barely function, and I'd waste a huge amount of energy on that anxiety. Putting glitter on was a special reminder to myself that I didn't need to worry about the outcome of the race, but only to focus on giving it my absolute best effort and enjoying the process. Sparkling up before my race is also a salute to the little girl in me who just wants to "go super speed!" To my team, it's become a habit of mine that everyone is now used to. I glitter up any of my teammates who come to my hotel door before we take off for the race venue. It's a special time, when everyone is nervous and excited to be representing our country. We get together early in the morning to help each other get ready and deal with our own pre-race nerves. It's a little bit like our special striped relay socks, which have been kicking around our team since 2012. The knee-highs with red and white stripes on one leg and blue and white stripes on the other are worn only on relay days, and I suppose every racer attaches their own meaning to them. For me, they signify how hard we've worked and how much fun we have as one team unit. They're a reminder to race with heart, to give it absolutely everything I have, because my teammates' dreams are on the line.

•   •   •

Seeing my fellow teammates along the sidelines, I'm reminded that I wouldn't be here without their support and help. My teammates were there for me in the good times and, most important, in the bad times. I hear Liz's words once again: "Don't worry about anyone else. Don't worry about a medal. Just go do this one thing. Go ski as fast as you can."

I can feel the clock ticking now, and we're just a few minutes to race time. I take off my warm-ups, throwing them over the fence to Cork. Looking across the starting area, I see my competition, the best sprinters in the world. I bounce back and forth, grinning ear to ear. Kikkan and all the other leg-one skiers line up at the starting line and exhale.

We have a chance to do the impossible. Don't worry about anyone else. Don't worry about a medal. I took all my excitement and nerves and tucked them away in a little corner of my mind.

Just do this one thing. Go as fast as I can.

•   •   •

When Kikkan was done with her first lap, she would ski into the tag zone alongside all the other racers and touch her hand on any part of my body. Then I could start the second lap. We didn't have to pass a baton. We didn't have a physical item to hand off. Once she touched me, I would be in the race.

The tag zone is the hectic and bewildering race within the race. At only thirty meters long, it doesn't give racers any room to make mistakes. Anticipating which side of the tag zone your teammate will enter and getting into a position where she can quickly find you and make the tag is one of the more anxiety-producing moments of a team sprint.

Our team sprint final was comprised of three laps per person on a 1.2K course, so each team would complete six laps total. Team sprinting is like Formula 1 racing, with tight-turning tracks, except that there are two race cars that are on the same team. There's a tag zone and a pit—a place where the skis get worked on, and athletes can quickly talk strategy with coaches. Each lap, the skier finishing the leg tags her partner, who is waiting in the tag zone. After checking right and left to make sure she won't interfere with other racers coming by, the finishing skier swoops off the side of the course into the pit to get her skis worked on and gets ready for the next lap, while her partner completes a lap.

Adjacent to the tag zone were a line of boards on the skier's left-hand side. Behind the line of boards were all the team pits. Each country got a pit box that was exactly the same size—just big enough to fit a wax table and a few bodies. In each pit box stood a coach, the two ski techs, who worked on the skis between laps, and a waxing table, so that the skis could get touched up between laps. The line of boards ended a little bit before the tag zone so that skiers could not accidentally step into the tag zone and get annihilated. Techs and athletes waiting to enter the race cannot get in the way of the field of play.

Since we had won our semifinal heat and had the best overall time, Kikkan started the team sprint finals in the lead position. The other leg-one skiers were staggered behind her and fanned out in a chevron start. The aerial view of their starting positions looked exactly like an arrowhead. Kikkan was in the top spot, and she was the sharp point of our team attack.

Halfway through Kikkan's first lap, she hung tight to the leaders and held an amazing pace. While Kikkan and the other skiers were busy racing, the leg-two skiers (that's me!) got ready in the tag zone.

• • •

I lined up with the other leg-two skiers near a line of tiny pine branches that marked the start of the thirty-meter zone. They use pine so that if you ski over them, the base of your ski won't get scratched. Also, they smell great! When we line up, we stagger ourselves out, jockeying for a good position. You trust that your teammate will find you and be able to tag you, but it's also up to you to make yourself available. I put my hand up and yell, "Kikkan!" just so she can see me. This is where those striped relay socks really come in handy!

Despite all this, the actual tag off can be extremely tricky. We practice tags with our teammates so that we can get a feel for how fast they're going to blow by, and it's *always* faster than we think. The ideal tag for us is when Kikkan tags me at the moment we're both going the same speed. If Kikkan tags me and then glides past me, it means I should have started double poling sooner and faster. We make those notes in practice, but even so, we have to instantly judge how fast our teammate is moving and get up to speed accordingly.

I saw Kikkan coming in, and you know my girl can bring it! She was in the lead pack. She did exactly what she was supposed to do. Storming into the tag zone, she headed straight for me.

It was go time.

As Kikkan approached, I started furiously double poling, hammering my poles into the snow with my arms and propelling myself forward. Surrounded on all sides by skiers making their tags, I kept my tight position, double poling my little heart out, and moved down the tag zone, getting up to speed. By the time I was halfway down the zone, Kikkan had pulled up next to me, stopped skating, and pulled her poles in tight so she could reach over to tag me without getting any of our equipment tangled. When a skier tags her teammate, she can't push the other skier, just a hand-to-body tap. So, usually, it's this overly dramatic touch, like pushing a big red game buzzer. Bam! *Got it!*

I was finally in the race.

CHAPTER 21

LET'S GO GET IT

The racecourse at the Alpensia Cross-Country Centre was a beast. There was a short, flat stretch leading out of the tag zone, followed by a fairly long grinder of a hill—not crazy steep but a place where you could easily give up time if you didn't have the pedal down. At the top of that was a tight left-hand 180-degree turn into a downhill, which in the early legs was a place to be especially careful—it would be easy to get tangled up with another skier and fall. That first downhill led into a tight right-hand corner, where we'd seen falls in previous races, and then immediately pitched into a hard climb, which got progressively steeper as you climbed. The first uphill ensured that the course was challenging, but the second, increasingly steep hill made this a course more friendly to hybrid distance-sprinters than to pure sprinters. Skiers were doing a lot of hard climbing each lap, and the pure sprinters might not be able to recover as quickly between laps.

At the top, the course dropped left into a fast downhill, with a series of S turns winding down the hill toward the stadium. With the speed of the downhill, the drafting effect could be huge, but with the turns, passing was difficult. At the bottom of the main downhill, where the speed was the highest, the course veered right and hit the skiers with one last, short bump of an uphill that flowed up and over the tunnel the athletes, techs, and coaches used to enter the stadium. From there, a sweeping left-hand turn led to the tag zone, which was set to parallel the finishing lane. On the last lap of the race, the anchor skiers would take a slightly longer left-hander into the finishing stretch that flowed right in front of the stadium stands to the finish line. Loud fans filled the stands to watch racers navigate the banked downhill corner at around thirty miles per hour, on skinny skis without metal edges. The bright stadium lights illuminated the arena for the ultimate sprint to the finish line.

Once I cleared the tag zone and entered the race, I skied as if I had been shot full of adrenaline. I was so excited! I felt that I was in the best shape of my life, and I was ready to get after it. But on that first lap, my strategy was to not lead the pack. The course was so demanding, I knew I was going to have to conserve my energy, and I wanted to be able to observe the other skiers to take notes for the final lap, the way I had in the semifinals. But all the other skiers must have been thinking the same thing, too, because we were moving at a pretty pedestrian pace. I don't mean that in an insulting way. We were moving fast, but we weren't all-out sprinting on the first lap. As we made our way through the loop, I thought, *Wow, I feel good. Too good. I bet everyone else probably feels too good as well.*

On my first hill, I was pushed to the inside. Norwegian skier Maiken Caspersen Falla was in front of me, and Swedish skier Stina Nilsson was on my right side. The three of us jockeyed for position almost the whole way.

As I moved through my first lap, I took note and began to formulate my strategy for lap two. Back at the bench in the pits, one piece of feedback Cork and Marek (Kikkan's ski tech) were getting from coaches around the course was that the skis were running very well. Our other techs outside the pit had tested waxes, structures, and application methods right up until five minutes before the race start, and it was great that their hard work was paying off.

• • •

As I finished the end of my first lap, our tag came down to the wire. Unbeknownst to me, Kikkan was still getting clipped into her skis as I was about to make the left-hand turn that led me to the tag zone! She had only twenty seconds to clip in and get into position, which is not that much time when you're knocking snow out of boots. I'm sure it was pretty sweet from an adrenaline perspective, but it was also very nerve wracking, and she handled it really well. I didn't even know that shit had almost, as they say, hit the fan until we were huddled up after the race, and Kikkan casually mentioned, "Oh yeah, that tag almost didn't happen!"

As Kikkan headed out for lap two, I held my poles up in the air, close to my body, so that no other skier could accidentally run into them or break them. I moved to the left-hand side of the tag zone and rounded the corner of the V boards separating the course from the pit zone. Cork ran over as I unclipped my bindings, jumping off my skis before I had even come to a stop. Snatching my skis from the snow, he ran to the bench and handed one ski to Marek.

In just two and a half minutes, they each clamped a ski to the bench, brushed them out with a nylon brush, wiped them down with a cloth, tapped out the powder we were using for wax, hand-corked it in, brushed that out with another brush, and put the skis on the snow so that I could snap back into my bindings. Sounds exhausting? Just try watching them do it sometime! With the quick turnaround, neither he nor Marek could actually see the race, and they were relying on what they heard on the radio to judge how much time they had to get the skis ready.

While they were working at warp speed, I was jogging around, thinking of my tactics for the following lap. Sometimes you'd see athletes conferring with their coaches, talking over strategy, but by this point I was ready to trust my instincts and years of experience and not risk overthinking it. All of my fellow anchor skiers were doing different things to stay loose: some of them were vigorously slapping their legs, trying to force the lactic acid to move; some of them were windmilling their arms; some of them were swinging their legs; some were jogging; and some were doing jumps. We all have our own game plan for how to handle time in the pit.

However, I may have been the only one out there doing happy little skips back and forth! I was so psyched, full of adrenaline and pure joy that I was here, in this moment, competing for my country at the highest level. *And wow, this is going so well.* I was happy with my first lap. I felt confident. I felt unstoppable. I should point out that even with years of World Cup races under my belt, it's rare to feel "unstoppable." You don't have to feel like a rock star to win a race, but if you happen to notice that feeling, you've got to take it and run like hell, because it's incredibly rare.

I began to get my mind straight. Sprinting is about confidence; you have to truly believe you're the best one out there, or you definitely won't be. From a strategic standpoint, I instinctively knew I had to go for it. I had to push the pace. There were still way too many skiers in the lead pack, and it felt too risky to not push the pace and try to string it out. Sure, if I fell to the middle of the pack, I would get the benefit of a huge draft. But when I tried to make a move and get to the front, the chances were quite high that someone might block me, crash, get tangled up, or jockey me out of position. I didn't like those odds.

Just then a tiny, nagging seed of doubt crept back into my mind. *What if I tire myself out, don't have enough energy at the end, and lose a sprint?* I quickly told myself to forget that line of negative thinking. I was in the best shape of my life. I told myself that it would make my opponents as tired as I was, and would even out the sprinting field when it came down to the last lap, or at least push them out of their comfort zones and make them waste a lot of energy that they didn't want to waste. I was literally going up against the best sprinters in the world. If I had any shot at outsprinting them, I would have to empty their tanks just a little on our second lap. Then hopefully my style of "sprinting when everyone is already tired" would play out for the better.

In that moment, it was all about having confidence in myself. It was about believing in my ability to withstand pain. That was what tipped the scales in the decision making. I was not going to worry about Nilsson and Falla and what they could do. I knew they were the best sprinters in the world. But I also knew what I *could* do.

I could grind.

•   •   •

I made the decision in my head but wanted to hear a positive affirmation from a coach. I didn't want them to see me pushing the pace on my second lap, panic, and go, "What is she *doing*?"

I jogged and found coach Chris Grover.

"Grover, my first lap felt great. But we're moving too slow," I said. "I'm going to move to the front and up the pace, try to string it out a bit."

Grover looked at me and said, "That's a great plan." Pause. "Go for it!"

He said it with full confidence. The coaches at every point during the Olympics were saying that they trusted us. This wasn't football or basketball, where the coach drew up a game plan and the athletes followed. We were drawing up our own game plans and changing them on the fly. The coaches fully believed that I knew what I was doing. They've seen me in hundreds of competitions. They trusted my body and my brain. They knew that I would figure out how to get us into the medals if they let me work my plan, but equally as important, they knew I needed to hear that they were with me all the way.

I jogged back toward the pit. Cork put my skis down in the snow. Then he knocked the snow off my boots and got ready to repeat the rewaxing process on Kikkan's skis. Every pit around me was buzzing with activity, everyone furiously working on equipment. All the skiers were getting into place. Nerves and stress were high, and you could practically hear the tension crackling in the air. I could hear the crowd in the stadium going wild. But as I clipped into my skis, I tuned it all out. I knew that my family was out there somewhere, and they were screaming and supporting me, and that was enough for me.

I scooched around the side of the fencing into the tag zone, lining up again for the next tag. Kikkan was now in sight and was hanging strong in third place, keeping us in medal contention right behind Sweden and Norway.

I was saying only positive things to myself. *Wow, I feel great. I'm going to go crush this next lap as fast as I can. It's going to be awesome.*

I focused in on my race plan and got ready to rock and roll.

• • •

On my second lap, I shot to the front, increasing the pace. Norway and Sweden followed immediately behind me, but just as planned, the pack started to string out, countries dropping off the back. We had finally come down to just the three of us, and I took the lead. This was the crucial point of the race where the medals were decided; with the gap we created on this lap, we knew that Norway, Sweden, and the USA would all get a medal if no crazy race accidents ensued. We just didn't know what order we'd come in. Kikkan and I were a team, and together we were putting our team into medal contention. She was still the tip of our spear, the sharp point of our attack. And I was the blunt force behind it. We both did our part.

There are different ways you can try to drop skiers. When you're racing, all skiers are in Level 4 (which is our label for race pace). On a really hard point of the course like the big hill, you could make a surge. So, a skier could suddenly up the tempo at a strategic part of the course with the intent to make their competitors fall behind. Another way to drop people is to up the tempo from the start of a lap, which is what I did. I started my lap one notch higher and held it. The pace was so intense that the entire second lap resembled the VO_2 max treadmill testing we go through at the U.S. Ski Team headquarters. It's hard from the very start, and by the end of the first minute you're thinking, "Oh, shit." I was setting a pace that was, for me, at the very edge of unsustainable. But I was peaking, and I was in the best shape of my life.

I was so pumped because Falla and Nilsson had picked up my pace too. They both were clearly comfortable with what I was doing. They answered my drive. I pushed the pace and then pushed some more. On the big steep climb, Falla pulled into the front and drove the pace, ensuring that our bid to become just three in the lead pack would stick.

I came into the tag zone with a slight lead, having drafted Falla on the downhill. Since it was just three countries in the lead, the tag zone was much less chaotic this time. Kikkan saw me flying in so she was already double poling hard through the tag zone. We made the tag, and in seconds she was off, racing down the course.

• • •

The fifth lap of the team sprint in PyeongChang was Kikkan's last Olympic race for our country. And there she was, storming into her last lap, going up against the giants of the sport. After skiing in five Olympics, Kikkan still had one last big move to make: she had to work with the other race leaders and make the gap we had just created stick. Kikkan made her Olympic debut when she was nineteen years old at the 2002 Winter Olympics at Salt Lake City. Now, here she was at thirty-seven years old, down to her last lap on her last race. She would have to dig deep and hold tight, one last time, if we were going to medal.

Kikkan and I did have a history of winning, just not at the Olympics. For years, we had battled against the legends of the sport on their home turf all over Europe. In 2013 in Val di Fiemme, Italy, we were the first American team to win a gold medal in the World Championships. In 2017, we both won individual medals in the individual sprint at the World Championships. We had both won individual World Cups and stood on the World Cup podium in relay teams together.

We had won . . . but not where it counted, according to the American media.

I stood at the end of the tag zone waiting for Kikkan to come around, pumping my arms back and forth to drain lactic acid, and also because I was so excited! I wasn't even nervous. You can even see in the video of that moment, I mouth the words, "Let's go." I was ready. I was stoked to finish this.

• • •

Kikkan came roaring down the final straightaway heading into the tag zone, her beautiful technique easy to pick out. She had raced the perfect race. She had hung on to the leaders. She had used all of her technical skills and tenacity to stay on them, and she handed the race over to me in exactly the position I'd hoped for.

I don't know what Kikkan's exact mental processes were at the time. I hate it when announcers, writers, and sports commentators try to put words in our mouths and guess what we were thinking at the time we were in a competition. I hate that, because you know what? Only *Kikkan* knows what *Kikkan* was thinking! I'm not going to try to tell you; that would be incredibly presumptuous of me. But what I was thinking was that I was so proud of her. My heart was bursting with pride because there she was, doing what needed to be done, executing the plan, completing her job, and doing it beautifully. When I looked up and saw her kicking ass, refusing to give an inch, I was filled with pride.

It lit a fire in me because we were teammates, and I wanted to do my part now too. I wanted to give it my all for her, because I knew she gave it all for me. She helped put our team in a position to win, and now I wanted to go out and win it: for her, for our team, for all the athletes who had come before us and helped us get here.

I looked up and told myself, *All right. Let's go get it.*

• • •

By this point in the race, Nilsson, Falla, and I had not had much rest. Our legs were still full of lactic acid, we were breathing hard from the last lap, and our batteries were nowhere near fully charged. But we were all in the same boat! Kikkan tagged me, and once again, we had a great exchange. I was able to get to the front of the lead pack straight out of the tag zone. I was filled with positivity, and it burned like rocket fuel inside of me.

I went out, guns blazing, and shot up the first, long, gradual hill. I felt confident, like this was a day when nothing could go wrong (to be sure, this isn't a common occurrence when you're racing against the top skiers in the world!). The coaches yelling on the course were stationed there with spare poles in case someone snapped one, and possibly to offer strategic advice. But at this point, all they were doing was cheering. Hard! They were so stoked because they knew it was going well.

I was not thinking about winning. I wasn't thinking about the gold medal. It wasn't about any medal. I was zoned in to the task at hand.

Keep racing as hard as you can.

There was still a race to the finish. Yeah, I felt great. But it wasn't close to being over.

• • •

I made the 180-degree turn and started down the first hill. Maiken caught my draft, came around and moved slightly ahead of me. We were at the bottom of the epically large uphill, and we fanned out. Maiken was in the left side of the lane, which was the most direct line as the hill curved to the left. I was two feet to her right and three feet behind her. Stina was two feet to my left and three feet behind me. Although we were packed tight together, I knew I still had options to move.

I could try to scooch my way in behind Maiken and kind of cut in front of Stina. I could do that, but Stina traditionally skies very aggressively, so I was just asking for a tangle if I moved left. I could've stayed wide on the outside and tried to sprint around Maiken. But at that point, all of us were sprinting all out. If I swung wide, I thought I might burn all of my matches and lose all of my energy, and if I tried to pass too early, I would be dead. Plus, I would immediately be leading into a tricky downhill without the benefit of the draft.

I went with a third option: I eased up ever so slightly. I'm talking the tiniest of easings up, so slight you'd never notice it. I eased off my internal gas pedal and pulled back into third place over the top of the hill. By doing that, I was able to draft both women on the downhill. When you're drafting other skiers, you'll be going the same speed but without needing to get as low and tight in your tuck. I could stand up a little more, let my legs flush themselves out slightly more, and feel fresher without losing speed.

Then we hit the patch of ice that was opening up on the first corner of the S turn, and both Maiken and Stina almost fell. I saw that happen in slow motion and decided in an instant to swing out a little wider. Every movement at that point in the race was hard: my limbs were stiff; I was tasting copper, which meant I was deep inside the pain cave; and I was pushing my body to its breaking point. But not having the near fall saved me some precious adrenaline.

Right when Stina and Maiken hit the ice on the corner, I was in the process of deciding when to pass them. My speed was steady, and I was gaining on them because I was in their draft, but I decided to not try to pass right in that moment. Then all three of us swung wide out of the second S turn, our speed faster than our flooded muscles could handle. There were pine boughs stuck in the snow, serving as course markings, which we were allowed to cross as long as we crossed back onto the course before the V boards began. They're marked like that specifically because skiers might swing wide right at that spot, just as we did. It was a wider line down the hill and not an advantage, but it was better than skidding and checking our speed.

I crossed back over onto the course and swung wide, passing Maiken. I slotted in behind Stina, right before the V boards started.

Cork had a hard time watching this sequence because I squeaked in at the last possible second! Stina was skiing without using her poles, swinging her arms for momentum, and her poles were flicking up and catching me in the face. Her pole tip glanced off my glasses, and I held my hand up instinctively to protect my face as I kept pace behind her. We don't race with sunglasses on at night just to look cool, you know. (*Is that even cool? Sunglasses at night?*) They are serious protective gear!

Skiing toward the left-hand turn before the home stretch, I felt like a coiled spring. I was thinking about passing Stina at that point, but I stopped myself because if I showed her I was passing, she'd just swing wide and pinch me out toward the boards. I decided to wait to make my final move until the last second of that last turn just before the lanes started. I wanted to wait as long as I could to accelerate and then make it powerful. If I waited to make my move, I would get to pick my lane.

I was ready. I had the energy. I knew when and where I was going to make my move.

We came into the final stretch, and I swung out wide, upping my tempo to the highest gear I possessed. I gave every ounce of energy I had left and then dug deep to pull out even more.

• • •

I've often been asked what I was thinking in that moment when I came racing down the last hundred meters. In front of that roaring crowd under those bright stadium lights, it's a picture-perfect setting for making history. My arms and legs were firing away as fast as they could go. The TV announcer was bellowing, "Here! Comes! Diggins!" There I was, a dorky kid from a tiny town in the Midwest going ski to ski with the best sprinter in the world, and hanging in the balance was the chance of earning one of the most iconic awards in the world of sports. I wish I could tell you that I was having a profound thought in that very cinematic scene.

But sorry to be such a buzzkill, I wasn't thinking about anything at all. I know that's not what you wanted to read! I know it's more exciting and dramatic for me to write that in that moment when I chased down Stina and took the lead, I had a profound, life-changing, out-of-body experience. It truly would be more cinematic if I told you that my entire life flashed before my eyes as I thought about my childhood in Afton and my parents, my sister, my grandparents, and all the hours spent training for me to get to that exact moment in time.

But that's not the case at all. How lame is that!

Honestly, I wasn't thinking about anything. I was in that space athletes call "the zone," that special place where you don't overthink anything, you just let your body take over the way you've trained it to. Instead of overanalyzing and getting in my own way, I stepped outside my head and let my muscles do their job, laying it all out there. My mind emptied. I did not hear the crowd. I did not see the lights. It was as though I had suddenly developed tunnel vision and someone had turned the volume down low. The deafening roar of the crowd became a light buzz, the cameras flashing by on their automated tracks and Stina to my left became a blur. I saw only the space between me and the finish line.

I can only remember one thought, and it echoed around inside my head.

Go! Go! Go!

I did not have any more tactical decisions to make. I was executing my plan. I was going as hard as I could. I was not thinking about anything anymore, and that was exactly why it was working so well. All those years of sports psychology and hours spent training kicked in as I let muscle memory take over. I allowed my body to do what it naturally does.

Go! Go! Go!

That was it.

•   •   •

We came to the final few meters, and I surged forward, running on fumes, my body digging deeper than ever before for any last ounce of energy. Out of the corner of my eye, I could see that Stina surged too. She wasn't going down without a fight! But I knew that I had it. Even though it looks close on TV, we both have had closer lunges in regular sprint races before. I mean, we've seen lunges where it comes down to the officials reviewing the video frame by frame and seeing the exact moment when the toe of the ski boot crosses first (the finish is not judged by the tip of the ski but by the toe of the boot).

The finish line was in sight, and once again, I let my body take over, trusting that all the hundreds of lunges I had practiced over the years would tell my body when it was the right moment to shoot my foot forward.

Then I lunged for the finish line.

• • •

My toe slid across the red line in the snow, my leg reaching out in front of me, my opposite arm raised high in the air, fingers curled into a fist. In that moment, I knew we had just won. But the enormity of winning the Olympics did not register. Not yet. When I crossed the finish line, I just felt the simple exhilaration that comes with having won a race— any race! I felt the adrenaline rush of having pushed my body to its limits, then pushed a little farther, and the euphoria of having achieved a goal, the satisfaction of having completed a race. It was the relief of being able to let my guard down after having this close emotional race, being at the top of my game, making real-time tactical decisions, handling the crushing amount of pressure, and getting to the line first. In those first seconds after crossing the finish line, capturing the gold medal and Olympic history never entered my mind.

I screamed. That seemed like the only way I could let out all that amazing emotion and that complicated mix of feelings. And as usual, I had to scream because I felt that, physically, I was going to die. I was in so much pain. I had pushed my body far past its limits, and now it was pushing back.

I collapsed into the snow just like I always have done at the end of all of my races. As the snow started to melt against my race suit, the mental zone that I was locked into started to wash away ever so slightly. The edges started to peel back, and my physical reality started to creep back in.

Within seconds, Kikkan was on top of me. She hugged me and screamed. I'd never heard her like that before! She was beside herself with emotion. As the leg-one skier, she had just watched the entire thing unfold, yelling and screaming for me from behind the finish line. The emotions of watching her teammate race, knowing her personal dream was also on the line, must have been excruciating for her. When you're the one racing, you're giving it your all, and you're preoccupied with the task at hand. You're in the zone, you're not thinking anymore.

But when you're on a team sprint, it is a whole different scenario. When you're part of a relay and your race is done, all you can do is sit back and watch and cheer . . . and hope. But you have no control. I'm not even going to hazard a guess as to how excruciating watching from the stands must have been for my family and Wade!

Kikkan hugged me tight as we lay there in the snow. Seeing her face, hearing her screaming and crying, feeling her hug brought me back to reality even more. Inside her hug, it started to dawn on me that we had just won the gold medal. I realized for the first time that we, as a team, had actually won the Olympics, the first gold medal and the first medal in forty-four years.

At that moment, I had no idea what that meant. I didn't know that the race would change my life. I didn't know the magnitude of what it would mean to my hometown of Afton, to my home state of Minnesota, to my club team in Stratton, Vermont, and to the United States of America. I didn't know what it would mean to all of the thousands of people who were watching on TV, screaming in their pajamas, running around their living rooms, jumping on their beds, jumping on their couches. I had no idea all of that was happening.

I just lay wrapped in Kikkan's hug, hugging her right back.

Then she started to sit up, to help me take my poles off.

I looked up at her, needing confirmation that this was real.

"Did we just win the Olympics?" I asked.

CHAPTER 22

ONE TEAM

All of a sudden, the volume turned on.

For the first time since I had crossed the finish line, the roar from the crowd became audible. It rose and rose until it was a wall of sound that surrounded us. I heard people screaming and cheering and clapping. I could hear my name being called out.

I looked up at the stands. The bleachers were alive with a mass of people moving and swaying. The ground felt like it was shaking.

Hearing the noise, feeling the vibration, and seeing the crowd made me realize that it wasn't a dream.

It was all happening.

We had just won the gosh darn Olympics.

The moment really sank in when Kikkan and I sat up. All the other teams came over to congratulate us. That little act spoke to the character of cross-country skiers and the relationships that we have with other athletes within our sport. The fact that every other athlete—from countries we had just competed tooth and nail against—came over to hug us and that they were genuinely happy for us was such a beautiful thing. You could see it on their faces. Everyone understood what it meant for us and our country to win a medal.

I was still sitting on the snow, holding onto my shins, and just beginning to process what happened. In those seconds that I sat there curled up, I thought of my family and Wade, and what this might mean to them, supporting me through so many ups and downs. I thought of my friends and high school coaches back home, watching this at 3 a.m., and what this would mean to them, too, having been by my side through my career. I felt like I couldn't catch my breath, that the many different emotions flooding in were somehow crushing my lungs. The raucous ovation was crashing down all around me. All the lights were on us, video camera crews circling, camera flashes popping off around us. I had no idea how to process it all. Kikkan and I had three seconds to ourselves before everything rushed in and we were swept up into this incredible wave.

Somehow, I got to my feet and was immediately enveloped in a sincere hug from Marit Bjørgen. This might have been our USA moment, but she was still one of my idols, and I fan-girled on the inside hard core. *Woooo! I'm getting hugged by Marit Bjørgen!* My emotions started to break open a little more when I looked up and saw the entire U.S. cross-country ski team standing along the boards in front of me. This was my team. All of my coaches, ski techs, the entire men's and women's ski teams, the people that had supported me for so many years. These were the people who had sweat through grueling training sessions by my side, pushed me to be better, supported me through wild ups and downs. There they were, a wall of blue jackets lining the boards right next to the red finish line in the snow. The entire team. And they were going nuts.

• • •

I saw that everyone was crying, screaming, and cheering, and I finally couldn't contain my tears any longer. Some of the staff were on their knees, openly bawling, the years of work and hoping and dreaming coming true right in front of them. The total raw emotion of the moment was so powerful and overwhelming. It was the kind of moment I knew I wouldn't forget my entire life, more so than the race itself.

When there is a team sprint, the harsh reality is that only two American men and two American women are selected to ski in the competition. Because only four people from the entire country are picked to race, the day of the team sprint finals can be extremely hard emotionally for the skiers that haven't been selected to compete. That's brutal. It was emotionally hard for me as well in the days leading up to the race, knowing that many people had earned this start and weren't going to get it. But on this day, every skier on the team who wasn't racing that day was out there supporting us. That sense of selflessness, camaraderie, and commitment to the team was so amazing to see, although entirely unsurprising given the character of the team and the individuals that comprised it.

The entire team had on face paint, glitter, crazy patriotic scarves, or the striped relay socks to support us. We were the only country that had their entire team out there cheering on their skiers. They were right up against the boards, and if a skier reached out, they could high-five them as they skied by. That's how close they were. That's how much they were a part of our team and our effort.

I got right in there and started hugging all of them, happy tears rolling down my cheeks. Hugging each team member, I'd start crying even harder as I realized the sacrifices each had made for the team to reach this opportunity. Underneath the pandemonium of celebration, though, were two things about the U.S. cross-country ski team that had largely gone unnoticed. These two things were monumental in helping us win the gold medal.

• • •

The first thing that has been largely underappreciated was how well the U.S. men's cross-country team did in their team sprint. In recent years, the media hasn't given the U.S. men's team a lot of credit. Throughout the year, they work just as hard as the women's team. They go through all the same travel days, all of the brutal months and months of training, and all of the same races in Europe. They have all of the same hopes and dreams. I want to point out how absolutely amazing our guys were on the same day that we won the gold medal.

The racing schedule for the team sprint finals had a huge impact on the outcome of my race. The course schedule was such that the women's team sprint semifinals went first, with the men's semis to follow. Then the women's final, with a gap before the men's final. In cross-country ski racing, the women almost always go first. After our semifinals race, in the gap before our final race, I was underneath the stands, getting ready. As I warmed up, I watched the men's race playing live on the TV.

The men's sprint team of Simi Hamilton and Erik Bjornsen (Sadie's younger brother) had been doing fantastic the entire day. I was awestruck by how well they were skiing. They were smooth and cool and confident. They skied powerfully and were making such smart tactical decisions. I remember thinking, *My God, they're going to have an amazing day.*

As I watched the U.S. men's team kick ass, I was reminded of one of my most crucial goals when I compete: we need to recognize and celebrate more than just the moments where we win. We need to also celebrate *every* breakthrough moment and the moments of incredibly good skiing, whether or not they resulted in a medal. It can be dangerous to forget to celebrate all the steps along the way, every "small win" that we check off the list on the way to our biggest and most daunting goals.

As I watched our guys race, I took that time underneath the stands to remind myself that my good friends, training partners, and "older brothers" were having these amazing moments on their way to the finals. Regardless of whether their efforts resulted in a medal, they did so well, and it was an incredible inspiration for me. Simi and Erik gave their all, and that motivated me even more to just go out there and race my heart out, regardless of the outcome. Unfortunately, though, in the men's team sprint final there was a crash, and they went down. It took them out of medal contention, but until that crash, they were in the lead pack. Yet that crash doesn't take anything away from how they skied with guts and heart, and their performance was extraordinary.

The second thing that slid under the radar was the ultimate sacrifice and contribution that my teammate Sadie Bjornsen gave for our victory. Although she didn't ski in the team sprint final, Sadie had a massive influence on the outcome. When I found Sadie along the boards at the finish line, it was one of the most emotional hugs that I've ever had in my life because I felt that she had been skiing every step alongside me in that race.

"I believe in you," I told her. They were the only four words I could manage, but I put the weight of my entire being behind them because I meant every bit of it. I fully believe in Sadie as a person, as a racer, as a teammate, and as an unstoppable force who can achieve amazing things in this life! We shared in the joy of the race, but I also shared the pain of her having fully earned the right to start, and the heartbreak of her not being given that chance completely broke my heart too.

"Thanks, Diggy," Sadie replied, as we both burst into tears all over again.

We both knew that the gold medal could just as easily have been hers. As I mentioned earlier, the harsh reality of the team sprint is that only two skiers get picked to race. Sadie was one of the finalists. She was one of our best all-round racers to ever compete for this country and had finished as one of the top two American women in pretty much every race that year. But it was splitting hairs for the coaches to decide on leg one, without taking anything away from either of these remarkable, strong women. Sadie handled the absolute heartbreak of Kikkan being selected over her to compete in the team sprint like a true pro, and the first thing she said was, "I believe in Kikkan, and I know she will have a great race." And of course, Kikkan delivered.

The choice came down to the two of them, and the brutal reality was that someone was going to have their lifelong dream taken away from them. They were both world-class skiers. The single most impressive moment of the entire Olympics for me was when Sadie lined up on the side of the race in the finals and cheered us on with all her heart, holding nothing back, holding no bitter feelings. What an amazing person Sadie was to be able to do that. It would only be human nature to feel scorned and secretly hope that the team would fail because you thought the coaches made a mistake and didn't pick you.

But Sadie didn't do that. She did the opposite. Sadie rallied.

One of the points I want to make here is that Sadie's absolute strength and grace were such an inspirational thing to me. She was the picture of true humility and modesty and an example of how our entire team acts every day. She is an amazing athlete but an even better person. I believe with all my heart that Sadie also deserves a medal. Obviously, there is no way I can give her the experience that I went through. But I hope that she knows she's part of it, because her reaction to not being selected for the team sprint was what allowed us to go out and ski that race without any reservations. Her reaction was what allowed us to ski full of confidence, to go out and win.

In that moment, Sadie's show of support had the weight of our team history behind it too. Her sacrifice went back to one of the defining moments of the U.S. women's cross-country ski team. In 2012, when Ida Sargent wasn't selected for the 4 × 5K relay in Gallivare, instead of pouting she became our biggest cheerleader. Ida became the fifth leg in that relay, setting an incredible example and team standard for years to come. A huge part of our gold medal moment is owed to Sadie and the culture of the entire U.S. cross-country team.

• • •

I worked my way down the hug line and finally came to Cork. This moment was as much his as it was mine, and I'm not even going to try to imagine what it meant for him. After years of patient coaching, dealing with my tired and frustrated tears after hours and hours of trying to fine-tune a technique problem, supporting me emotionally through the highest of highs and lowest of lows, having coached me throughout my entire professional career from the moment I stepped out of my high school graduation, we had made it. He was my coach, tech, friend, mentor, and "ski dad," and he had just witnessed all those years of literal blood, sweat, and tears pay off on the biggest stage possible.

Not one for public attention and cameras, Cork tried to sneak away to go wax my skis! I had to call after him.

"Get back here!" I yelled. "I need a hug!" (See what I mean? I'm demanding, and I need a lot of emotional support.)

"I've got to take care of your skis," Cork said, still trying to get out of the spotlight. "I have to get your skis ready for your next race, and I need to make sure they don't disappear!"

I did, in fact, have one more race to compete in at the Olympics. That was what Cork was focused on, how he was processing it all. Cork has an absolutely incredible work ethic and always gets the job done. But I wasn't taking no for an answer. Not in that moment!

"No, you don't. The job can get done later," I said to him. "Come here, I need a hug."

. . .

Cork was right, though. (Dang it! He's always right!) A half hour after winning the gold, I started to think about my next race. It wasn't at the forefront of my mind, but it was creeping in. The reality was that I had another race to prepare for. That's what I've always done during race season—I finish a race and immediately start preparing for the next. It's both a good thing and a bad thing, because I often don't let myself fully celebrate the moment I'm in, worried that I'll expend too much energy and not start the next race with a full tank! I was competing in the 30K, and that race was going to be a true mental and physical test of endurance. I needed to get my mind and body straight, and to do that, I felt that I had to leave the chaos of celebrating our historic gold medal.

I went back to the holding pen area, where there were two tents with heaters. In the midst of the race-day spectacle, the tent was where athletes could find a quiet, safe space to change out of wet boots and race suits and have some privacy. Inside the tent, we could take a moment to process our race, whether it was good or bad, away from the media. There weren't any private stalls, but there were no cameras, press, or fans allowed. Only athletes, physios, trainers, coaches, and press officers go into the tent, and generally, most of the coaches are men, and they stay out of the tent out of courtesy.

I found a little space in the corner of the tent where I could gather my wits and change out of my race suit into dry clothes. I started to think about the next race, trying to stay on task, trying to stay focused. I'm very process oriented, and I needed to trust that I had prepared for each race in the best way I knew how, so that I could come to the start line confident that I had done everything I could to find success. The 30K classic was a big one, the last race of the entire Olympics. I needed to chug my shake, get some extra calories in. I needed to get my dry clothes on. I needed to step away from all of the buzz and hype that was going on outside and prepare for my next race. Some serious type-A, single-minded focus going on right then and there? Yeah, you betcha.

But I was a mess.

I was all a flutter. I was dropping things. I was losing things! *What the heck! Where are my socks?* My brain was spinning.

I lost my race bib and was frantically searching for it.

I couldn't even undo the laces on my boots because my hands were shaking so much.

My mind and body were finally realizing what had happened.

I was going through everything all at once. I was surging with adrenaline and riddled with exhaustion. I was on an athlete's high and simultaneously starting to crash. I was filled with unbridled joy and race-day jitters. I felt as through I'd drunk an entire pot of coffee (and possibly one that was laced with cocaine, at that).

I started to freak out a little bit inside the tent. All of a sudden, I heard my sister's voice.

"Jessie!" Mackenzie called out. "Jessie!"

I couldn't see her. Athletes and staff were milling about around me.

"Jessie! Hey, where are you?" Mackenzie yelled.

I looked toward the entrance of the tent incredulously.

"Mackenzie? You're . . . here?" I reached out and grabbed her.

"There you are!" Mackenzie said. Then she turned back toward the tent entrance. "Mom! Mom! She's in here!"

Then both my mom and sister were standing in front of me inside the restricted tent, traditionally a very sacred area. Before this, I don't know if any family members have ever been in there! But the Diggins clan from Afton, Minnesota, came right on in. They put aside their usual Minnesota niceness for a hot second and budged their way inside, blowing right through security. The entirely-too-nice South Korean guards did not stand a chance. My mom and my sister were right there when I needed them the most.

They weren't exactly inconspicuous, decked out in USA glitz and glitter to the nines. Completely covered in red, white, and blue with USA scarves and sparkly "Go Jessie!" hats that they had had specially made by Podiumwear, it was obvious to the other athletes whom they were there to support. They were wearing temporary tattoos of the American flag. They had on glitter and face paint. Their nails were painted patriotic red, white, and blue. I mean, every detail that they could possibly come up with had been taken care of. They had been having so much fun.

My mom could see that I was shaking and frazzled, cold and wet.

She found my jacket and instinctively held it up. I stepped into it, and Mackenzie wrapped her arms around me to warm me up.

"Where's my race bib?" I asked frantically. "I can't find my bib."

"Oh, I'll find it for you," my mom said calmly.

She went full into mom mode and took care of her baby, who was clearly overwhelmed. I was still processing it all and really didn't know what was happening. I had just won the gold medal, but in that moment all I wanted was a dry pair of socks.

My mom found the socks, organized a change of clothes, and I started to calm down.

Mackenzie was the quintessential proud sister, and she was cracking me up.

"OMG, LOL. I'm going to text this to everyone. You just won the Olympics. YUS!" Mackenzie screamed.

I finally came out of the tent, and the rest of my family was right there, waiting for me. I got hugs from all of them. Everyone was so proud and amazed.

But I was still flustered.

"Oh my gosh. I have to take care of myself," I said, snapping myself back to reality. "I need to make sure that I do well in my next race. I need to prepare."

"Hey, slow down," my dad said, as he stepped closer to me. He hugged me again. Then he said, "You need to enjoy this. I know you have a race coming up. You're going to do great. But you have three days to recover."

That was when I realized that I was being ridiculous. My next race was a whole three days away. I could actually let my guard down a bit without feeling like I was sacrificing performance in the 30K.

"You need to calm down and enjoy this," my mom said. "Enjoy this moment, Jessie. Take it all in."

I let go of my stress and started to fully enjoy the absolute chaos that was starting to ensue. But first, I needed one very important thing: a big hug from my boyfriend! Wade had been waiting patiently to one side, wanting to give my family some time alone with me. I turned, searching for him, and found him with a big smile on. He was also wearing a huge red felt fake mustache. He hadn't quite gone the whole glitter route, but he did embrace the fun, silly, cheering atmosphere with my family, a Team USA hat on his head, a USA scarf around his neck, and jeans rolled up to show his striped socks poking up above his Steger mukluk boots, which matched mine and my family's. It was hilarious, and in all my photos from the finish zone with him, he's sporting this "three-musketeers" mustache! I jumped into his arms for a very special hug and stayed there until I was told by our press officer that it was time for the awards.

• • •

After the men had finished their final, the flower ceremony began. Since our race didn't end until 8:30 p.m., our official ceremony in the medal plaza was the next day. I think if we had rushed off and gotten our medals right away, I still wouldn't have realized what it meant. An athlete has no way of knowing what it will feel like to win a gold medal until it happens. I'm so glad we got the actual medals the next day, or I would have still been in shock from the actual race, and I wouldn't have been able to soak it all in.

As we marched to the flower ceremony, I was skipping and dancing my way out there. Every time Kikkan and I looked at each other, we'd burst into ear-splitting grins because we couldn't believe what was happening. The Norwegians and the Swedes were so happy for us too. Everyone wanted to win the gold, but they couldn't have been happier for us and more genuine about it.

They put the podium blocks in the open space between the finishing lanes and the tag zone. It was sort of a practice run for the medal ceremony the next day, which was a good thing because I was still somewhat numb, trying to take it all in. I was seeing everything and feeling everything, but it was hard for me to process what it all meant. Luckily, I'd have time later to remember the details.

Then the announcer finally called out our country. Kikkan and I reached out and held hands. We raised our arms triumphantly in the air. Then we jumped onto the podium. "The Star-Spangled Banner" played over the sound system, and the American flag was raised for the first time in forty years at the Olympics at a cross-country ski event.

It was an amazing feeling seeing our flag being raised. I hadn't expected that part to be emotional, but that's when the realization that this had never been done before started to sink in, and I thought about all the generations of skiers who had worked to make this happen. We looked at the flag and then out at our team and our families in the crowd. Kikkan's family was out there in full force in Kikkan's favorite shade of pink. We made eye contact with them and saw their big smiles, and our smiles got even bigger.

Kikkan and I may have won the gold medal together. But we accomplished it with our team and families too. We did this together, and knowing that they were there and a part of the ceremony was so special. They know that the gold medal wouldn't have happened without them.

• • •

After the flower ceremony, the entire U.S. cross-country ski team ran out to us in a celebration that swallowed us whole. The team was together, although we were missing a few people. Mainly, Cork was gone because at that point he was waxing my skis in the wax cabin. We huddled together for a team photo across the finish line. Everyone's faces were bursting with joy and the feeling of absolute happiness.

That team photo means so much to me because all the people in the photo deserved a medal just as much Kikkan and I did. So many people outside that photo deserved it too! I thought it was ridiculous that only two people could go up onto the medal stand, but we could at least bring everyone into the finish pen to share this moment together. All the people in the photo helped us accomplish something that had never been done, something that the world largely thought was impossible. The sheer force of will and positivity from every person there helped make it a reality.

Women, men, coaches, techs, volunteer staff, we were all the same. We were one collective effort. So many people there were such a huge part of the moment, and there were so many people not present who were equally part of that moment. It's funny, because, for me, that team photo in a lot of ways was more important than the actual medal. Someday, when I have a home of my own, I'm going to frame that team photo and put it up in my house. Right now, as I write this, the medal is sitting in a hat in a drawer. I don't look at it or take it out except for parades (literally). But that team photo captures the memory and the emotion of a team winning together and celebrating together, and it's the memory of that team celebration that brings back goosebumps every time.

We were one team.

CHAPTER 23

HERE BE DRAGONS

The morning after, I sat in bed trying to make sense of it all. It was like trying to stitch a dream back together, desperately trying to remember all the details before they slipped my mind like sand sliding through my fingers. Before I fully woke up, I tried to decipher what was real and what was imagined. For as long as I could remember, I had dreamed of someday winning an Olympic medal. Overnight, that lifelong dream was given oxygen and a heartbeat and was now a living thing.

I was living in a new reality.

After the flower ceremony the night before, things got out of control pretty quickly. I underwent anti-doping tests—unceremoniously peeing in front of a total stranger for the fifth time during the Olympics, because personal boundaries don't mean anything when you decide to become a pro athlete—and then immediately stepped into a swirling media tornado. Kikkan and I were shuttled through one interview after the next. We did multiple television appearances, and before each one, we sat in hair and makeup chairs in a cloud of hair spray. Powder was brushed on our faces so we didn't look shiny and greasy. As you might imagine, I pretty much bankrupted the anti-grease powder budget that night. NBC . . . feel free to send me the bill that my shiny, sweaty face incurred. At one point, Hershey's gave us these giant chocolate golden medals, and Cork still has it tucked away in the back of his fridge for an especially rainy day. However, I couldn't enjoy any of these giant chocolate medals, because I had this sinking feeling in the pit of my stomach, knowing I had the 30K race coming up, knowing I should be horizontal in bed, eating a lot of carbohydrates right now. (Oops, now Cork knows the *real* reason I gave the chocolate to him.)

At some point in the night, someone placed a giant slice of greasy pizza in my hand, and I remember thinking that it was the single greatest gift that I'd ever received (and I'm only half joking). You know why the cameras don't follow every second of what happens when you win the Olympics? Because it looks something like this: Kikkan and I slumped in the back of a big black car, shoving pizza in our faces, tired, overwhelmed, and in total sensory overload. We were giggling at nothing, totally punch drunk.

We finally got back to the Olympic Village just before midnight. I sat on my yoga mat on the floor with a little paper to-go tray of food that Liz and Sadie had so thoughtfully gotten for me from the cafeteria. I was absentmindedly shoving dry chicken in my mouth while looking through photos of the night, trying to visually piece together what had happened.

I saw a video of one of my teammates watching the race and bursting into tears. Seeing somebody else react to what we'd done, seeing the emotions through someone else's eyes . . . that put it together for me. That was the first time I started to cry outside the stadium. I experienced this powerful little moment of *Holy shit! We won the Olympics!* sitting by myself on my yoga mat at midnight.

I came across a Comcast commercial that had been filmed before the Olympics but aired nationwide throughout the Games. They had managed to edit the commercial within hours of our win, splicing in race footage. For the first time, I saw myself crossing the finish line. It was surreal to see actual footage of my lifelong dream come to life.

I searched through texts and emails from the night before. Everything was set up to capitalize on the moment. Press officers with the ski team and United States Olympic Committee had set up everything to immediately get as much press as possible. We were just little player pieces on a game board being put through moves planned out long before we even got on the board.

They built a schedule that would help guide me through the next couple of days. There were more interviews, photoshoots, and television appearances on the horizon. Dotted throughout this map of events were possible points of peril because I was bone tired and anxious. My body was starting to rebel against me, and I still had the 30K race to go, which I was excited for and wanted to race to the best of my ability.

I thought about everything that had led up to the team sprint. In the weeks and months before the race, I had prepared for pretty much everything to go right. Every detail had been covered. From my pre-race meal, to the wax on my skis, to the mental visualization of the course, it had all been thought through. But I had no plan for what would happen if we actually won. Nobody did! This was uncharted territory. *Here be dragons.*

•   •   •

The night of the medal ceremony, Kikkan and I decided that we were going to do a dance on the medal podium. I'd taught the team a hip-hop dance at the start of the World Cup season, thinking we might make another one of our funny music videos. We never made the video, but the whole team had learned this funny, funky dance, and the laughs we got out of it were well worth the time.

We walked onto the stage, and the crowd erupted. I saw my mom and Wade right near the front (they were the only two members of my family who were able to reschedule flights to stay with me). I made eye contact with them and started to tear up immediately, and so, of course, I had to look away! We waited for the other athletes to be called up, and then it was our turn. We clasped hands, jumped up onto the platform, and immediately went into part of our dance. It was one of the most joyful but bizarre moments of my life, doing this silly little hip-hop dance with Kikkan on the stage. During the anthem I was scared to sing along for fear that I would somehow forget the words or say them wrong, so I was just smiling and humming, trying not to cry, and realizing that under no circumstance could I lock eyes with either my mom or Wade because I'd immediately burst into tears.

After the ceremony, all I wanted to do was spend some time with my mom and Wade. So instead of going down to the coast and doing more media, I busted out of there as quickly as possible, jumping into a taxi that took me right to their condo. Walking in the door felt like taking a huge weight off my shoulders. For the first time in days, I didn't have any cameras or videos screens on me, there weren't any more questions, and I could just be myself.

I finally exhaled.

We foraged around in the fridge, found leftover salad and sausage, and cooked pasta. It was a sure sign that my Auntie Holly had been there because she always has a backup dinner ready and waiting! We ate spaghetti at the table together. Afterward, I remember being indescribably happy, lying on the couch with Wade's arms around me and feeling in that moment that there was nothing I had to do and nowhere I had to be. I was exactly where I belonged. I realized that the moments that made me feel truly fulfilled and joyful were moments that I have all the time in my life, regardless of a medal. Simply being with the love of my life and my mom and getting to spend time with them—that was when I felt the happiest.

I remember having a talk with Wade about all the media, saying that if any of this started to even slightly change who I am in any way, he had to tell me. My exact words may have been something like "If I get a big head, you go right ahead and kick my ass, OK babe?" We had to reassure one another that we were going to find opportunities to have our time together. Maybe this is how it has to be now with this many commitments, but it won't be this way forever. I think maybe that's how life is when you're working a strange job and in a long-distance relationship. But one of many, many things I love about this man is that he's always willing to find a way for us to make it work.

At the end of the night, at the end of a forty-eight-hour whirlwind of media attention brought on by our historic gold medal, there was one more thing I had to do: dirty dishes.

My mom offered to do them, but I sprang up from the couch. "*No!* I have to do them! I can't get a big head!"

I put the gold medal around Wade's neck, and he wore it while he dried the dishes . . . making him, yes, my gold medal dish dryer!

• • •

The day after the medal ceremony, we were able to present the Order of Ikkos medal to our coaches. When you win a medal at the Olympics as part of Team USA, you're given this special medallion to present to somebody who inspired you or helped you get there, or someone you want to thank. And usually, you get one medal. Wikipedia that thing, and it says in all caps, you get one. But Kikkan and I decided that we needed four, thank you very much. We felt that we couldn't thank only one person! There were so many people who had helped get us there! Honestly, we needed about a thousand. But they granted us four.

We thanked Jason Cork, Chris Grover, Matt Whitcomb, and Erik Flora, our coaches who had been there with us during our entire national team careers. It was really special to see them awarded, to be able to talk about them and thank them, and recognize them in front of everyone for how instrumental they were.

After we presented the medals, Reese Brown, our communications press officer for the Olympics, pulled me aside.

"I have a phone call for you," Reese said with a great deal of urgency.

"Really? Right now?" I replied, motioning to the goings-on all around me.

"No, you're going to want to take this, trust me," Reese said.

He pulled me out of the house, and I put the phone to my ear. The director of the United States Olympic Committee introduced himself. Then he told me that all the winter athletes had voted on which athlete would carry the American flag at the closing ceremonies, and he said, "They picked you. How you raced with so much energy and heart, your gutsy performance in the team sprint, but also every race you did, it really moved people. I'm proud to let you know you'll be carrying the flag and leading the entire team out at closing ceremonies."

I thought I was being pranked. I looked all around for a camera! Reese had the biggest grin on his face because he knew what was happening. Getting the news was such a surreal moment. But I had something else on my mind, because, well, I'm me, and I'm type A whether there is a once-in-a-lifetime opportunity in front of me or not.

"I'm doing the 30K! It finishes only hours before closing ceremony! How am I going to get there in time? What if I get pulled for anti-doping again and I'm late?" I asked.

"Don't you worry," Reese said. "I'll take care of getting you there in time—you just focus on your race."

. . .

I was ready for the 30K classic. I had some nerves, but I was ready to race as hard as I could, and try one more time to land an individual skier from Team USA on the podium. This was also the last competition of the entire Olympics! It was a beautiful and warm sunny day. So warm, in fact, that I kind of panicked at the start and stole the scissors from the med kit to cut the arms off my race suit. To me, the worst thing in the world was overheating! If the World Cup had a yearbook, I'd get nominated for "most likely to race naked."

My spirit was willing. But my body had simply had enough. We didn't have the best wax of our lives that day, which of course made it more difficult, but I also think that I was depleted on a physical, emotional, and mental level. It had been such a long Olympics, I had raced every race, and during the 30K I felt like I was sprinting the entire time. I pushed my body as hard as it would go, and my body pushed right and told me, "Dude, enough! I'm freaking *done*, OK?"

When I crossed the finish line, the exhaustion of the entire Games hit me all at once. Not a ton of bricks but more like an entire dump truck of bricks. I just lay there, curled up into a ball (probably choking on my own spit, if we're being totally honest). It had been my worst race of the Olympics by far in terms of time back and placing, and I was a little frustrated by not having wax that was on par with the girls I was competitive with. But I was still in seventh place. At the previous Olympics in 2014 my best result had been eighth, and that felt like such a miracle. Suddenly, the bar had been raised.

I remember thinking that I may have created a monster. We had created a situation where now a race without a medal, a championship without multiple top-ten results, might seem from the outside like a failure. On the one hand, you're so happy to have raised the bar to be racing at that level. But on the other hand, you feel the pressure rising. It's so much easier to make improvements in leaps and bounds when you're going from fortieth to thirtieth, but once you're racing among the top ten in the world, fighting for that tiny improvement gets harder and harder every time. And don't forget, you're fighting for those minute improvements under a media microscope. In the back of my mind, I became aware that my time for sneaking in there unannounced and having a good race without any pressure was at an end, and it was by my own doing.

I could barely walk at the finish line. My mind and body were so depleted from having been pushed past their limits for an hour and fifteen minutes. I had to rally. I pushed myself to my hands and knees, then got up from the snow, and Reese was waiting for me as soon as I exited the finish area. He swept me back to the village, where I had about an hour to shower, eat, and get ready for the night ahead. I put on the only makeup that I knew how to put on (which is, still to this day, mascara).

I clipped on my credentials and got on a bus with all the other flag bearers. We went to a staging tent outside the opening and closing ceremony stadium and were escorted to a hidden area in the back. I looked around and immediately spotted other cross-country skiers who were voted by their countries to carry their flag: Charlotte Kalla from Sweden and Marit Bjørgen from Norway! Marit, by the way, had just gotten her fifteenth Olympic medal that day. In a sport that has only six events every Olympics, that is astronomical. I was absolutely in awe of her, and, as a matter of fact, I still am and always will be.

We moved outside, and each flag bearer had a volunteer from South Korea with them. My volunteer guy was super friendly, and I enjoyed chatting with him about the Games and what it meant for him to have them in his country. The energy outside the stadium in the line was crackling; you could almost feel the electricity. The energy at the closing ceremony is, in my opinion, vastly different than the opening ceremony's. At the opening, all the athletes are full of hope and nerves, pressure and excitement, but also stressed about performing their absolute best in the days to come. The atmosphere at the closing ceremonies was tangibly different. There was a real sense of relief that it was over, a release of stress and pressure and expectations. It was giddy excitement from some, and those who had won medals were encouraged to wear them around their necks during closing. I didn't know that was a thing, and honestly, I felt kind of uncomfortable about standing out that way. If Marit Bjørgen didn't feel the need to parade her *fifteen* medals around, then I could not be a tool about the puny one medal that I had, you know what I mean?

For me, the closing ceremonies felt like a huge celebration. I was humbled to have been chosen as flag bearer, and I thought it was so cool that the biathlon team had nominated me. It was even cooler that the Team USA athletes had picked someone who wasn't from one of the mainstream sports but had voted based only on joy of competition and gutsy racing. It was the highest honor to have been recognized by my peers. I just felt lucky to be there in that arena, surrounded by athletes from around the world. As a team, as individuals, there was a recognition that people had gone out there and fought their hardest and either gotten what they'd trained for, or not. Either way, it was a journey to get to that point where you could march out of the Olympics with your head held high.

The Games had felt like such a success for me on a personal level, and now that all that stress was over, I was just levitating! I could finally quit worrying about the next race to come. That was the first time that I felt that I could truly celebrate the gold medal. I didn't need to wear the medal to celebrate it either. I *definitely* didn't want to be the jerk celebrating in front of other people who perhaps hadn't had a great few weeks. I just needed the knowledge that there was nothing else I had to be preparing for to let my guard down. Standing in the line as we got ready to carry our flags in to close out the Games, I finally let myself smile freely and revel in what I had done in those last 150 meters of the race. I let myself replay it in my mind and silently shout for joy and feel the rush of adrenaline.

We marched in around the circle and came to our individual stops for each country. I was standing next to the guy from Bermuda, who was, of course, wearing Bermuda shorts, and he was freezing and miserable. In stark contrast, I was bouncing up and down, smiling ear to ear, and soon all the athletes walked in. After waving the flag for what felt like an hour (hey, my arms were tired from the 30K that day, don't judge me!), the march was over. Then we got to sit down in the seats, relax, and enjoy the show. For me, that was special because for opening ceremonies there is this amazing, incredible show, and I'd never gotten to sit down and enjoy it, because I was racing the next day. This time I got to oooh and ahhh and enjoy every second. I didn't want to blink.

• • •

I headed back to the village, trying to frantically organize my jumbled life. Sitting there packing my bags, I took stock of what had happened. As awesome as the Olympics had been, I was finally facing the fact that my body was falling apart from physical toll, nerves, and stress. I had one finger where the skin was inexplicably peeling off the fingertip. I literally didn't have a fingerprint anymore! I had so many other weird things going on with my body too. For almost the entirety of the Games, I had been hungry. But as soon as I would start to eat, I'd lose my appetite. The only thing I *truly* wanted was chocolate, so I guess my true self came out. I had basically run on Hershey's Kisses for the entire Olympics. I remember sitting in the Team USA house, eating the most amazing Reese's Peanut Butter Cups I'd ever had in my life because those were just about the only thing I could reliably eat. (Special thanks to Wade and my mom for finding them for me and smuggling them out of the Team USA house.) I'd gotten pretty skinny, and we were all a little worried about me getting sick before the Olympics were over.

As I packed, I was a little scared of what was going to happen next. Our agents were awesome, and they had lined up some amazing experiences for me and Kikkan in New York City. But it was such a fluid situation that schedules were shifting and changing all the time, and that made me nervous. I'm an athlete that thrives on schedules and detailed plans, and the media whirlwind had thrown my life into a chaotic space. There were dragon symbols all over the map that was now in front of me.

Part of me was seriously questioning whether I should do all the media stuff. I wanted to keep things as normal as possible. To do what I've always done and simply rest and prepare for the World Cup races in Europe, which were starting back up after the Olympics.

But the other half of me was thinking, "*Don't be stupid.*"

I desperately wanted a World Cup to take place in the United States. Specifically, I wanted it to happen in my home state of Minnesota. That had been my mission for so long, to give back to the ski community by inspiring thousands of skiing families with the chance to see a World Cup race live. Doing all the media was how I could potentially help make that happen. I knew also that cross-country skiing wasn't one of the big attractions at the Winter Olympics. It's not nearly as popular as snowboarding, downhill skiing, ice hockey, and figure skating. I knew that my media exposure would help grow this tiny sport of mine and would create more opportunities for the young skiers coming up behind me. If I didn't do the interviews, if I didn't go on the television shows, if I didn't make the long journey to New York City for more media just because I was *tired,* I could deny our sport an opportunity for growth. I told myself, *No, sorry honey, you're doing all the interviews.* I was going to sit in the cloud of hair spray and have all the anti-grease powder shellacked to my nose that it took to help move Nordic skiing forward.

In the end, it wasn't about me. It was about the next me. Maybe there was a young athlete out there who was worried about not having natural ability and needed to know that an athlete's heart and grit are what really matters most. Maybe there was a young girl out there who was struggling with body image and needed to know that she was OK just the way she was, that being tall or skinny or short or round did not matter. If I could help inspire those young athletes to gear up and go for it, to try their best and work hard regardless of their body shape and innate talent level, then I needed to do just that.

I packed my bags and let the media tornado blow me all the way to New York City.

CHAPTER 24

COMING HOME
OR, THE WEEK I MASQUERADED
AS A ROCK STAR

I was as jet-lagged as I've ever been, turned totally upside down. I was sleep-deprived and starving. My body was now seriously pushing back with some attitude, screaming at me, *You need to feed me and take care of me. After everything you've put me through, you owe me that!* So Wade, who had flown in to spend a day with me, and I left our hotel at 5:30 a.m. in search of a perfect lox bagel. We walked around New York City at dawn, watching the sunrise flash across the windows of the tall buildings in fragments like a kaleidoscope. It was such a simple act, just two dorks going for a morning walk looking for bagels. But for me, it felt like the most glorious vacation in the world, and a highly romantic one at that, now that I was finally getting some time with Wade.

Later that morning, we met Kikkan to go for a run in Central Park. Even though I felt like I was on vacation and honoring that feeling in my mind, I knew I still needed to keep up some level of training, even if a one-hour easy run didn't feel like anything compared to the training we usually do. This, by the way, is why cross-country skiing is so crazy. A one-hour run makes you feel guilty. We think there's no way we're possibly training enough that day. We're kind of messed up.

The first sign that my life had truly changed because of what it meant to win a gold medal as an American athlete was when Wade and I went to dinner. On the plane ride to New York City, Delta had congratulated us on the plane, giving every passenger on board a glass of champagne for a full-plane, rousing victory toast. Flight attendants would stop by my seat, slip an extra piece of candy into my pocket, and wink. As amazing as this was, I figured this royalty treatment was because the Olympics had just ended. There was *no way* people would remember who we were in a week.

Wade and I wanted a romantic restaurant somewhere near the Broadway area so we could simply talk and decompress. We found a beautiful little Italian place. We had a candlelit table in the corner for two, and it all felt very *Lady and the Tramp*. We were enjoying this wonderful meal and were planning to finish and walk over to see the play *Hamilton*. My agent's company, CSEP (thanks, you guys!), had gotten us a steal of a deal for Kikkan, her brother Tanner, Wade, and me on the condition that we bring our medals and let *Hamilton* media do some promotion with them. Being relatively smart individuals, we said, "Yes, please, we will absolutely whore out our medals for *Hamilton*."

The owner of the restaurant figured out who I was. Which was weird because normally no one noticed me and Wade. The owner came over to our table and started talking animatedly about his family in Italy. He spoke passionately about us going to visit them someday.

"Oh, you *must* come, you really must come some time to visit," he said, waving his hands with gusto. "But first! You *must* have the tiramisu!"

Wade and I were both full, and we protested, trying to explain that we couldn't eat any more and were also going to be late to *Hamilton*.

"*No!* You *must*! And moscato! Bring the moscato!"

So, we found ourselves with more dessert, wine, and a plate full of tiramisu and making plans to visit a total stranger in Italy.

This was not normal.

●　●　●

The *Hamilton* media manager showed us to our seats. Kikkan and I didn't have our medals visible, but we were wearing the easily recognizable white closing-ceremony jackets (so that the media manager could find us on the sidewalk outside). People slowly realized who we were, because at this point it had been only a week since we had won and only a few days since I was all over TV as the closing-ceremony flag bearer.

People started to clap for us. I'm sure most of the people had no idea who we were or what was going on, but the audience started to clap, because other people were clapping! Suddenly, the entire theater was giving us a standing ovation. As the thunderous applause came roaring down, we all stopped in our tracks, looking at each other, stunned.

Cross-country skiers don't get standing ovations on Broadway before the show!

Unreal.

Audience members started coming over. Although it was only fifteen minutes until the show started, people were asking for photos and autographs. We signed their *Hamilton* playbills, as though we were some of the actual talents about to perform. The crowd was crushing us, getting closer and closer. Eventually, a bouncer came and told people to start taking their seats because the show was about to start. We finally took our seats, the show began, and the play was the most amazing thing I've ever seen. I was totally blown away and instantly in love with the entire show.

At intermission, we were crushed once again by audience members. I *really* had to pee, but I could not take one step, as we were surrounded on all sides by people wanting photos. I was so confused! I felt like I was living someone else's life, as though I'd stolen a snippet of some celebrity's glamorous, amazing life and at any moment I'd have to give it back, so I just had to laugh and enjoy every second of the crazy ride.

Finally the same bouncer rescued me—he must have realized that this wasn't really *my* life I was living. Unlike a real celebrity, I can't hold it forever.

"I'd be happy to escort you backstage to the actors' restroom if you'd like," he said.

After the show ended, we went to see the backstage staging area and marveled over their amazing organization for each show. We met all the actors in the greenroom, as they were having a little après-show drink to celebrate. The whole room was buzzing with a joyful energy. It was clear how much they loved their job. I admired their passion and charisma, soaking in the happy energy. Next, we were shown the King's Wall, a backstage area on the left-hand side where they hang up the king's costume between shows. The wall behind it has hundreds of signatures from celebrities, and in an incredible lapse of judgment, they gave us a Sharpie and let us sign it.

We went outside into the fresh air to walk off the adrenaline. The lights of Times Square were all around us, vivid and bright and blinking. As we walked under the neon lights, I looked up at this huge billboard advertising a new TV show that had just come out, called *Good Girls*. The three actresses on the show—Christina Hendricks, Mae Whitman, Retta Ruby Hill—were towering over us.

"You guys didn't recognize them? Those three actresses were in the row right behind us!" Tanner, Kikkan's brother, exclaimed.

The next day on *Late Night with Seth Meyers*, Mae Whitman (huge fan of her, by the way) was a guest on the show to promote *Good Girls*. As she talked to Meyers, she told a cute, funny, and self-deprecating story about going to see *Hamilton* with her castmates the night before and how it was a great bonding experience—until they were shoved out of the way by autograph hounds trying to get at "these Olympians from the cross-country skiing team."

Famous actresses pushed aside by cross-country skiers! Whose life am I living right now? This led to another talk about how an ass kicking would be imminently forthcoming if my "little peanut head," as Wade calls it, grew even a millimeter.

• • •

The next morning, the "glam squad" (another term I didn't know until after the Olympics) arrived at our room at 6:00 a.m. for hair and makeup. I still couldn't believe how much work went into a five-minute TV appearance. Behind those little clips of video was roughly an hour and a half of makeup. You know what's even weirder? A "natural" look takes even more time in the makeup chair. Go figure.

One thing I came to understand was that when you look at a magazine at that beautiful and flawless human gracing the cover and think to yourself, *Wow, I'll never look that good . . .* it's true. You won't. Not because you're not fabulous, darling, but because it's not real. *Nobody* looks like that in real life! Unless you're reading this right now, Beyoncé, in which case I totally take it back. You *do* look that good in real life.

After a few photo shoots throughout the year, I recognized that they all shared a pattern. Each shoot was usually really fun and involved an incredible level of self-delusion. I had to truly believe that I looked like a rock star because how confident I felt would come out in my body language. And if the designers and stylists were putting clothes on me for the shoot, it was more of an arts and crafts project than a high-fashion statement. The clothes would likely be pulled from runway sample sizes, and they wouldn't come anywhere close to fitting. This was disconcerting at first, until I learned that someone is hired for the entire day whose only job is to pin the clothes on you and make every tiny wrinkle disappear. There are photos of me that look great from the front . . . because you can't see the three clothespins, the plastic chip-bag holder, and the five safety pins that are all keeping the open back of the dress on me. Also, I'm probably wearing jeans underneath it. Unfortunately, you don't get to keep the clothes even if they do fit you, and I know this because I've tried to get away with it many times. Thousands of photos are taken from every possible angle, in every possible pose, to find the exact right one. So that one perfect photo you see in an ad? It took about three hours to get it.

There is an incredible gap between what you look like every day and what you'll most certainly look like if a team of professionals spend sixty to ninety minutes on your makeup and hair. It's still fun to get dressed up, but the greatest joy comes from recognizing that, truly, what you see in magazines, TV, and advertisements is far from reality. When people tell me, "Don't compare yourself to that Photoshop photo," I really do believe them now, having seen the other side.

The reality was, at least for that time, my life didn't feel real. For two long days, Kikkan and I were shuttled from one thing to the next. Between every TV appearance, we were taking calls and doing interviews over the phone for newspapers and magazines. Of course, I got desperately carsick because New York City has the most herky-jerky driving that I've ever experienced, so for many of the TV shows I'd show up looking a little green!

We went on the show *LIVE with Kelly and Ryan*. What a world. Cross-country skiers don't go on megapopular morning talk shows, everybody knows that. The stage manager said that our segment would be short because they put another ad in, so when we went down the catwalk between aisles of people in the audience, we would have to run. Apparently, people would try to grab us to shake our hands, and it would slow down the show, so we were told to *run!* What was happening? My biggest concern for the hour was being slowed down by fans on a catwalk in a television studio?

I remember feeling severe anxiety through many of these appearances, specifically in the moments leading up to them. My whole mission for the time that I was in New York was to gain traction and support for a World Cup in the United States. I had never been able to compete in a World Cup in my own country, and I knew that a race could create a lot of opportunities for skiers as well as inspire the next generation. A lot of people were pulling for a World Cup to be in New York City, but I knew in my heart that it had to be Minneapolis if we ever wanted to get this done while I was still competing. Minnesota was the only place equipped to make it happen in the next two or three years. It was all pointless stress though. I got to talk about how great it would be to have a World Cup in the United States, specifically, how great it would be in Minnesota and how much that would mean for the community there. In the end, all of the media was worth it because after months and months of negotiations and hard work behind the scenes, Minneapolis secured the bid to host the first World Cup event in the United States in nineteen years in March 2020.

• • •

I spent a day with Ice Breakers, under the Hershey company, because they were a sponsor of mine through the Games. (I'm shamelessly plugging them in this book in hopes that a gigantic box of Reese's Peanut Butter Cups will land on my doorstep.) The day ended in the New York City Hershey's store, and it was amazing. I had to wipe the drool off my face in between camera flashes. They made gigantic s'mores—four normal-size s'mores stuck together into one beautiful, gooey, dripping biscuit of awesomeness. They also let me go on a shopping spree. Seriously. A chocolate shopping spree. Here was a company after my own heart.

Later that night as I was hopped up on a sugar rush in my hotel room, I was a guest on the popular National Public Radio show *Wait Wait . . . Don't Tell Me!* The show was live in Chicago, and I was to call in at a certain time. There had been a little miscommunication about the calling number and when exactly I was supposed to call in . . . and by that, I mean that I was scatterbrained and exhausted and forgot. Right as I was crawling into bed in my pajamas, I got a text that asked if I'd called in yet. *Oh, shit.* I scrambled around and found the number, but I couldn't call in from the landline, because I couldn't get out of the hotel phone system. I was panicking, and panic makes me stupid, so I called in from my cell phone with my Bose headphones connected. I was just praying that the cell service was good enough for them and didn't cut out halfway through! I called in with about thirty seconds to spare, and I did the entire interview lying in bed with my feet propped up against the wall because they hurt from walking around all day. Behind the scenes, it was about as unglamorous as it gets!

The interview was fun, especially the back and forth with Paula Poundstone. Earlier in the year on another *Wait Wait . . . Don't Tell Me!* episode she had said cross-country skiing wasn't even a spectator sport. She went on to mock the U.S. women's team, saying that we were getting our asses kicked so badly that we were in the back of the pack texting one another. This remark came during a year when we won the Olympics, I placed second in the World Cup overall, and as a team we had more than fifteen individual World Cup podium finishes. So while she intended to be funny, she came off pretty uneducated and mean because it wasn't even close to true. Just saying.

I knew Paula was a comedian and her job was to be funny, usually at the expense of others. But she was just *so* wrong. We work so much harder than anyone knows. To say that we're texting each other in the back of the race felt like such a slap to our 850 plus hours of sweating and training throughout the year to prepare for what we do. Anyone who had seen us collapse across the finish line with not an ounce of energy to spare would never say that about us. Obviously, she hadn't seen it.

They had me on the show so I could make my peace with Paula on air, as it were. It was pretty funny, but the best part came after my segment ended, in moments that were never put on the on-air replay. The host, Peter Sagal, said goodbye to me. I said goodbye and thank you for having me. But then I hesitated, waiting on my phone in my hotel room in my pj's, unsure of what to do. When you call in to a radio show, a producer behind the scenes normally patches you in and out. So I waited for the producer to patch me out, holding my breath, waiting for something to happen. But then I heard the cast of *Wait Wait . . . Don't Tell Me!* start to talk again. I figured they were giving me a free bedtime listen-in, so I didn't hang up.

But they didn't know that.

"She's so nice," Paula said sarcastically about me. "What an *asshole!*"

It was a joke about this sort of imagined rivalry between us, and how she hated that I was a nice Minnesota girl and killed her with kindness. She was upset because she couldn't even be mad at me. I burst out laughing, because I was supposedly signed off and then behind my back she called me an asshole.

Suddenly, I heard the audience roar with laughter. Not only was I still connected . . . but I was still *live*. The entire theater heard my hysterical little chipmunk laugh.

"Oh, shit!" Paula snapped in horror.

Peter Sagal jumped in and said, "Jessie, how fast can you get to Chicago right now? I bet you could be on the next plane to duke it out with Paula."

After a little ribbing about Paula's faux pas, they said goodbye again. This time I was disconnected immediately.

I was in sleep-deprived stitches, exhausted after running myself into the ground going from one interview to the next, speaking passionately about the Olympics and the World Cup. I had experienced the entire range of emotions that week: the joy and wonder of winning the Olympics; the stress, pressure, and crushing nerves of knowing you have to compete; and now the sweaty palms, anxiety, and bewilderment of being on television. In the span of two days, I had a small glimpse of what life was like for a celebrity. I had gone from being an unrecognized athlete who competes in a small winter sport, to being crushed by attention and requests for autographs, pictures, and interviews. I felt incredibly out of place. While I learned that I love public speaking and the chance to create more opportunities for our sport, I also realized that you can't accept every invitation as a cross-country skier and still expect to *win* on the World Cup. Our training is so hard and so long that you have to be consistently willing to be an athlete first, and I found that I was quite all right with that. Having experimented with a taste of this other life, I understood how much I loved my simple days training in the woods with my team, baking muffins in the afternoons, and enjoying every small moment. I was never cut out for this whole "famous" thing, as exciting as it sounded when I was younger!

I would later rejoin my teammates on the World Cup, end the most successful season I'd had to date with more podium finishes and "firsts" for Team USA, and wrap up the season by placing second in the overall World Cup standings. But for now, in this moment, I felt a little bit lost. I had been brought out from the quiet, snowy woods of my life and put under the hot lights of television studios and photo shoots. The entire scenario was just ridiculous. I was in my hotel room alone and surrounded by free chocolate—which was the only feeling of fame that I would ever truly need—and howling with laughter.

The mishap on *Wait Wait . . . Don't Tell Me!* was one of the funniest, most surreal moments of my entire life. I had been called an asshole in front of a live radio audience. And I had no one to tell! I was all alone, lying on my hotel bed, kicking my feet in the air, hysterically tired, and had no one to share the experience with. So I did what I've always done, whether I was a gold medalist or simply an excited young girl getting the chance to compete in her first varsity race.

I called home to tell my parents.

EPILOGUE

What I really want to do right now is curl up under a blanket on the couch in my condo in Stratton and watch *The Vampire Diaries* on Netflix (don't judge me). That's what I'd love to do, especially since it's raining outside. But the best and most addicting TV show ever will just have to wait.

There's work to do first.

I'm in the team van—squished into a seat between Paddy and Sophie Caldwell, next to a pile of roller skis and poles—and everything smells a little bit like dirty socks. SMST2 club coach Pat O'Brien is behind the wheel, and we're about to begin our morning workout: a forty-five-minute roller ski through the Green Mountains and then a set of intervals, followed by another thirty-minute ski as a cooldown. All told, we're going to be sweating out in the rain for at least two hours.

What's new, right?

Honestly, nothing has really changed since winning a gold medal. All the same people who were with me before the Olympics are still with me now. They are literally right beside me. Besides Paddy and Sophie, all my SMST2 teammates are here: Simi, Ben, Kelsey, Alayna, Kyle and Julia, KO and her brother Ben. Cork is here too. He's been with me for the past decade, right there beside me during all of my highs and lows, and he's here now.

The one thing that isn't here with me in the van, though, is the gold medal. After the whirlwind of publicity and attention, all of that hoopla has died down, and now I'm back to simply doing what I do best: training hard.

The medal stays in a sock drawer, out of sight and out of mind, because for me, skiing has always been about more than victories. As awesome as the 2018 Olympics were, they will ultimately not define me. I'm made up of many experiences and emotions, and I play many roles: a daughter, an advocate for causes I care about, a teammate, a speaker, a girlfriend, a sister, an adventurous adrenaline idiot, and hopefully someday a mother. "Gold medalist" is one of those roles, but it's not the only role in my life. I have the ability to have a positive impact on the lives of the people around me, and that's always been the case, with or without a medal. So yes, although it's cool, I never look at that thing. I only bring it out for times when it can inspire others. I want to earn the right to be proud of who I am every day, not forever falling back on those fourteen minutes on a Thursday night in South Korea.

In the end, when you strip away that shiny moment, I'm right back to where it all started. I'm still out here in the sun and rain and putting in the work. This is who I really am.

• • •

We unload our skis and poles in the pouring rain.

"Supposed to rain all day," coach Pat says to no one in particular.

There is a collective shrug from all of us. We clip into our roller skis and get on with it. We set off down the road toward the official Town of Stratton. It's new pavement, twisting and turning through the vividly green forest. There are no cars on the road, but we're all wearing various shades of neon and reflective material anyway. We roll in a single-file line, Cork on a bike behind us. Through sheets of rain, we ski through the rolling countryside, cracking jokes, catching up, and laughing at the ridiculousness of skiing uphill through so much water that it's running down the pavement in glossy sheets. We eventually stop on a deserted mountain road with a steep grade.

Pat pulls up in the team van, and we toss our water packs in the back so he can drive them up to the top for us. On either side of the road there are markers for the Appalachian Trail, which cuts through the deep woods and crosses the empty road. Off in the distance, the sound of a gun firing crackles through the mountains. It's rural Vermont, so we're not really surprised. Pat takes a closer listen to the interval of the gun shots.

"Someone is shooting target practice," Pat says with a shrug. Then he cracks a grin, "Pretend it's the start gun!"

Skiing uphill, we begin our set of intervals, racing across the countryside together. Cork sprints ahead of us to stand on the side of the road, rain cascading off his hood, to film our technique so we can watch later. With each interval, it gets harder to breathe, and the lactic acid builds. But we keep going, giving each other high fives and cheers after each one, switching leads so we can continue learning from each other's technique.

Winter skiers are made in the summer. And they're not made alone.

•   •   •

The clock finally ticks down, and we finish the interval set, hanging on our poles and gasping for air. The familiar feeling of hard-earned endorphins floods in, and I'm sure my teammates are feeling it too: the rush of satisfaction in a job well done. Pat has the drink belts lined up in the back of the van, and we buckle them around our waists, heading back down the road to ski our cooldown.

As we're rolling back down the mountain road, wind and rain whipping against our glasses, I let my mind wander. For a stretch of several miles, I think about all that has happened in the past year. I'm still very much the same skier who just wants to race fast, and I don't think that medals have changed who I am in any way. But I have to admit to myself that since the Olympics, there are parts of my life where opportunities have changed, and there are definitely perks to having a greater platform available to make a difference in the world.

Since that day in South Korea, I've been blessed with new opportunities, and I'm not just talking about getting last-minute tickets to Broadway shows. I've had the chance to make deep connections with a few foundations that mean so much to me. I've experienced moments that I never thought were possible.

Admittedly, I never thought I'd ski naked through the woods of Vermont, but many good things have come from doing the Body Issue photo shoot with *ESPN the Magazine*. I decided to open up and talk about my history with an eating disorder in the hopes of bringing awareness to coaches, teachers, and parents but ultimately to let people struggling through a rough time know that they're not alone, that it's never too late to turn it around, and that asking for help is brave.

I was scared to admit that my past wasn't always pretty and that I wasn't always proud of how I acted. But once I revealed the most vulnerable part of myself, the most amazing thing happened. I partnered with The Emily Program as a spokesperson and began to receive letter after letter from young athletes, both boys and girls, letting me know that my words had helped them find the courage to tell their parents they needed help. We still have a long way to go, but the goal is to take away the stigma from eating disorders and empower people who are suffering from them to reach out for help.

I can't plan a party to save my life, but somehow I managed to squeeze my way into helping plan a World Cup event in Minneapolis. The ski community in the Midwest has given me so much throughout my life. After the Olympics, I figured it was my chance to ride that momentum and give something back, to help inspire the next generation of athletes, dreamers, and recreational skiers. After a whirlwind spring immediately following the Olympics, and the work of about a hundred people who tirelessly poured their heart into this enormous project, we had a bid. The day I got the confirmation that we were officially hosting a World Cup race in Minneapolis, I was jumping up and down, flailing my arms, running in circles around my kitchen, totally unsure of what to do with my joy!

Speaking of joy, if you're ever having a downer of a day, try being hugged by about three hundred little kids in the span of thirty minutes. It'll really lift your spirits for at least a month! One of my favorite things I got to do the spring after the Games was visit my old elementary school, Valley Crossing. I gave a presentation for the entire school, but the best part was on our way out of the gym, when I stood by the door so every kid could touch the medal. But then, because little kids are the best, most of them decided to throw a big ol' hug into the mix as well! It was so cool to see their eyes light up when I talked of traveling the world, setting goals and a game plan, and working hard to get one step closer. That's why I joined the board of Share Winter, a grant-giving nonprofit that seeks to give as many kids as possible the chance to learn a snow sport for the first time.

I wish the very best for anyone who wants to become a skier, but I'm worried about the amount of opportunities they'll have in the future if climate change isn't taken seriously. Besides not having snow to race on anymore, these kids won't have a *planet* to *live* on. Which is why I'm now an ambassador for Protect Our Winters, to continue to raise awareness of the dangers of climate change. Does it sometimes feel hopeless? Yes, of course. But I have to believe that if enough people care, we can change the world by saving the world.

There was a point in my twenties when the only household item I owned was an (adorable) owl coffee mug. I was traveling too much to carry anything bigger than that! Eventually creating a home base in Vermont was incredibly grounding for me, and being able to put down roots—metaphorically and literally, since I love growing vegetables— has made months of travel easier now that I have someplace where I can fully unpack my suitcase. Perhaps the part of my life where I feel I've been the bravest is starting a life with someone I love. Building a life with Wade has been one of the biggest sources of joy and fulfill- ment. The unconditional giving and receiving of love lift me through tough times and long periods when we're apart while I'm traveling. And I've gone from living out of a suitcase to having multiple places I call home: Minnesota, where my family lives; Vermont, where my team lives; and Boston, where Wade and I are building a home together.

• • •

As we finish our cooldown and wrap up our workout, we load our gear back into the van. Rainwater and sweat drip down my back as I pull a dry shirt over my head, snagging a bar from my drink belt before jump- ing in.

Inside the van on our way back to Stratton, I wipe away the conden- sation on the window and stare out at the soggy, rolling Vermont land- scape. In the happy, contented haze that follows a hard workout, my mind drifts back to PyeongChang. I realize that maybe the Olympics really *did* change my life after all. They gave me memories of a moment when I was brave and went after what I wanted, holding nothing back. I'll always have that feeling to hold on to during tough times and, ultimately, to chase after during good times. I hope to live every day with the kind of bravery that I showed in PyeongChang when I attempted something that had never been done before.

I remind myself that I'm still the little girl who only skied to go super speed through the snowy woods, looking forward to the downhills. I still have some of the spontaneity and pure energy of the junior high school student who got called into action and joyously and spastically entered her first varsity high school race hopped up on candy bars. I've still got some of the guts of the teenager who moved away from home with nothing more than a duffel bag and a dream to be on the U.S. national team. I will always carry with me the young woman who fought through an eating disorder, bullying, anxiety, self-doubt, injury, accidents, fear, and weird travel incidents to pursue this crazy dream. And no matter what the future may hold, I'll always be the skier who found success at the World Cup races and the Olympics with grit and glitter. These pieces of my past, both the good and the bad, have shaped me into the person I am today. I carry them proudly, especially the tough parts.

I still possess that fierce joy that I had when I first started racing, which is why I continue to work toward a new best. Whether it's training with my teammates or traveling the world in pursuit of an even better "runner's high," I'll continue to set new goals and chase them down. If I don't catch them immediately, I'll dust myself off and try again. One of my favorite quotes is from artist and author Mary Anne Radmacher, and she sums it up best: *Courage doesn't always roar. Sometimes courage is the quiet voice at the end of the day saying, "I will try again tomorrow."*

• • •

The van pulls into the deserted school lot, and we unload the equipment, poles and skis sticking out every which way like a game of pick-up sticks. I'm soaked to the bone and getting hangry, so I drive home, take a hot shower, and eat lunch. Then I answer some emails, foam roll, and take a quick nap. But at 3:45 p.m. I'm headed back to the school gym for my second workout because, in the end, nothing has changed.

I wander into the empty gym. My teammates will be here any minute. The sweaty chorus of cheering, plates thudding to the ground, and weight bars being racked will start. But for now, it's as quiet and still as a church. The rain has stopped, and sunlight pours in from a wall of windows. It's steamy and hot, and there's no air conditioning, just two giant fans. I never have figured out what the deal is with Vermont refusing to use air conditioning. I walk across the rubber gym floor, turn on the stereo, and crank up Taylor Swift. As I approach the row of spin bikes to begin my workout, I empty my mind of all of my emails, sponsor shoots I'll do later in the week, and all of my outside commitments. Right here, right now, it's just me and my training and my will to get better. Nothing more, nothing less.

I begin pedaling on the spin bike and slowly start warming up. Five minutes in, and I'm already covered in sweat! Hip-hop bass from the top-40 playlist I'm hopelessly addicted to pulses through the room like a heartbeat. My teammates file into the gym and exuberant high fives are exchanged as we begin our workout. I push through hex bar dead lifts and explosive jumps, pulling my focus back in for each set. Sweat drips down my face, and I get ready to go again. In that split second when I want to give up and back down, I dig a little deeper and remind myself that I'm still the little girl who carried a canoe through the wilderness "all by herself."

I got this.

I am brave enough.

ACKNOWLEDGMENTS

FROM JESSIE

If skiing has shown me anything, it's that nothing important in life is ever accomplished alone. It's taken a whole lot of people to make this book possible, just as it's taken a whole lot of people to make ski racing possible. I find that it's somewhat impossible to tease the two apart, so my acknowledgments are coming in as one big, happy, puppy pile of thank-yous.

I am who I am because of my family: Deb, Clay, and Mackenzie Diggins . . . and our adorable dogs over the years. Thank you for being the people I want to call first whenever anything happens in life. I am so incredibly grateful for how close we are and for all the unconditional love, hugs, support, and laughter you bring to my life. Thank you for getting me through my hardest years and for celebrating with me in the happiest moments.

Wade, I love you so much. I can't wait to keep making you laugh and to go on camping trips all around the world with you. Thank you for putting up with all my stress while putting this book together and for helping me along the way.

To all the coaches in my life but specifically Jason Cork, Matt Whitcomb, Chris Grover, Pat O'Brien, and Kris Hansen, thank you. You

coached me in skiing but also in life, and you taught me to be a better
person as well as quick on skis. You are all examples of coaches who
have gone above and beyond, looking to coach the human behind the
results. Also, you all had to be my "ski dad or mom" at one point or
another, so thanks for letting me cry on you.

To all my teammates, from MYSL days through high school to
SMST2 and the national team: you are the reason I'm in this crazy
sport. You motivated me from the start, made me want to show up to
practice every day, laughed and celebrated the good times, and hugged
me right through the hard times. Love you all, so much.

To my sponsors through the years, thank you, thank you, thank you.
You allow me to pursue my biggest dreams, to be able to give back to the
community that raised me, to help inspire the next generation. Your
support and belief mean the world to me.

To the ski community in the Midwest, you have something truly
special going on. Thank you for supporting me and cheering me on all
these years . . . even when in Europe, I feel those cheers!

There are so many people I want to thank, and honestly it's impossible to fit everyone into one book, but here are a few who have helped
me immeasurably: Lauren Loberg, my sports psychologist, for years
of being my brain when my own decided to go on vacation; Tschana
Schiller, the most badass strength coach one could ever wish for; Susie
Parker-Simmons, for helping me learn proper sports nutrition but also
regain a healthy relationship to fueling once more. To all our volunteer physical therapists and massage therapists, thank you for keeping
my body together when it was trying to fall apart. To our wax techs,
I cannot say thank you enough; I'm convinced this is the hardest job
ever, but you do it with good humor and a smile and throw down some
pretty magical shit in that wax bus. We've had many volunteers and
full-time techs over the years, but I'd like to be sure and recognize Jason
Cork, Oleg Ragilo, Peter Johansson, Jean-Pascal Laurin, Tim Baucom,
Andrew Morehouse, and Eli Brown for your years of being our "boys in
the bus." And a special thank you to Liz Arky for your rock-solid belief,
your years of tireless support, and your mentorship.

To Jillian Lampert at The Emily Program, your expertise and
research as I attempted to fill the gaps in time have been immeasurably

helpful. To Angie Scott and Rasa Troup, and in loving memory of Joan Caillier, for their time, effort, unconditional support, and understanding as they saved my life, together with The Emily Program staff and brave girls in my group. You all not only saved my life in the moment when I needed it most but gave me the tools to charge forward and be excited about each and every day.

Erik Anderson, your guidance, cheering, words of wisdom, and belief in this book helped bring it to life! Thank you for all your time spent sitting late at the kitchen table, going over this darn thing line by line. Mary Keirstead, thank you for your attention to detail and for being my fantastic copy editor. Thank you to the entire team at the University of Minnesota Press—thank you for believing in us and helping me tell my story. You all had to teach me how to write a book even as I was writing it, and your patient coaching and belief made all the difference! Michael Croy of the Northstar Literary Agency and Patrick Quinn of Chicago Sports and Entertainment Partners, you both made this project a reality. Thank you for all your hard work, and, Patrick, thank you and your team for years of helping me tell my story to the world with our partners. To my fun and hardworking teammate Julia Kern, thank you for all the giggles during the sunset walks we took in New Zealand while you shot the cover image.

Finally, this book would not be in your hands if not for one Mr. Todd Smith. Todd, the moment we bonded over our shared love of Tina Fey, I knew you were the one to help me tell my story. Your hard work, endless enthusiasm, cheering when I needed it, epic writing sessions, and sense of humor made this journey a fun one, even when it was hard. Thank you for helping me bring these pages to life!

FROM TODD

First and foremost, a huge thank you to my wife, Sarah, and son, Murphy, for their love, support, and patience throughout my life and most certainly when I'm writing. A lifetime of thanks to my parents, Gary and Linda, brother Tony, and sister Becky. A special thanks and warm Minnesota hug to Clay and Deb Diggins for graciously welcoming me into their home. A big thanks to Jason Cork of the U.S. Ski Team for all of his insight, humility, and background information. This book would not exist without all of the hard work behind the scenes done by Michael Croy of the Northstar Literary Agency and Patrick Quinn of Chicago Sports and Entertainment Partners. A huge thanks to Erik Anderson, Kristian Tvedten, and all of the staff at the University of Minnesota Press for their understanding, professionalism, deft touch, and support along the winding road from writing to editing to publication. A sincere thank you to Jillian Lampert at The Emily Program for all of her knowledge, research, and time.

I'd like to personally thank the following writers and authors for their help over the course of this project: John Branch, for his encouragement; Chris Jones, for his inspiration; Wayne Coffey, for his advice and mentorship; and Quinton Skinner, for his literary friendship. A special acknowledgment goes out to Jessie for her positivity, unbreakable work ethic, and honesty. You're an elite athlete but an even better person, and it was a true honor for me to help give the stories of your life a home.

Finally, I recognize my loving memory of Katherine Noland and Jay Aydinalp-Mathews.

JESSIE DIGGINS was raised in Afton, Minnesota, and became a professional skier at the age of nineteen. A two-time Olympian and four-time World Championship medalist, she is the most decorated U.S. cross-country athlete in World Championship history. She and teammate Kikkan Randall became the first Olympic gold medalists in U.S. cross-country history when Jessie edged her ski across the line in the 2018 PyeongChang team sprint. Although she lives out of a suitcase, she resides at least part-time in Stratton, Vermont, where she is a member of the Stratton Mountain School T2 elite team.

TODD SMITH is a freelance writer and author of *Hockey Strong: Stories of Sacrifice from Inside the NHL*. He lives in Minneapolis.